Fear of the Dark

As film has become a major component of popular culture, so the portrayal of black people on cinema screens has evolved in an apparently non-systematic, erratic manner. Critical reactions to films with black characters have tended to concentrate on the ideological correctness of depictions of black people and on the extent to which they rely on stereotypes. In contrast, *Fear of the Dark* develops a particular critical perspective on the film portrayal of black female sexuality and questions the extent to which both white and black film-makers have challenged stereotypical images, examining the historical function of the myths around black female sexuality.

Films such as *Sapphine* (1959), *Flame in the Streets* (1961), *Leo the Last* (1969), *Pressure* (1974), *Black Joy* (1977), *Burning an Illusion* (1981), *Playing Away* (1986), and *Mona Lisa* (1986) are closely examined and situated in their historical and social context. There are several themes which provide the focus for the analysis of the films: anxieties about interracial sexual relations; the assumption of an oppositional relation between black and white people; fears about the instability of the family unit and its effect in black and white communities; and social relations between black and white women.

Fear of the Dark will be invaluable reading for students, lecturers and researchers of visual anthropology and cultural and media studies.

Lola Young is a former professional actress and currently is Principal Lecturer in Media and Cultural Studies at Middlesex University.

Gender, Racism, Ethnicity
Series editors: Kum-Kum Bhavnani, Avtar Brah, Ann Phoenix, Gail Lewis

Gender, Racism, Ethnicity is a new series whose main concern is to promote rigorous feminist analysis of the intersections between gender, racism, ethnicity, class and sexuality within the contexts of imperialism, colonialism and neo-colonialism. Intended to contribute new perspectives to current debates and to introduce fresh analysis, it will provide valuable teaching texts for undergraduates, lecturers and researchers in anthropology, women's studies, cultural studies and sociology.

Other titles in the series:

White Women, Race Matters
Ruth Frankenberg

Gendering Orientation
Reina Lewis

Fear of the Dark

'Race', Gender and Sexuality in the Cinema

Lola Young

ROUTLEDGE

London and New York

First published 1996
by Routledge
11 New Fetter Lane, London EC4P 4EE

Simultaneously published in the USA and Canada
by Routledge
29 West 35th Street, New York, NY 10001

Typeset in Times by Computerset, Harmondsworth
Printed and bound in Great Britain by
TJ Press (Padstow) Ltd, Padstow, Cornwall

British Library Cataloguing in Publication Data
A catalogue record for this book is available from the British Library.

Library of Congress Cataloging in Publication Data
Young, Lola, 1951–
    Fear of the dark: 'race', gender, and sexuality in the cinema/
Lola Young.
    p. cm. – (Gender, racism, ethnicity series)
    "Films cited": p.
    Includes bibliographical references and index.
    ISBN 0–415–09709–6. – ISBN 0–415–09710–X (pbk.)
    1. Blacks in motion pictures. 2. Women in motion pictures.
3. Sex in motion pictures. I. Title. II. Series.
PN1995.9.N4Y68 1995
791.43'652042'08996–dc20   95–17135
                                                                CIP

ISBN 0–415–09709–6 (hbk)
ISBN 0–415–09710–X (pbk)

Contents

Acknowledgements

Some of the ideas and research contained in this book have been documented elsewhere in a different form: in particular the work on *Mona Lisa* in chapter 7 was first explored in the essay 'A Nasty Piece of Work: A Psychoanalytic Study of Sexual and Racial Difference in *Mona Lisa*' (Young, 1990).

It is impossible to list all those who have contributed to the completion of this book and to detail the nature of that contribution (sometimes they wouldn't have known how and what they did to keep me going). I will simply list some of the many people who have, at some stage or other, and in some way, helped me to continue with my work: Gregg Birch, Betty Birch, Barrie Birch, Jo Sullivan, Anne Kauder, Dolly Kauder, Mark Sealy, David A. Bailey, Ola Franklin, Karen Alexander, Margaret Tovey, Lynda Dyson, Reina Lewis, Jonathan Rutherford, Sally Gran, Michael Dawney, Barry Curtis, Jon Bird, Angela MacRobbie, David Lusted, Claire Pajaczkowska, Avtar Brah, Gail Lewis, Ann Phoenix, and Delia Jarret-MacCauley.

This book is dedicated to Gregg, and to those whom I wish were here: Ben Birch, Femi Franklin, Bobby Kauder, Albert Kauder and Maxwell Fela Young.

Introduction

When I was a little girl at primary school, I was always asked to play the witch in playground fantasies. I felt uneasy but wanted to have friends so I did. Much later, after having several years experience as a professional actor in a children's television series, I was asked to play a bus conductor, a prostitute, a nurse. Later still I was asked to play a witch in *Macbeth*: I wanted to act in Shakespeare, so I did. Eventually I didn't enjoy these limited roles, so I stopped acting.

The research and writing of this book has to a large extent been a personal project as well as a political one, since I have been trying to make sense of some of my experiences of growing up in Britain during a large part of the period covered by the films discussed. In particular, the experience of being a black woman acting in Britain was a salutary one, where my aspirations were not met by the opportunities offered. Looking at contemporary popular cinema and television, I see little to make me regret my decision to leave acting: there seems to be little scope for the talents of middle-aged black women to be displayed. I remember many conversations with acting friends and colleagues about the situation, and committees were formed and papers written. There was much talk in the 1970s and 1980s of positive images, role models and stereotypes, but for me, there was never enough detail, or a sense of the histories involved. The desire to find out more about the 'how did these stereotypes about blackness start and why?' has been a significant impetus in developing the themes of this book.

AIMS AND SCOPE OF THIS STUDY

The aim of this book is to examine the conjunction of 'race', gender and sexuality in British films. The themes and preoccupations of black and white film-makers in Britain suggest the existence of several histories of interracial social and sexual relations and constitute an invaluable resource indicative of a variety of experiences and interpretations of experiences. However, the films under discussion in this book are not taken to be transparently readable historical documents 'reflecting' past and contemporary racial issues: rather, they are seen as a means through which issues specifically related to notions of racial difference, gender and sexuality are mediated and articulated.

In comparison with work carried out on 'race' and representation in the USA, the amount of theoretical and critical work which focuses on images of black people and white ethnicity in British cinema is small. One relevant factor is that the number of films produced here is very much smaller, as is the proportion of black people in the population. The situation also reflects the relatively small numbers of black people writing in the fields of cultural and film studies, especially women. Since the discourse of 'race' has primarily been seen as a problem for black people to engage with until relatively recently, white academics and film scholars have only rarely addressed the question of white racial identities and the relationship with gendered identities. It should be noted that the use of the terms 'black' and 'white' in this book does not imply essential properties and characteristics or indicate acceptance of racial categorizations (the problematic nature of racialized discourse is discussed in some detail in chapter 2).

SCOPE OF THE STUDY

The films selected are feature length (at least 90 minutes long) and originally made for cinematic release, although I have viewed them on a variety of formats. Some of the films were viewed on 35mm and 16mm at the British Film Institute (BFI); others were on VHS and borrowed or bought.[1] The principal films discussed are: *Sapphire* (1959), *Flame in the Streets* (1961), *Leo the Last* (1969), *Pressure* (1974), *Black Joy* (1977), *Burning an Illusion* (1981), *Playing Away* (1986), and *Mona Lisa* (1987). The main focus then, is an examination of the impact of a generation (approximately 30 years) of post-war black settlement on representations of racial difference.

There are several films featuring black characters that I have not examined or mentioned: this book is not an attempt to compile a definitive, comprehensive catalogue of every film in which black actors have performed or every film which engages with racial issues. The study is restricted to a small number of texts on the basis that the understanding of these specific examples may facilitate the understanding of other, similar instances. The films here are regarded as a series of representative illustrations indicative of general ideological positions and discursive practices.

In the context of this book, films designated 'white' are those which were made under the artistic control of a predominantly white creative team: that is mainly as writers and directors. By 'black' films I mean films to which black people have made a substantial contribution in those creative roles. Although this criterion may be seen as rather elastic in its operation, I do not, at this stage want to go beyond that into extended debates about what constitutes a 'black' film: this book is not primarily concerned with attempting to make definitive comparisons between 'black' and 'white' films or to resolve debates about what a 'black aesthetic' practice might be.

With reference to the issue of audience and spectatorship, there is no attempt to factor in actual audience responses to these films since no empirical research was carried out to support any assertions about viewers. Instead, on several occasions, attention is drawn to the ways in which audiences may be positioned, or encouraged to identify with particular situations and in the main, an 'imaginary' audience is inferred.

There are substantial numbers of black people living in Britain who feel their cultures to be at best marginalized, and at worst, continually undermined and denigrated by popular media (mis)representations. However, the approach taken to analysing the films in this book will not involve making explicit value judgements about the quality of the work discussed: the objective is not to condemn the films, or to label them racist or sexist, their imagery negative or positive.

METHODOLOGY

This study is concerned with an examination of black people's often problematic status in Britain through a detailed critical analysis of a number of feature length films produced mainly between 1959 and 1986. There are, in addition, a small number of films prior to 1959 which are discussed: these analyses are undertaken in order to indicate some of the cinematic themes prevalent before the peak of black immigration to Britain in the late 1950s and to suggest how the issues changed subsequently.

There are several themes which provide the focus for the analyses of the films: anxieties about interracial sexual relations; the assumption of an oppositional relation between black and white people; fears about the instability of the family unit and its effect in black and white communities and social relations between black and white women. The questions raised regarding these films are to do with the ways in which they represent racial and sexual difference and how film-makers engage with issues arising from the construction of these differences.

This book is also implicitly concerned with the development of appropriate methodologies for the analysis of discourses of 'race', gender and sexuality in British film. The study was initially undertaken because of a feeling that conventional film studies had not developed an appropriate critical framework for the detailed study of representations of racial difference in British cinema.

I argue that an adequate analysis of the complex issue of racial representation involves a consideration of the relationship between Britain's colonial past and the terms in which ideologies of racial and sexual difference are expressed in the cinema. A basic premise of this study is that in order to consider properly cinematic images of racial difference it is necessary to recognize and identify the extent to which, historically, discourses of gender and sexuality have been racialized. Thus, each film analysis is either informed by or directly refers to this history.

The films examined are situated in their own immediate historical context and the relevant social issues foregrounded or suggested by the film in question are highlighted. Thus although the central concern is with the cinematic representation of racial and sexual difference, the close textual analyses frequently refer to issues of history, and to social and political contexts: in particular, the historical shifts in attitudes towards racial difference and sexuality, and the relations of dominance and subordination between white and black people are considered.

It is argued that there is no single theoretical framework able to address all the issues raised by the combination of racial, sexual and gender issues and the pertinent historical developments. It is necessary, therefore, to draw on a number of different concepts in order to examine the films, and thus the textual analyses draw on theories regarding ideology and discourse in order to elicit some of the meanings attached to images of blackness and whiteness. In particular, use is made of principles drawn from psychoanalytic theory in order to explore notions of Otherness as suggested by images of black and female sexuality. This study is then, based on a Cultural Studies, interdisciplinary approach rather than being located in a more orthodox 'Film Studies' paradigm.

PRINCIPAL ISSUES TO BE DISCUSSED

The problems inherent in regarding representations as truthful, positive, distorted or negative, are discussed in some detail in chapter 1, where an account of the main theoretical issues involved in this study is given. Included in this chapter is a critical review of relevant literature and an explanation of the key terms used during the course of the book. In the second chapter racist ideologies concerned with the pathologization of black sexuality and interracial sexual relations, which were evolving during the eighteenth and nineteenth centuries are discussed in order to establish how such beliefs came to be naturalized. This historical account of the principal themes embedded in images of racial and sexual difference extends into the twentieth century and discusses three issues in detail: sexual activity as pathology, attitudes towards, and taboos about, interracial sexual relations and the scrutiny to which black bodies have been subjected. In addition, the terms 'black' and 'white' are located as politically expedient constructions within the discourse of 'race'. This examination is carried out in order to clarify the historical issues involved in the cinematic representations of black sexuality, and social and sexual relations between black and white people.

In chapter 3, films made during the 1930s and 1940s are considered in order to introduce and contextualize the thematic concerns of the book. Chapters 4, 5, 6 and 7 are substantially comprised of detailed examinations of specific films from the late 1950s through to the late 1980s. In each chapter, I discuss the reasons for selecting the films and locate them in the historical and social circumstances of their production and consumption. The concluding chapter is a summary of the main arguments contained in the book, a clarification of the contribution to knowledge in the field, and a consideration of how these issues and themes might be developed and expanded in the future.

To summarize then, the aim of this book is to establish a field of enquiry in British cinema which has been largely neglected: that is, to indicate areas of interest regarding the complex interaction between ideologies which have emerged in regard to gender, 'race' and sexuality, and to note some of the continuities, discontinuities and contradictions which have marked representations of both whiteness and blackness.

The book is intended as exploratory rather than exhaustive and represents an attempt to articulate problems and contradictions, not to supply solutions. It is intended as a contribution to ongoing critical debates about representation, theory and 'race' in visual culture and other related issues to do with film criticism, feminism and ethnocentrism.

Chapter 1

Themes and issues

The aim of this chapter is to indicate the major theories and concepts which have informed the textual analyses which follow. To this end, it begins with an examination of some of the literature concerned with representations of 'race' and racial issues in the context of North American popular cinema. I will argue that underpinning much of this material is the contention that the black people in these texts are inaccurately represented. There follows a schematic account of theories relating to ideology and realism which serve to problematize the position which considers black people to be 'misrepresented' in mainstream cinema.

This study draws on insights developed by black and white feminists: I will refer to these analyses under the general heading of 'Feminist Issues'. This is followed by a more specific consideration of feminist film scholarship and its relationship to racial issues. Subsequently, I will examine some of the work which draws on psychoanalytic theory for an understanding of racial difference and the links with sexual and racial anxiety, dwelling in some detail on the concepts of Otherness and 'difference' in psychoanalytic discourse.

'RACE', COLONIALISM AND REPRESENTATION

The question of images – their construction and their histories – and the meanings which accrue to them is central to a discussion of any visual text: when it comes to carrying out work which involves representations of black people, the analysis of images has a heightened political inflection, since representations of black people are always deemed to 'mean' something, to be laden with symbolism in regard to 'race' in racially stratified societies.

A great deal of critical work has been concerned with representation and the relationship between the external reality referred to and the image constructed of it. This relationship is problematic if it is implied that there is some direct transfer of material reality from the object to the image. It is a difficult and complex subject which extends and problematizes debates about producing positive images or combatting stereotypical imagery.

First published in *Screen* in 1983, and concerned with moving beyond the 'negative/positive' images debate, Robert Stam and Louise Spence open their analysis of colonialism and representation by highlighting some of the problems associated with previous studies of racism in the cinema (Stam and Spence, 1985: 632). As Stam and Spence point out, texts such as *Slow Fade to Black* (Cripps, 1977), *From Sambo to Superspade* (Leab, 1975), and *Toms, Coons, Mammies, Mulattoes and Bucks* (Bogle, 1991),[1] have in the main limited their analyses to discussion about the degree of correspondence of the images to their referents through the examination of stereotypes. In these studies it is assumed that stereotyping is an inherently negative practice.[2][3]

Stam's and Spence's essay demonstrates the shortcomings of earlier efforts to understand the complex articulations of racist and colonial ideologies in film. They reject texts which put the 'emphasis on realism' and betray 'an exaggerated faith in the possibilities of verisimilitude in art in general and the cinema in particular' (Stam and Spence, 1985: 637). These films, they argue, avoid 'the fact that films are inevitably constructs, fabrications, representations' (ibid.: 637). Nonetheless, Stam and Spence are prone to this tendency to desire some correspondence with reality themselves. This is illustrated by the comment:

> Countless safari films present Africa as the land of 'lions in the jungle' when in fact only a tiny proportion of the African land mass could be called 'jungle' and when lions do not live in the jungle but in grassland.
>
> (ibid.: 637)

This may be read as theoretical inconsistency, but it may also be seen as an unconscious acknowledgement of the investment that audiences have in realist texts and it is not as easy to dismiss the potency of such a desire as perhaps Stam and Spence would like to believe. The desire for 'authentic' representations which depict life 'as it really is' is strong and it is a desire encouraged by the continued use of those forms of realism which purport to be a 'window on the world'.

Stam and Spence warn of the dangers of overemphasis on the study of the images themselves, which they claim may lead to:

> both the privileging of characterological concerns (to the detriment of other important considerations) and also to a kind of essentialism, as the critic reduces a complex diversity of portrayals to a limited set of reified stereotypes. Behind every black child performer, from Farina to Gary Coleman, the critic discerns a 'pickaninny', behind every sexually attractive black actor a 'buck' and behind every attractive black actress a 'whore'. Such reductionist simplifications run the risk of reproducing the very racism they were initially designed to combat.
>
> (ibid.: 640)

It is important to argue for complexity rather than over-simplification, and there is a problem with continually labelling particular images as 'pickanniny' or 'whore' without regard to their historical and cultural specificity: however rather than considering this identification of particular images to be a reification of stereotypes, it might be thought of as the identification of tropes which have evolved out of the 'master' discourses of colonialism. It is argued here that it is imperative to trace the development of these images, to place them in their historical context and to question whether it is possible to identify shifts in the reworking of the themes and metaphors. Indeed, there is an implicit admission of this in Stam's and Spence's comments regarding *The Birth of a Nation*, for their description of Gus as '*the* sexually aggressive black man' (my emphasis) suggests an acceptance of the 'brute, black buck' stereotype elaborated on by Donald Bogle, amongst others (ibid.: 644).

In asking that 'the analysis of stereotypes must also take cultural specificity into account' (ibid.: 640), Stam and Spence are actually referring to a national specificity, since they consider stereotypes as they relate to the beliefs and attitudes of different countries. The cultural specificity of groups within, for example, the USA does not seem to be an issue.

There is also evidence of a reluctance to recognize the implications of their statements about reductionism and essentialism. For example, they write of how a North American spectator taking a different reading from the text's preferred meaning is deemed to have misread a scene from a Brazilian film, rather than to have made sense of the scene in terms of their own cultural context. This is inconsistent with their use of the more favourable, more academic term 'aberrant reading' to refer to Latin American audiences' interpretations of a Hollywood text. This latter point indicates the tendency to consider audiences in an undifferentiated manner, as in the statement regarding point-of-view conventions in images of encirclement in Western films. Stam and Spence claim that the 'spectator is unwittingly sutured into a colonialist perspective' (ibid.: 641). However, it is doubtful that audience identification is so uniformly achieved as suggested here. It may well be the case that such texts attempt to position the spectator on the side of the colonizer – to interpellate the viewer thus – but meanings are unstable and cannot easily be controlled. Even though the 'colonizer's' perspective is foregrounded, any number of spectators may consciously choose to side with those Indians located as exterior to the besieged white Europeans.

Stam's and Spence's basic aim is to attempt to construct a critical methodology which must:

> pay attention to the *mediations* which intervene between "reality" and its representation. Its emphasis should be on narrative structure, genre conventions, and cinematic style.
>
> (Stam and Spence, 1985: 641)

In regard to this study, such a methodology is inadequate without a historical perspective on the representation of reality: any such endeavour should be concerned with the historicity of cinematic representation.

Another important point which is raised by Stam's and Spence's work is, to what extent is the North American experience of racial differentiation applicable elsewhere, and in particular to Britain? To refer back to Donald Bogle's *Toms, Coons, Mammies, Mulattoes and Bucks* (Bogle, 1991): some of Bogle's memorable list of black stereotypes are specific to North American experiences of slavery and its consequences. Although there are many similarities, it is important to remember that British experiences were dissimilar in important respects and colonialism and imperial conquest have operated quite differently from the USA. I draw on that which is applicable from the USA whilst recognizing the specificity of British cinema, society and history, and conceptualizations of racial difference.

Having worked on North American racial imagery in the cinema (Pines, 1975), Jim Pines engages with racial difference in British cinema (Pines, 1981). His essay examines black people's positioning in British cinema, and there is an explicit comparison made to images of blackness in North American popular cinema. The essay is not solely concerned with film as Pines discusses documentary television too: the comparison of themes and textual strategies across the media is interesting but serves to gloss over the specificity of cinematic discursive practices. Unlike much of the black critical writing on film of the 1970s and early 1980s, Pines' work is clearly informed by structuralist and semiotic analyses such as those which developed in the pages of *Screen* during the 1970s.

Another point which marks out Pines' contribution from that of other black male critics writing during this period is his indication of the importance of gender issues. Although this aspect of his essay is underdeveloped, he does at least acknowledge that black women and men are differentially inscribed in films such as *Sapphire* (1959) and *Flame in the Streets* (1961). Pines also indicates the problematic cinematic identification of white women as irrational, racially prejudiced white people in these two texts but does not develop this aspect of his analysis. He identifies the extent to which black young men's experiences are foregrounded in black-focused texts such as *Pressure* (1974), *Black Joy* (1977) and *Babylon* (1980). These themes – the place of black women in cinematic representations, the textual status of white women, and the privileging of young black male experiences – suggested briefly by Pines in his essay are all further developed during the course of this study.

Chris Vieler-Porter recognizes Jim Pines' critical contribution when he suggests four categories of mainstream cinematic representations of black people in British cinema, since 'colonial-based' and 'ethnic' dramas are categories suggested by Pines (Vieler-Porter, 1992: 238), although of Vieler-Porter's nine bibliographic references, only one refers specifically to British cinema.[4] The full list of categories are as follows:

1 *Colonial-based dramas*: these are films which are located 'out there' in the colonies and serve to reinforce notions of white and/or British cultural superiority.
2 *'Race-based' dramas*: these are racial problem films mainly made in the 1950s and 1960s.
3 *'Race' assemblage dramas*: Vieler-Porter places the films in this

category into three sub-categories. The first category of films is where the black presence is simply a backdrop for white centred dramas. The second is where black people are there to provide the source of comic action. His third sub-category is where blacks are used as a marker for racial difference within the team of the male action adventure.

4 *'Ethnic' dramas*; the most opaque of the categories described since it is not clear what criteria is used to identify films included here.

The examples Vieler-Porter gives cover a wide range of settings, genres, themes and subjects, and under the heading of 'ethnic drama' he juxtaposes such diverse texts as *Burning an Illusion* (1981), *Countryman* (1982), *My Beautiful Launderette* (1985) and *Mona Lisa* (1986). There are films which do not fit easily into any category, those which appear to be in the wrong category and some which straddle categories. Such a schema is no substitute for serious study of individual texts and their relationship to others across different periods. One of the major drawbacks of this type of analysis is the concentration on the surface content for the purposes of categorization. This form of taxonomic reduction is only helpful in so far as it is not considered binding and is used as a starting point for consideration. To be fair to Vieler-Porter, it is offered as an outline, a tentative contribution to an underdeveloped area of study and appears in a low key BFI publication.

Although John Hill's book-length study of 1950s and 1960s films contains some interesting material on moral authority and patri- archy, and the role of the family and racism especially in *Sapphire* and *Flame in the Streets*, the primary emphases of his work are signalled by the title, *Sex, Class and Realism* (Hill, 1986). His unproblematized use of the term 'half-caste' is worrying and because he discusses so many films, those which are directly concerned with racial issues do not receive much attention. However, his methodology provides a useful model in terms of its theoretical eclecticism. The combination of the latter and his location of the films in their social and cultural context means that this work is more constructive than a collection of textual analyses of films which have been abstracted from their conditions of production and consumption.

FEMINIST ISSUES

The arguments and observations offered come from a feminist perspective which sees it as essential to identify the extent to which gender and sexuality may be seen as racialized discourses in the cinema: a major concern throughout is to draw attention to both the presence and the absence of black women and to try and account for these instances of visibility and invisibility. The ways in which texts by both black and white film-makers indicate contrasting notions of black and white femininities and masculinities are also analysed.

During the 1960s and 1970s, white feminists made claims for an undifferentiated international sisterhood in the name of women's liberation (Friedan, 1963; Mitchell, 1971; Millett, 1972; Oakley, 1974). This approach failed to realize its potential as a mobilizing, revolutionary force, partly due to its lack of racial awareness, and the conscious and unconscious racism within the movement which undermined the notion of a universal women's program for liberation. While insights into patriarchal systems were developed, the potential for examining racism in the same moment was not exploited.

Publicly exposing these issues within feminism absorbed the energies of many African–American and black British female writers who concerned themselves with examining the racially defined aspirations of black women living under both patriarchy and racism. Angela Davis' *Women, Race and Class* (1981), is a key text: it was an early piece of African–American feminist criticism which sought to establish as a field of study the interplay between 'race', gender and class. This was one of the primary texts which helped black women to make sense of their predicaments as a doubly oppressed group but although her remarks on 'race' and feminism are wide in scope, taking a historical perspective on contemporary issues, Davis does not explore representation, or engage with cultural/theoretical positions on these issues. It is a substantial empirical work about the material effects of racism and the implications for European and African–American feminism.

The extent to which African–American feminism is applicable in a British context is dependent on how far it is possible to generalize from the particular predicaments of African-American women (Wallace, 1979; hooks, 1982; hooks, 1989). The class system in Britain has developed differently: it is far more institutionalized than it is in the USA, and closely connected to notions of community and national identity. Also, historically, the way in which social and sexual relations and hierarchies under slavery were organized differed in significant ways and legislative aspects of the control of black sexuality have not been enacted in Britain.[5] Nonetheless African–American feminism has had a substantial impact on the analysis of racism and sexism in Britain. One of the key texts here is a black British feminist perspective proposed by Valerie Amos and Pratibha Parmar in 'Challenging Imperialist Feminism' which was published in an issue of *Feminist Review* devoted to black feminism (Amos and Parmar, 1984). Again, this was primarily concerned with an analysis of black women's struggle for recognition within what was perceived as a largely racist women's movement rather than with cinematic or media racist representations. Similarly, Stella Dadzie, Suzanne Scafe and Stella Bryan criticise women's liberation movements for their racial myopia and failure to develop policies and practices which recognise the specificity of black women's experiences. Although the criticisms are not specifically concerned with film, the authors also indicate the extent to which stereotypes of black women inform the way in which white professionals – mainly in social work situations – view their black 'clients' (Bryan *et al.*, 1985). Major areas of disagreement in these debates were white feminists condemnation of the family as the locus of women's oppression and their insistence on contraception and abortion on demand. Dissent from the latter point came from the knowledge that black women had been used as guinea pigs for contraceptives and that social and welfare programmes in the USA and elsewhere sought to control black women's fertility with compulsory sterilization, abortions and so on.

For the purposes of this study, the issue of the supportive role of black families and their cinematic representation is of particular note since it is a point which is raised in chapters 4, 5 and 6 in relation to representations of black and white families in several films. At this stage attention is drawn to the fact that the work of black feminists cited argues that far from being an oppressive institution, for many black people, the family has been a source of strength in hostile situations.

In terms of British-based black female interventions in the analysis of cinematic images of black people in general or black women in particular, there is little sustained analysis of images underpinned by a consistent conceptual framework. Critical writing by black women about gender, 'race' and sexuality is largely directed toward addressing issues raised by a more sociologically, inclined feminism rather than being concerned with film and cultural production (Bryan *et al.*, 1985; Carby, 1986).

FEMINISM AND FILM THEORY

White feminist film scholars' lack of engagement with racial issues has often been located in feminism's controversial relationship with psychoanalytic theory. For the purposes of this critical review, feminist appropriations of psychoanalytic theory are important although not many have identified 'race' as a specific problematic related to gender (Kaplan, 1983; Johnston, 1985; Modleski, 1988). Much feminist cultural theory has been castigated by black feminists for its general lack of attention to racial issues and such critiques have begun to have an impact on white feminist film scholars. I argue that notions of femininity and feminism itself, are intimately connected to slavery and colonialism although this is only just beginning to be addressed in feminist film scholarship.

Although originally published in 1974, and despite continuing critiques since then, Laura Mulvey's essay 'Visual Pleasure and Narrative Cinema' remains a significant reference point for feminist film criticism (Mulvey, 1985). This influential essay noted the re-presentation of the heterosexualized female body as an essential component of most mainstream cinema, a re-presentation for male consumption. Mulvey described and analysed the gendering of the look but did not suggest how this might be racially differentiated.

Drawing on Freud's theory of infantile sexuality, and later Lacanian developments, Mulvey sought to explain the pleasure gained from looking at films in the cinema. Freud posited that the pleasure in looking – referred to as scopophilia – is a fundamental component of humans' sexual disposition and that it is related to the child's desire to observe the primal scene (Freud, 1977). Mulvey related scopophilia to the process of watching films by suggesting a link between the self-contained private world as played out in front of the audience on the cinema screen, and the pleasure and desire invoked by the forbidden looking carried out as infants.

Mulvey noted that men are the major protagonists in most mainstream films and it is through the man's motivations, actions and thoughts that sense is made of the narrative: most often the woman is there to stimulate the man into taking action. Fear, anxiety and desire are activated by the appearance of the female body and it

is these psychic drives which propel the male character towards
action stimulated by desire or aggression.

Mulvey posited that the male unconscious has two possible
modes of escape from the castration anxiety stimulated by the
woman's 'lack' of a penis. In terms of the representation of women
on film, one route is continually to investigate 'woman' in an
attempt to demystify and control her: in most mainstream films it is
the female who is subjected to and subordinated by the male look.
The woman is scrutinized by the man as he attempts to assert control
and to punish her for evoking and provoking (forbidden) desire.

Another possible strategy for dealing with castration anxiety
suggested by Mulvey is that of fetishistic scopophilia which results
in an overvaluation of the image, hence the cult of the glamorous
female star the physical beauty of whose body parts provides the
sexual satisfaction. This notion goes some way towards explaining
why it is that white female stars, although often peripheral to the
action, are physically foregrounded and idealized, with emphasis on
particular parts of the body. The woman herself may be set up as a
fetish – as a substitute for the penis she 'lacks' – or some part of her,
such as her legs, or her breasts. According to Mulvey, women's
sexuality represents a threat and a way of countering this threat is to
locate the woman within the confines of the containing patriarchal
structure of the monogamous heterosexual couple or family.

The question of the 'race' of the characters and the viewers was
not an issue for Mulvey, although there are some interesting points
to be raised about the avoidance of castration anxiety in regard to
black women on film. The first strategy of the male unconscious to
which Mulvey refers, that of cinematically investigating the woman
in order to demystify her, is analogous to nineteenth century medical
approaches to racial and sexual difference: this will be analysed in
some detail in chapter 2. As regards Mulvey's second assertion, that
of the valorization of the beauty of the female star, this is a position
that has not been available to women of African descent to the same
extent as it has to white European women. Historically, black
women have not been subject to overvaluation in the same sense that
white women have and comparatively few may be described as
being part of the 'cult of the female star'.

Mulvey's hypothesis is problematic for a number of reasons: of
particular importance to this study is that her analysis does not take
a historical perspective. In her description of the way in which
women were subjected to and subordinated by the male gaze,

Mulvey did not differentiate between women, thereby denying intra-group diversity, apparent even if restricted to white women, because of class differences, physical appearance and so on. It is also the case that black women of African or Asian descent, Chinese and Japanese women, Arab women, although all designated Other have their own representational specificity. It is important to consider why and how it is that disproportionate numbers of white women function as emblematic objects of heterosexual desire and to examine historical precedents.

There is ample evidence to indicate that when it comes to the cinematic aestheticization of the feminine, white women's faces and bodies are privileged signifiers of female beauty and desire. [6] Although not specifically articulated, Mulvey's essay is about white people's relationship to the look and cinema, and this is something which continually occurs in academic, as well as common-sense discourses – the implicit assumptions being that white experiences are representative human experiences. The meaning of whiteness and notions of white identity are discussed further later on in this chapter.

It has been suggested by Jane Gaines, in her essay 'White Privilege and Looking Relations', that a materialist approach to racially differentiated representation would be more productive than feminist theorists' emphasis on psychoanalytic interpretations of texts because the stress on sexual difference has led to a privileging of gender as the locus of oppression. Gaines forcefully argues that materialist explanations of racism are a crucial component of any holistic analysis involving 'race' although such arguments are insufficient on their own. Gaines does not indicate the extent to which materialist explanations of racial subordination have privileged class, nor does she indicate the limitations in considering racism solely as the product of the economic structure of western societies. The problem of discrimination in non-capitalist societies and the many forms which racism may take are not addressed. Although it may be politically essential to analyse racism as a strategy of capitalism, and to analyse the way in which it is institutionalized and systemic, this form of analysis has not been able to account for and to clarify how the power relations embedded in textual systems and forms of representation may be unconsciously sustained.

Gaines posits that:

Framing the question of male privilege and viewing pleasure as the 'right to look' may help us to rethink film theory along more materialist lines, considering, for instance, how some groups have historically had the licence to 'look' openly while other groups have 'looked' illicitly.

(Gaines, 1988: 24)

Although critical of the universalist tendencies of feminist film theory, Gaines is herself prone to this as she curiously homogenizes the experiences of black women and white women. Nonetheless, I agree with Gaines that the privileging of gender in a hierarchy of oppression where the primacy of 'race', gender and class are seen as being in contestation with each other has been a contributory factor in the stifling of white feminist discussions of 'race'. Interestingly, although Gaines quotes from Fanon, she does not emphasize that it is, in large part, his understanding of psychoanalysis which enabled him to pinpoint that for white people, blackness represents a troublesome Otherness which is not able to be assimilated (Gaines, 1988: 17). Freud's attempt to describe and explain the infant's struggle to enter into subjectivity and adulthood indicates a more complex picture than Gaines allows in her essay. The question of the oscillation of both women and men between 'female' and 'male' positions of identification suggests the possibility of also regarding racialized looking as a non-fixed position of identification.

Ambivalence about the use of psychoanalytic theory for discussing 'race' is evidenced by Mary Ann Doane in 'Dark Continents: Epistemologies of Racial and Sexual difference in Psychoanalysis and the Cinema' (Doane, 1991: 209). Significantly, this chapter occurs in the last section of the book entitled, 'At the *Edges* [my emphasis] of Psychoanalysis'. Doane acknowledges that:

The force of the category of race in the constitution of Otherness within psychoanalysis should not be underestimated. When Freud needs a trope for the unknowability of female sexuality, the dark continent is close at hand. Psychoanalysis can, from this point of view, be seen as a quite elaborate form of ethnography – as a writing of the ethnicity of the white Western psyche. Repression becomes the prerequisite for the construction of a white culture which stipulates that feminine sexuality act as the trace within of what has been excluded.

(Doane, 1991: 211)

Thus although the foregrounding of gender and sexuality in white

feminist discourse has been attributed to the predominance of
psychoanalytic theory as an explanatory model for women's
oppression, such an exclusion is unwarranted. The ideological and
discursive systems which produce and reproduce notions of
blackness and whiteness are implicated in Freud's use of the trope of
the 'dark continent'.

Doane does not adequately elaborate on or clarify her argument
for considering psychoanalysis as an 'ethnography of whiteness'. In
any case, if psychoanalytic theory is to be seen as a tool for the study
of the construction of white racial identities, the question of how –
if indeed it is possible or desirable – black people fit into this
analytic paradigm requires some thought. Doane states:

> If certain races (associated with the 'primitive') are constituted as
> outside or beyond the territory of the psychoanalytic endeavour –
> insofar as they lack repression or neurosis (perhaps even the
> unconscious) – the solution cannot be simply to take this system
> which posits their exclusion and apply it to them....
> Psychoanalysis, unshaken in its premises, cannot be *applied* to
> issues of racial difference, but must be radically destabilized by
> them.
>
> (Doane, 1991: 216)

Implicit in Doane's contention is the assumption that psychoanalytic
theory is a universalized account of human psychical development,
rather than an account of white racial identity. There is also an implication that issues of racial difference relate solely to the context of
discussions of the 'primitive'. This raises the question of the place
of those diaspora blacks who have for several generations resided in
predominantly white societies in Europe and the USA. It is
necessary to radically interrogate the ways in which psychoanalytic
theory may be able to contribute to the construction and maintenance of racial hierarchies and to examine the reluctance so often
encountered in this endeavour, particularly amongst white feminist
theorists. To claim that psychoanalytic theory cannot be applied to
racial difference implies that racial difference can only be explored
in the context of the analysis of blackness and black identities. In
relation to this, Frantz Fanon, Joel Kovel, and Sander L. Gilman
have argued convincingly that psychoanalytic theories regarding
repression and projection may be used as a theoretical framework
for analyses of white supremacist conceptualizations of difference
and identity.

Although Doane's contribution to discussions of racial and sexual difference is welcomed, there is still the question of black women's representational status. If feminist psychoanalytic theory holds that (white) women's bodies represent a lack for the (white) male unconscious, and if, as argued by Doane, black men's bodies represent a hyperbolic sexual presence, then how are black women situated? Doane claims that the trope of the 'dark continent' relegates black women to non-existence (Doane, 1991: 212). It would seem that the enactment of this trope in representational terms bears this out since black women are more likely to be absent or insignificant in popular cinema. I argue in chapter 2 that this may be attributed to the problem which black women constitute for white men: a double negation of the white, male self which underlines the notions of sexual and racial difference.

Although there is still relatively little acknowledgement by white feminist academics working on film that the histories of racism, colonialism and slavery connect historically with gender and notions of femininity, these repressed histories are available for analysis in a range of historical and contemporary cinematic images. In her essay 'Gender and the Culture of Empire: Toward a Feminist Ethnography of the Cinema' Ella Shohat demonstrates how 'race' and racism are implicated in conceptualizations of 'woman' and the 'feminine' and thus feminism (Shohat, 1991). Shohat identifies:

> the role of sexual difference in the construction of superimposed oppositions – West/East, North/South – not only on a narratological level but also on the level of the implicit structuring metaphors undergirding colonial discourse.
>
> (Shohat, 1991: 45)

Shohat follows with an extensive examination of eroticized cinematic encounters featuring more or less explicit representations of sexual and racial anxieties.

Speaking of how veiled women of the Orient in Western paintings, photographs and films manage to expose more flesh than they conceal, Shohat goes on to reveal Freud's implication in the 'dark continent' trope by referring to examples of the terms used in his investigations of the female psyche:

> this process of exposing the female Other, of literally denuding her ... comes to allegorize the Western masculinist power of possession ... she, as a metaphor for her land, becomes available

for Western penetration and knowledge. This intersection of the epistemological and the sexual in colonial discourse echoes Freud's metaphor of the 'dark continent'. Freud speaks of female sexuality in metaphors of darkness and obscurity often drawn from the realms of archaeology and exploration – the metaphor of the 'dark continent', for example, deriving from a book by the Victorian explorer Stanley. Seeing himself as explorer and discoverer of new worlds, Freud . . . compared the role of the psychoanalyst to that of the archaeologist 'clearing away the pathogenic psychical material layer by layer' which is analogous 'with the technique of excavating a buried city'.

(Shohat, 1991: 57)

In attempting to engage with such a broad range of texts – her historical sweep encompasses the novel *Robinson Crusoe* and the film, *Raiders of the Lost Ark* (1981) – Shohat does not adequately differentiate between orientalist imagery and images of Africa and Africans, and thus is unable to account for the absence of black African women in all but a handful of colonialist texts. Although both 'oriental' and African women have been fantasized as hyper-sexual, this has manifested itself quite differently in representational terms. Whereas in the orientalist imagination, women of the East have a mystique, signified by the veil, black women's alleged hyper-sexuality is constructed as animalistic and voracious, as will be argued in chapter 2.

Shohat's essay is also unable to engage with what happens when 'out there' becomes 'over here' as in the case of Britain when settlers from the former colonies came to live in this country. The analysis is most useful in its discussion of how Hollywood has continued to produce orientalist fantasies where Other lands and peoples are feminized and still imagined as 'ripe' for 'penetration' and exploration. Although her discussion of the orient as a metaphor for sexuality is of interest, it does not quite fit the focus of this study on images of black Otherness.

BLACK WOMEN ON FILM

Much of the recent academic writing available on black women and their images in the cinema is from the USA and concerned with North American examples (Gaines, 1988; Bobo, 1988; Larkin, 1988; Wallace, 1990; hooks, 1991 and 1992; Jewell, 1993). An exception is bell hooks' discussions of various British films including, *Looking for Langston* (1988), *Dreaming Rivers* (1988), *The Passion of Remembrance* (1986) and *My Beautiful Launderette* (1985) in *Yearnings* (hooks, 1991) and of *The Cook, The Thief, His Wife, Her Lover* (1989) in *Black Looks* (hooks, 1992). However, most of the specific texts she cites fall outside of the parameters established by this study, as they are mainly products of the independent cinema circuit, although her comments on *Mona Lisa* (1986), and her more general remarks are useful for thinking through the relationship between 'race' and gender in contemporary representations. One other problem in her work is that she deliberately eschews a sustained methodological approach, and her film critiques are in the form of relatively short essays without conventional referencing systems which make it difficult to follow up some of the points raised.

Although black women writers based in Britain have made occasional forays into the examination of racial and gender issues raised in North American film, this is again in the form of short, more journalistically orientated analysis as opposed to sustained theoretical investigation (Stuart, 1988). Felly Nkweto Simmonds' critique of representations of black women's sexuality – centred on African–American film director Spike Lee's *She's Gotta Have It* (1986) – although it attempts to articulate a black feminist position, is really an elaboration on the notion of negative images of black female sexuality which does not have the time to develop into a more substantial argument (Simmonds, 1992). Also, its orientation is not only North American in regard to the film under consideration but also in regard to the historical context for examining representations of black women's sexuality. This scarcity of specifically British material would appear to be indicative of the lack of involvement of black women in the academy in this country and the priorities of those who do have a presence.

PSYCHOANALYTIC THEORY AND 'RACE'

There are a number of studies which indicate a potential for a productive relationship between psychoanalytic theory, historical representations and 'race' although sometimes with reservations. This is of significance to a discussion of film theory which was, particularly during the 1970s, heavily influenced by both Freudian and later, Lacanian developments in psychoanalytic theory.

An important issue to raise here is that the psychical processes and mechanisms which Freud described were considered as transcultural and ubiquitous, although there is clearly some ambivalence which relates to the Otherness of the 'primitive'. Interestingly, there is an affiliation between the Otherness of the 'primitive' and the Otherness of 'woman' and in Freud's work it is possible to detect the conflation of (white) female sexuality – particularly of those of the 'lower' social orders – with that of the unknowable and fathomless sexuality of the primitive (Freud, 1986: 313). Freud posits that sexual control is contingent on a 'civilized' social structure, whereas sexual freedom is equated with the more 'primitive' peoples who are regarded as atavistic. Thus excessive, or at least less rigorously controlled sexual expression and activity, was mapped onto the 'dark continent' by Freud. In fact, it is in that over-used, under-analysed trope of 'the dark continent' which Freud invoked to describe (European) women's sexuality, that the Otherness of the sexuality of women and that of the Africans coalesces.

Freud observes that the sexuality of children in societies at 'a low level of civilization . . . seems to be given free rein' (ibid.: 318). He notes that although this may result in communities free of neuroses, he speculates that this advantage may 'involve an extraordinary loss of the aptitude for cultural achievements' (ibid.: 318). Freud's last point is particularly interesting knowing that he had an extensive collection of artifacts and antiquities belonging to some of those 'lower races'. The work of both Mary Ann Doane and Ella Shohat points to the desirability of undertaking a study of Freud's relationship to colonialism and the ways in which his attitudes to 'race' and cultural identity might be inflected in his work on sexual difference.

An example of relatively early 'race-relations' literature which demonstrates an awareness of the deeply embedded anxieties regarding racial difference and the association with sexual fears in Britain is that written by Kenneth Little (Little, 1948). He observed the linguistic associations of black with evil and negativity and also suggested that a psychoanalytic theory of racism might be useful:

> On a psychoanalytic plane . . . it would appear as if the Negro stereotype provides a small section of English society with a convenient scapegoat and symbol into which various repressed desires and longings, and sometimes irritations, can be injected with impunity. There is a fund of risqué stories which circulate

readily in English society, in which the sexual propensities of the black man play a prominent part.

(Little, 1948: 230)

Racism, fantasy and representation have been tackled within a psychoanalytic framework by both black and white writers: of particular relevance to this study are Frantz Fanon (Martinique and France), Joel Kovel (USA), Sander L Gilman (USA) and Homi Bhabha (Britain) (Fanon, 1986; Bhabha, 1983; Gilman, 1985; Kovel, 1988). Although neither Fanon, Gilman nor Kovel write from British perspectives, it is possible to extrapolate from their particular hypotheses because they each indicate general tendencies connected with 'whiteness' as well as with the specifics of the national identities they examine.

Although Frantz Fanon – who was a trained psychiatrist – felt that psychoanalytic theory could be of use to black people he was distrustful of the uses to which it might be put: he also observed and was critical of the absence of a consideration of 'race' issues in the work of Freud, Jung and Adler. He wrote in France in the early 1950s that: 'If one wants to understand the racial situation psycho-analytically . . . as it is experienced by individual consciousness, considerable importance must be given to sexual phenomena' (Fanon, 1986: 160). His *Black Skin, White Masks* was primarily concerned with the feelings of inadequacy and inferiority to which blacks were prone as a result of colonial rule and he used psycho-analysis and psychology to describe and explain the effects of colonization and oppression on the black psyche: this study has been a reference point for those seeking to explain how some black people oppress and denigrate other black people.

However, Fanon did not restrict his enquiry to an examination of black people's internalization of racial oppression: he proposed a two-part study containing both a 'psychoanalytic interpretation of the life experience of the black man' and a 'psychoanalytic interpre-tation of the Negro myth', although he had doubts about how such a study could actually be made to work (ibid.: 151). He used psycho-analytic theory to try to analyse and understand the psychic processes which underpin white people's fantasies about black women and men (ibid.: 151).

Significantly, Fanon argues that neurosis is not a universal, fundamental component of the human psyche and that the Oedipus complex is absent among 'Negroes' (ibid.: 151). There is also a level on which Fanon concurs with Freud as he claims: 'Every intellectual gain requires a loss in sexual potency' (ibid.: 165). This is interesting because despite having set out on separate paths, both Freud and Fanon posit that the colonial subject may be without the neuroses which plague the colonizer.

However, for black people, the psychological problems which result from the encounter with white racism structure their experience of the world. Indeed, as the category 'black' is a white supremacist construction, '*It is the racist who creates his inferior*' (his italics) (ibid.: 93). Fanon argues that: 'As long as the black man is among his own, he will have no occasion, except in minor conflicts, to experience his being through others. (ibid.: 109).

During the 1960s there was a surge of interest in Fanon's work; certainly the Black Power Movement and other oppressed groups who were organizing politically gained valuable insights from his writing. In the USA, during the late 1960s, black power activist Stokely Carmichael advised white psychologists to 'stop investigating and examining people of colour, they ought to investigate and examine their own corrupt society.'[7] Joel Kovel, the white radical psychologist, took up the challenge issued by Stokely Carmichael, writing *White Racism: A Psychohistory*, first published in 1970 (Kovel, 1988).

Kovel describes two main types of racist: the dominative racist who acts out her or his supremacist beliefs with the overt intention of subjugating blacks; and the aversive racist. Kovel did not consider these types to be definitive, inasmuch as he recognized the shifting nature of bigoted beliefs and that there were bound to be overlapping psychological and behavioural features.

The aversive racist is a complex 'ideal type' according to Kovel and may experience a range of feelings and actions which vary in intensity and level of development. If an aversive racist perceives a threat from blacks because they are getting too close – for example, too many moving into a neighbourhood or too frequent socializing with young white people – action, motivated by a deep-seated belief in white superiority will follow. Disconcertingly, aversive racists frequently appear 'liberal' and 'tolerant', seemingly supporting struggles for black liberation: yet beneath this veneer of ideologically correct activity, they maintain the features of aversion, avoiding intimate contact with black people (Kovel, 1988; 60).

Avoiding issues raised by interracial sexual relationships and maintaining a distance from any activity which may be interpreted as interracial intimacy is one of the manifestations of a strategy of aversion. This can be identified as a consistent feature of films made by white people: there is a constant refusal to relate intimately to black people's knowledge and experiences, despite protestations to the contrary.

Although these types have been developed in the context of a history of 'race' relations in the USA, it is worth noting how such observations may be re-inflected in a British context. For example, I would argue that in relation to cinematic representation, aversive racism is clearly evidenced by the continuing absence of significant black characters in contemporary settings and the frequent refuge taken in period pieces where, presumably in ignorance, white writers and directors still seem unable to grasp the point that black people have been living in this country, undergoing a full spectrum of emotional experiences, for several hundred years. Kovel's formulation of aversive racism echoes Fanon's description of black people as phobogenic – stimuli to anxiety in white people, and for most white film-makers it would appear that 'distance becomes a singularly effective mode of defensive adaptation'(Kovel, 1988: 61): an effective strategy for avoiding confronting racial anxieties. There are many creative opportunities afforded by the long history of a culturally plural society to depict the diversity of black experiences which are avoided. The practice of aversive racism may be seen as a significant feature of white British mainstream, independent and 'art' cinema.

Progress in understanding the deep structures of the mind which contribute to the perpetuation of racism has been slow and the questions that Fanon posed have direct relevance to the way in which racial positions are conceptualized in British society today. As previously indicated, in regard to the cinema Mulvey pointed out that in most mainstream films it is the female who is subjected to and subordinated by the male look: as Bhabha demonstrates, reference back to Fanon reminds us that looking has been racialized too.

Homi K. Bhabha's essay 'The Other Question. . .' represents a significant shift in terms and methodology from earlier discussions about Otherness and its articulation in colonialist cinematic discourses. Using film, but also referring to the administrative and juridical spheres, he suggests that the stereotype is the major discursive strategy of colonial discourse. It is a form of knowledge that oscillates between what is already 'known' and is always in place, and something which must be constantly and anxiously repeated in order to sustain its credibility. Bhabha points to the way in which colonial discourse is marked by the recognition and disavowal of racial, cultural and historical differences, and he poses a series of questions:

> What is this theory of encapsulation or fixation which moves between the recognition of cultural and racial difference and its disavowal, by affixing the unfamiliar to something established, in a form that is repetitious and vacillates between delight and fear? Is it not analogous to the Freudian fable of fetishism (and disavowal) that circulates within the discourse of colonial power, requiring the articulation of modes of differentiation – sexual and racial – as well as different modes of discourse – psychoanalytic and historical?
>
> (Bhabha, 1983: 26)

There is an interesting slip in Bhabha's retelling of the verbal motif which runs through Fanon's chapter, 'The Fact of Blackness' (Fanon, 1986). Bhabha writes:

> On one occasion a white girl fixes Fanon in a look and word as she turns to identify with her mother . . . It is a scene which echoes endlessly through his essay *The Fact of Blackness*: "*Look*, a Negro . . . Mamma, *see* the Negro! I'm frightened. Frightened. Frightened."
>
> (ibid.: 28)

This is designated by Bhabha as a primal scene. Bhabha then goes on to say:

> The girl's gaze returns to her mother in the recognition and disavowal of the Negroid type; the black child turns away from himself in his total identification with the positivity of whiteness which is at once colour and no colour. In the act of disavowal and fixation the colonial subject is returned to the narcissism of the Imaginary and its identification of an ideal ego that is white and whole.
>
> (ibid.: 28)

Two points arise here, and I am raising them because they indicate some of crucial areas yet to be adequately addressed by male critics in their own work, and which compound the marginalization of black gender issues. First, Bhabha invests these scenes in Fanon's work with importance because they deal with looking and surveil-

lance and their role in the formation of racially defined subjectivities. Although he does not say so, the italics are his own and in each
reference, Bhabha refers to the white child who looks to confirm its
identity as white, as being female. However, the translation of
Fanon's text reads as follows:

> "Mama, see the Negro! I'm frightened!" Frightened! Frightened!
> Now they were beginning to be afraid of me ... "Look at the
> nigger! ... Mama, a Negro! ... Hell, he's getting mad .... Take
> no notice, sir, he does not know that you are as civilized as we
> ...."
>
> My body was given back to me sprawled out, distorted,
> recolored, clad in mourning in that white winter day. The Negro
> is an animal, the Negro is bad, the Negro is mean, the Negro is
> ugly; look, a nigger, it's cold, the nigger is shivering because he
> is cold, the little *boy* [my italics] is trembling because he is afraid
> of the nigger, the nigger is shivering with cold, that cold that goes
> through your bones, the handsome little *boy* [my italics] is
> trembling because he thinks that the nigger is quivering with rage,
> the little white *boy* [my italics] throws himself into his mother's
> arms: Mama, the nigger's going to eat me up.
>
> (Fanon, 1986: 112 – 114)

Bhabha quotes the section about the boy later and with no direct
commentary on it: why not? (Bhabha, 1983: 34). The gender
emphasis/change is significant because of the uneven way in which
power is distributed between white women and men.[8] The look is
held by the young white male, thereby underscoring the differential
power allocated to males in racially and sexually stratified societies.
The look is particularly charged when it crosses the colour line
because of its historical association with the regulation of sexual
activity between black and white (particularly in relation to black
men). This little white boy looks at this adult male who is black and
sees not a larger version of himself but a black phantasm that quivers
and sweats under his infantile but powerful gaze. It is important that
this is a white *boy* because in the next chapter, 'The Negro and
Psychopathology' Fanon writes, in a long footnote, about Lacan's
concept of the mirror phase thus:

> When one has grasped the mechanism described by Lacan, one
> can have no further doubt that the real Other for the white man is
> and will continue to be the black man. And conversely. Only for

the white man the Other is perceived on the level of the body image, absolutely as the not-self – that is, the unidentifiable, the unassimilable. For the black man, as we have shown, historical and economic realities come into the picture.

(Fanon, 1986: 161)

In this account of the relationship between the black male body and the threat it poses to white male subjectivity, Fanon identifies black men as being the white man's Other. This Other is necessary for self-definition and thus becomes an object used to nurture love of the self. In this context, the significance of the mirror phase is that it provides an illusory coherent identity for the white male ego. The sense of coherence provided during the mirror phase may be seen as analogous to the fallacy of wholeness that is provided through narcissistic identification in the cinema. Narratives which disrupt and undermine that sense of integrity do not provide the same kind of pleasures as those which affirm it.

In arguing for understanding and analysing stereotypes as a colonial discursive strategy from within a psychoanalytic framework, it is important to address some difficulties and contradictions concerning psychoanalytic theory and racial difference and which emerge from Bhabha's essay. Bhabha privileges discursive and psychical strategies and mechanisms without adequately indicating how the material reality of life under colonial rule was affected by the ideological work of stereotypes. Also, Bhabha privileges the colonizer's role without a consideration of either the effect on, or resistance offered by, the colonized subject.

Freud's challenge to the ideology of liberal humanism through the decentering of the subject from its pivotal position – the omniscient 'bourgeois' individual – constituted a major upheaval in the way in which the notion of subjectivity and consciousness were considered: it was a revolutionary thesis. However, psychoanalysis has frequently been appropriated to serve as an instrument of oppression and rehabilitation into social conformity by dominant forms of Western psychotherapeutic practice: there is plenty of evidence to suggest that many institutional procedures have oppressed black people in a number of ways. Bhabha does not express reservations about the use of psychoanalysis as a cultural theory: neither does he refer to any difficulty or tension which might exist because of what might be characterized as the cultural and temporal specificity of psychoanalytic theory or its lack of an historical and material base.

Importantly, psychoanalytic discourse is not subjected to a rigorous examination in terms of its own location within, and relationship to, colonial discourse.

With the exception of Sander L. Gilman – whose work will be examined in the context of a discussion of difference and Otherness which follows this section – none of these male writers has adequately engaged with the specific issues raised by gender and sexual difference in the discourse of 'race'. Fanon, although he occasionally discusses black and white women, does not identify the specificities of black women's experience of slavery and colonialism apart from in the context of a consideration of black women's alleged preference for white male sexual partners. His comments regarding white women's sexual desire will be discussed more fully in chapter 4.

Kovel does recognize particular characterizations of black women but these are dealt with within a Marxist/psychoanalytic framework which subsumes gender difference under class struggle and only spasmodically recognizes women as a different analytical category. Bhabha recognizes his lack of a gender-based analysis but does not suggest the extent to which this may undermine his approach.

CONCEPTUALIZING DIFFERENCE AND OTHERNESS

Crucial to the comprehension of how psychoanalytic theory describes the construction of Otherness is an understanding of projection and how it may be deployed to explicate racist attitudes.

According to Laplanche and Pontalis:

> Projection emerges . . . as the primal means of defence against those endogenous excitations whose intensity makes them too unpleasurable: the subject projects these outside so as to be able to flee from them (e.g. phobic avoidance) and protect himself from them . . . the subject now finds himself obliged to believe completely in something that is henceforth subject to the laws of external reality.
>
> (Laplanche and Pontalis, 1988: 352)

In Freudian terms then, projection describes the process whereby the subject attributes the intolerable passions and inclinations – intolerable because considered to be manifestations of the 'bad' self – to others that she or he is unable to accept in her- or himself. Thus the racist will deny or disavow her or his own fears and disposition, repressing them into the unconscious and projecting these intolerable feelings on to the despised racial group. Denial or disavowal, and projection are not to be considered as clearly delineated sequential phases of development but rather as a complex interweaving of overlapping processes.

In order to understand why difference is so important and how differentiation may develop as racism, it is necessary to understand the process of differentiation in early infancy and its place in the developing human being. Sander L. Gilman makes the point that the context for the process of differentiation in early infancy is similar to the context within which stereotypes are to be found and thus has important implications for this study (Gilman, 1985: 17).

According to psychoanalytic theory, in the very early stages of an infant's life, the baby has no conscious appreciation of itself as itself: once it becomes aware of the difference between itself and the world around it, the infant experiences anxiety as the result of a perception of a loss of control over the fulfilling of its needs and desires. The anxieties which arise from the perception of 'lost' control are repressed by mentally splitting the self and the world-picture of people and objects into 'good' and 'bad'. The 'good' self was originally in control of everything and thus free from anxiety: the 'bad' self has no control over the infant's environment and is prone to suffering apprehension. Contradictions raised by the confrontation between the 'good' and 'bad' facets of the self are painful and difficult to deal with, therefore:

> the 'bad' self is distanced and identified with the mental representation of the 'bad' object . . . The deep structure of our sense of self is built upon the illusionary image of the world divided into two camps, 'us' and 'them'. 'They' are either 'good' or 'bad'.
> (Gilman, 1985: 17)

The relationship between the construction of difference and general stereotyping is particularly potent when applied to notions of racial difference predicated on skin colour.

> In 'seeing' (constructing a representational system for) the Other, we search for anatomical signs of difference such as physiognomy and skin color. The Other's physical features, from skin colour to sexual structures such as the shape of the genitalia, are always the antithesis of the idealized self's.

(ibid.: 25)

Those who belong to a 'different' people are invested with all the qualities of the 'bad' or occasionally the 'good' (as in the colonial myth of the good native, loyal and submissive). Black people come to embody the threat to the illusion of order and control and represent the polar opposite to the white group.

According to Gilman, differences are constructed through the process of creating distinct categorizations which assist in the production and maintenance of an illusory order in a chaotic and fragmented world. People who appear to disturb the boundaries of those categorizations represent a further threat and are doubly problematic. It becomes difficult to pinpoint the qualities which constitute racial and sexual difference if the demarcation lines are unclear. The anxiety which the creation of the Other was initially intended to alleviate is reactivated and brought to bear on the phobogenic objects: these Others may often be people regarded as 'transgressive' in some way and recategorized as 'mixed race' or homosexual. Having constructed racial difference as Otherness, 'intermixing' becomes an unthinkable act, any desire for which has to be repressed.

Scientific racist ideologies, racial myths, and stereotypical characterizations in theatrical, literary and visual culture are enactments which materialize from the cycle of repression and projection, as are individual, institutional and state racisms. Embedded in this psychic process are distortion, ambivalence and contradiction and it is underpinned by guilt and denial. These processes interact in a complex manner with economic and other imperatives.[9]

WHITENESS, BLACKNESS AND FEMININITY

There has recently been a recognition of the need to undertake analyses of whiteness without maintaining and intensifying the privileged position assigned to it. White people in general are unused to regarding themselves as members of ethnic groups or as having an ethnic or racial identity beyond that of being superior in relation to Others. Richard Dyer's exploration of the trope of whiteness in British and North American cinema was instrumental in making whiteness on film visible. He suggests that within the cultural framework which sustains the construction of black as Other, white has no categorical status: it is the norm against which everything else is measured with no need of self-definition (Dyer, 1988). Although this deconstructive work on whiteness is necessary, it should not become yet another opportunity for white experiences and attitudes to be foregrounded.

White feminist cultural theorists have been slow to recognize the significance of the historical relationship between white women and black women. Indeed, feminism failed to make much impact upon the understanding of racism until very recently and then due largely to interventions made by African–American and black British-based feminists. It has been pointed out that privilege is unevenly distributed amongst white women and men, and lack of privilege is unequally spread amongst black women and men: there are, of course, differences regarding class, sexuality and physical appearance, thus analyses that engage with 'race', gender and class are necessary in order to address the interconnections between these aspects of human subjectivity. Gaps and absences in critical theory need to be exposed, one of which concerns the way in which white women's position as partners in ensuring the viability and health of the 'race', have afforded them a relatively privileged position both in reality and in cinematic representation.

To return to the subject of film theory, there are a number of inter-connected points I wish to make here. Without at least being informed by the issues raised in the material above regarding 'race', feminist film criticism is impoverished through being unable to take cognizance of white women's collusion in racial oppression, their relatively privileged social status and the ways in which this is manifested in visual culture, whether or not black people are present. White feminists have tended to deny that because of the histories of colonialism and imperialism, gender and sexuality are articulated through a racialized discursive field which renders any critical account of gender a racial issue as well.

If it is accepted, as feminists have argued, that cinematic forms connive in reproducing the ideology which underpins patriarchy, then it should also be recognized that cinema is complicit in the structuring and naturalizing of power relations between black and white people.

IDEOLOGY, REALISM AND BLACK CINEMA

Although the bulk of the films discussed have been written and directed by white men there are several films included which have involved the creative involvement of black men. Sustained critical work on these latter texts is minimal representing yet another instance of black people's work being excluded from serious critical consideration. The bulk of more recent critical work on the production of black film has concentrated on contemporary independent film production, though even this critical material has been sporadic and mainly in essay form.

A major piece of writing from this body of work is Kobena Mercer's essay, 'Diaspora Culture and the Dialogic Imagination' (Mercer, 1988). There is an underlying assumption in his commentary that the work of black film-makers should resist cultural and ideological assimilation in two respects. First, in terms of the content of their films, they should take a political position in opposition to the dominant, racist ideologies underpinning texts constructed by the 'white' mainstream. This action is deemed most productive politically if it is linked with a second level of resistance to dominant values: the problematization of realist aesthetics. Thus the form of a text should mark a distinctive break with the conventional ways of representing reality. These proscriptions echo those of the editorial collective of Cahiers du Cinema (Comolli and Narboni, 1976: 23).

These realist conventions are such as those discussed by Colin MacCabe in 'Realism and the Cinema: Notes on Some Brechtian Theses' in which he posited that realism should not be defined by its content or by its capacity to mirror reality but by the way in which the text's organization functions to position the spectator or reader (MacCabe, 1985). MacCabe also identified classic realism as a reactionary form of representation because of its discursive limitations. The classic realist text as described by MacCabe, is defined by a structure in which the various discourses within the text form a hierarchy: among these discourses – each one of which proposes a particular view of 'reality' – one is privileged as the bearer of truth and serves as a gauge by which the veracity or falsity of other, competing discourses are judged. Contradictory discourses are contained and framed by a dominant discourse and it is argued that in all cases, contradictory discourses are neutralized by the dominant, privileged discourse. MacCabe claims that in cinema, what is seen is privileged over what is heard. [10]

Monolithic views on realist aesthetics are problematic for a number of reasons. Perhaps most importantly, such positions deny the spectator autonomy, rendering her or him dependent on what is always an unstable and negotiable set of meanings. Such a view of realism does not allow for oppositional or contradictory meanings or misinterpretations of authors' work. Part of MacCabe's argument is that realism does not encourage the spectator to develop a perspective on struggle or conceptualize the possibility of transformation and this also needs interrogation. There is a tendency towards closure in realist narratives, an attempt to tell the 'truth' about a given situation, but this can never be consistently achieved, is always contested by the polysemic nature of the images and the process of image construction, analysis and interpretation. I would also argue that a discussion about the power of the text's metadiscourse without a recognition of the power relations that inform the construction and readings of the text, is incomplete. These aspects of textual analysis are underplayed by both Mercer and MacCabe.

The cinema is concerned – particularly in realist texts – with reproducing accounts and definitions which strive to sustain beliefs in particular ideas and institutions. Often these ideologies are not identified as such, but rather exist as common-sense notions which become 'naturalized' and to which people become habituated.

In his essay 'Ideology and Ideological State Apparatuses'(1988), Althusser names the cinema as one of the constituents of the Ideological State Apparatus (ISA). Althusser argues that the ISAs contribute to the process of reproducing the relations of production – that is the social relations necessary for the existence and continuation of the capitalist mode of production. It is held that the ISAs re-present the myths and the imaginary versions of real social relationships which constitute ideology. Also – and this is especially pertinent in relation to realist cinema – the text interpellates the reader or spectator and offers them the position from which the text is obviously comprehendible: thus the position of the reader is that of the subject in and of ideology (Belsey, 1980: 56). Althusser's work was particularly influential with film theorists from the mid to late 1970s as his work became available in Britain (Belsey, 1980: 56; Lovell, 1983; Lapsley and Westlake, 1983: 23; White, 1992: 161; Eagleton, 1992: 170). The potential for thinking about being positioned as a 'white' or 'black' subject was not explored. [11] This is surprising since it was argued that ideologies are concerned with images and myths, the 'languages' through which human beings are encouraged to make sense of the world and there are a multiplicity of myths and fantasies concerning 'race'. This lack of an examination of the extent to which people are interpellated as racialized subjects is indicative of a wider lack of awareness regarding the significance of Europe's colonial heritage and the extent to which issues of 'race' are implicated in discursive practices.

Notions of truth and reality may become established in society through being constantly reiterated and eventually naturalized through ideology and discourse. The Foucauldian concept of discourse is useful for identifying specific groupings of signs and ideologies which relate to particular fields of knowledge. The study of discourse concerns the ways in which forms of 'knowledge' are produced through language and other signifying systems: the most important aspect of discourse is that it is a socially constructed mode of speaking, writing or representation formed out of elements of ideology, backed by class or institutional power/dominance, and informed and circumscribed by the parameters of its historical usage. According to Michel Foucault, it is power rather than facts which give things the appearance of truth. Foucault argues that:

> We should admit that power produces knowledge . . . that power and knowledge directly imply one another; that there is no power relation without the correlative constitution of a field of knowledge, nor any knowledge that does not presuppose and constitute . . . power relations.

> (Foucault, 1977: 27)

What masquerades or becomes known as 'pure' knowledge or as 'fact', or – as is argued in chapter 2 – 'science', is often an ideology or ideologies articulated through a discourse or discursive practices.

It was suggested at the beginning of this chapter that the attempt to represent the reality of 'the black experience' needs to be interrogated. One important point to note here is that black women do not often have the power to contribute to dominant definitions of reality and black women have not made a significant contribution as writer or director to any of the films which fall inside the parameters of this study. The notion of a 'real' or 'authentic' black representation is especially problematic if it is posited that such a representation is possible from a singular, black perspective. This position is worrisome because such a stance implies that the answer to negative, stereotypical images is to produce 'truthful' or 'realistic' representations. The assumption here is that somehow it is possible to claim unmediated access to an essential black subjectivity, to speak with an 'authentic voice' of 'the black experience'. Although such subjectivities only exist in the realms of mythology, outside of the confines of academia and abstract intellectual debates, anecdotal evidence suggests that many black people still crave positive images and are disappointed with white and black film-makers who do not accommodate such ideas.

Theories of ideology, representation, reality and the diversity of black experiences were not addressed in most of the early critical work on 'race' and representation. These works are mainly concerned with the truthfulness of images of black people and do not attempt to analyse the complex interrelationship between text, representation, referent and viewers that more recent developments in theories of cultural reproduction have indicated.

SUMMARY

Many cinematic images of black women and men obsessively repeat well-worn stereotypes of black femininity and masculinity. Analyses of textual practices based solely on the text have often been inadequate: critical accounts of the functioning of film representations should consider the social and historical context within which the textual practice is located and this will be a constant concern of the analyses which follow.

In order to try and make sense of such images, it is necessary to be aware of, and examine historical instances of the process of racialization of discourses on 'woman' and 'man' and the complex interaction between these axes. Thus, in chapter 2, I consider the ways in which particular ideas about sexuality and 'race' have been conceptualized historically.

Chapter 2

Notes on the discourse of 'race'

In this chapter, by analysing discourses of 'race', gender and sexuality, I will establish the means by which language and other systems of representation have produced a specific set of 'knowledges' about 'race' and sex. I will draw on particular historical discourses in order to demonstrate the pervasiveness of manifestations of the fears and desires associated with black women and men. It is necessary to indicate how notions of racial difference came to be naturalized since I argue that it is these ideas which have informed the work of white film-makers and set the parameters for black film-makers' responses to their representation in the cinema.

The first section of this chapter problematizes the notion of 'race' and the assumptions which underpin its discourses. This is followed by a historical account of the development of racialized discourses with specific reference to eighteenth century philosophy and science and an indication of how ideologies about sex, 'race' and gender developed during this early colonialist period. Colonialism is here defined as the process by which European powers pursued economic, political and cultural dominance in Asia, Africa, Latin America and Ireland: it reached its peak during the early years of the twentieth century. From this I demonstrate that beliefs about the dangers of interracial sexual activity have been expressed over a period of at least two hundred years. The pathologization of interracial sex is further discussed in the context of eugenicist precepts up until the 1950s. The penultimate section is concerned with how these ideologies became embedded in the discursive practices of photography and cinema and their link with scientific discourses of the eighteenth century. This material serves both as a general introduction to the themes to be dealt with and also as a preamble to detailed analyses of the issues and predicaments located in the films that are discussed in later chapters.

WHAT IS 'RACE'?

Working with a concept such as 'race' is fraught with difficulties since although it is held that such a designation has no scientific value but is an ideological construct, racialized discourses are pervasive and have to be engaged with. It is a problem which goes beyond an issue of definition since it affects the way in which identities are formed and social interaction experienced on a day to day basis. Although the division of people into racial categories is often based on the valorization of the primacy of phenotypical features – the visual signifiers of difference – it is generally accepted that biological definitions of 'race' which date back to at least the eighteenth century are spurious.[1] 'Race' is not, then, an objective culture-free designation of difference and neither is the labelling of skin colour. Sander L. Gilman argues that 'the very concept of color is a quality of Otherness, not of reality' (Gilman, 1985: 30), since Jewish and Irish people have at various times been designated 'black'.

As Phil Cohen remarks:

> 'race' ... is an ideological construct, not an empirical social category; as such it signifies a set of imaginary properties of inheritance which fix and legitimate real positions of social domination or subordination in terms of genealogies of generic difference.
>
> (Cohen, 1988: 23)

However the belief that there are fundamental, essential differences between black and white people persists and is difficult to dispel, resulting in the ascription of particular psychological, physical and intellectual characteristics to different 'races'.

To further complicate the issue, the matrix of perceptions associated with these notions make it virtually impossible to separate the connotations of the word 'race' from its denotative meaning. These meanings are tangled together and locked into a value-laden system of binary oppositions. In this system, black is a potent signifier of evil, of dirt, of that which is alien: whereas white signifies goodness, purity and that which is familiar, the norm.

It would be unjustified to claim that it was simply because 'black' had an extensive set of negative connotations that Africans have been thought of as inferior: however, it is probable that the binarism of the signifiers 'black' and 'white' was sufficiently entrenched to facilitate a mode of thinking which justified an economically driven black enslavement, on moral grounds. The African's skin colour became the defining characteristic, and 'black', from operating at a connotative level shifted to a denotative plane: to be black was to *be* evil, to *be* hypersexual, to *be* morally debased, to *be* inferior.

A purely economic analysis of the defensive strategies of the slave-owning plantocracy and the emerging mercantile capitalists is unable to work through the complexities which developed in regard to 'race' during the eighteenth and nineteenth century and which have continued since then. As Albert Memmi states in his preface to *The Colonizer and the Colonized*:

> To observe the life of the colonizer and the colonized is to discover rapidly that the humiliation of the colonized, his objective subjugation, are not merely economic. Even the poorest colonizer thought himself to be – and was – superior to the colonized. This too was part of colonial privilege. The Marxist discovery of the importance of the economy in all oppressive relationships is not the point. This relationship has other characteristics.
>
> (Memmi, 1990: 10)

The institutionalization of racism, the scientific justifications for dominance seem to go beyond what is necessary in order to sustain the economic system, a point on which Frantz Fanon concurs.[2] The diversity of the sources of popular images of racial difference, the complexities of their development and the relationship between the past and contemporary political issues, means that it is impossible to produce a neat, seamless explanation for the maintenance of racist ideologies and their absorption into the fabric of this society. Racism is not attributable to a single factor such as capitalism, the colonial enterprise or personal prejudice. It appears to be a complex interweaving of all these factors, in a continual state of flux and subject to the political, social and economic imperatives of the particular moment.

'RACE' DISCOURSE AND THE DEVELOPMENT OF 'RACE THINKING'

Before the fifteenth century, people in Britain knew little about ancient African domains and the 'knowledge' disseminated about Africa was largely based on myths and fantastic travellers' tales (Fryer, 1984: 6). In addition, images of the 'good/white' overcoming the 'evil/black' were a recurring theme in Biblical art and images of blacks as lascivious, childlike and demonic, were derived, in part from the Bible itself. Indeed, one of the standard biblical 'explanations' for people having black skins originated from the story of the curse of Ham whom God made black-skinned for looking at his naked father lying drunk in a tent. The fabric of racist ideologies, and the justification for slavery and the brutal economic exploitation of African and other peoples was woven from this multifaceted concoction of fear, ignorance, myth and fable.

The emergence of a discursive field such as 'race' is dependent upon particular elements being in place at specific moments. The mid-eighteenth century through to the first decades of the nineteenth century are essential to an understanding of how various racisms became so fundamental to the self-perceptions of Britain and western Europe. Even before that, in the seventeenth century, for white Europeans in general, colour was considered to be an essential property of human subjectivity. Empirical observation provided 'evidence' of racial difference through skin colour and black skin was correlated with what was characterized as an incapacity for rational thought.

The idea that placing people into 'races' was a scientific mode of human classification can be traced back to the eighteenth century when science was emerging as an important discourse of 'truth' and:

> The neutrality and objectifying distantiation of the rational scientist created the theoretical space for a view to develop of subjectless bodies. Once objectified, these bodies could be analysed, categorized, classified, and ordered with the cold gaze of scientific distance.
>
> (Goldberg, 1993: 50)

For a study of the development of the racialization of scientific discourse, one of the most compelling characteristics of scientific enquiry of this period is this drive to order and to categorize. Empiricism contributed to the creation of the conditions whereby taxonomies and hierarchical ordering could flourish. This was due to its role in tabulating what were perceived as the essential, *visible* differences between different groups of human beings.[3] Important also was that Enlightenment thinkers thought it imperative to trace the evolutionary progress which was conceived of as a linear progression from primitive savagery to advanced civilization: they took themselves to be exemplars of the highest peak of cultivation.

An apparent contradiction of the eighteenth century is that, in an age when the notion of equality as a moral imperative was alleged to be pervasive, it seems anomalous that slavery, racial subordination and genocide were rampant. These two strands – egalitarianism and domination – were able to co-exist because Enlightenment philosophers who were ostensibly committed to the idea of equality, liberty and fraternity only extended this notion to those who were considered to be rational beings. A definition of rationality was constructed which excluded groups of people from outside of western Europe, excluded those considered to be low down in the social order, excluded those who did not own property and excluded women (Goldberg, 1993: 27). Thus, in addition to economic power – generated by a capitalism which was still at a developmental stage – the power to define which differences were important and which were not, combined with the power to produce 'knowledge' through empirical observations of difference, and provided the conceptual predicates for the rise of racist ideologies.

The body of ideas and writings which has become known as 'pseudoscientific' racism is important because it was not merely upheld by extremists existing on the margins of European society: it was the orthodox approach to explanations of difference and the justification of brutal economic exploitation (Gould, 1981; Stepan, 1982; Fryer, 1984; Gilman, 1985; Goldberg 1993).[4] It is also important because the idea of different, inferior 'races' established during the eighteenth century by scientists, philosophers and planters and so on systematized and legitimated racial prejudice and discrimination and enshrined it in social policies and in the law.

BEAUTY, RACE AND GENDER

Sander L. Gilman's work has also indicated the extent to which notions of black hypersexuality and its concomitant threat to white sexual propriety, became connected to conceptualizations of female sexuality: most notably to that of 'deviants' such as lesbians and 'lower class' female prostitutes (Gilman, 1985: 76). Thus class, gender, sexuality and racial difference can be seen as part of a matrix of ideas in which the white, bourgeois male at the centre was perceived as the norm and thus left unexamined, whilst the identities of those seen as 'Other' were constantly interrogated, investigated and monitored.

A number of feminist writers have identified:

> a set of conceptual dichotomies within which Enlightenment science and epistemology are constructed: reason vs. emotion and social value, mind vs. body, culture vs. nature, self vs. others, objectivity vs. subjectivity, knowing vs. being. In each dichotomy, the former is to control the latter lest the latter threaten to overwhelm the former, and the threatening 'latter' in each case appears to be systematically associated with 'the feminine'.
>
> (Harding, 1986: 165)

They have also recognized that this set of dichotomies holds true in regard to racial subjugation as well as patriarchal dominance. There is a congruence between the Otherness of the female, and the Otherness of the 'primitive' or the black for the white male, with the subordinated elements in the set of dichotomies referred to above being the property of the primitive black (Harding, 1986: 163; Torgovnick, 1990).[5] It would be reductive, however, to suggest that the two forms of oppression were the same. Both have their own specificities as well as intersecting at various points. It is important to consider the extent to which white women may become representatives of whiteness *qua* culture, rationality and so on in comparison to black men and women; and the intensified negation of whiteness and masculinity as embodied by black women. That such a combination of differences causes anxiety and confusion can be inferred from a significant number of literary and cinematic texts, from restrictive legislation and from the objectification of black – predominantly female – bodies for the purposes of scientific enquiry, as will be demonstrated.

The study of skull shapes – known as craniology – made a significant contribution to scientific racism and helped to consolidate notions of physical beauty. Such studies had started in the eighteenth century and the theory was initially advanced by Johann Blumenbach who thought the shape of the skulls of people he designated Caucasian to be the most beautiful form. The Dutch anatomist Pieter Camper, dissatisfied with Blumenbach's craniological methodology, concluded that the wider the angle, the higher the forehead, the bigger the brain, the more intelligent and beautiful. In a comparative study of African facial angles, there is a return to the animalistic, simian visual analogy with Camper finding 'a striking resemblance between the race of Monkies and of blacks' (quoted in Fryer, 1984: 167).

Notions of beauty were further racialized during the eighteenth century and there is evidence of a conjunction of ideas relating economic wealth to the 'wealth of good looks'. References to physical beauty have to be problematized as these have always been an oppressive concept particularly for women. Standardized notions of beauty are one reason why black women's appearances in mainstream cinema have been so limited. Images of white European women as the standard of beauty are pervasive: those images are the polar opposite of and yet dependent on images of black women's femininity and sexuality as I argue later in this chapter. The difficulty of beauty becomes even more acute when considered in relation to black women and the roots of the valorization of white skinned women over black go back many years.[6] Goldberg argues that in the nineteenth century the notion of beauty was linked to economic wealth and racialized:

> Beauty, for classical aesthetics, was a property, possession of which determined subjects' ontological value, just as possession of economic goods for classical economics created utility . . . To lack the 'natural' qualities of classical beauty was to be poor; and as with *laissez faire* economic theory, this was considered to be the subject's own responsibility. By the late eighteenth century, beauty was established in terms of racial properties: fair skin, straight hair, orgnathous jaw, skull shape and size, well-composed bodily proportions and so on.
>
> (Goldberg, 1993: 30)

It is at this moment that hierarchies founded on sexual, racial and class differences were systematised and intertwined (Goldberg, 1993: 28).

INTERRACIAL SEX: A SHORT HISTORY

As discussed in chapter 1, Fanon asserted that in order to understand 'Negrophobia', an investigation of the sexual predicates of this psychic phenomenon was necessary. In the initial research into the films produced by white film-makers, it became clear that the issue of interracial sexual activity constituted a significant taboo area, which although perhaps not quite as emotionally charged as in the

USA, has been – and continues to be – a powerful motif in British culture. An investigation of historical writing reveals that the set of ideas and myths attached to interracial sex go back centuries and appear to be founded on a number of justifications for keeping racial groups in their separate social, sexual and geographic spheres.[7]

To early white invaders, the most obvious and arresting features of Africans were their skin colour and their relatively exposed bodies. Due to the latter, freedom of sexual activity was assumed and Africans were considered to be on a par with animals in their inability to control their sexual desire and thus inferior to the civilized whites (Walvin, 1973; Jordan, 1974).[8] Abhorrence of interracial sexual relationships was evident during the sixteenth century, and predates the peak of slavery as this comment by George Best in 1578, clearly indicates:

> I myselfe have seen an Ethiopian as blacke as cole brought into England, who taking an English wife, begat a sonne in all respects as blacke as the father was ... whereby it seemeth that blackness proceedeth rather of some natural infection of that man, which was so strong, that neither the nature of the clime, neither the good complexion of the mother concurring, could anything alter, and therefore we cannot impute it to the nature of the clime.
> (Walvin, 1973: 20)

Even in this short passage, it is possible to discern the anxiety and fascination occasioned by this relationship, as well as the long history of interracial sexual relationships in what is almost always represented as an all-white Elizabethan England.[9] There is the compulsion to attribute a cause to differences in skin colouring (here, a rejection of climatic, in favour of biological determinism); there is the pathologization of blackness which posits that it is an infection, an idea which was still in existence some three hundred years later; and there is the attribution of 'good' to a white woman's complexion.[10] In addition, James Walvin argues that: 'Even before the European encroachment on West Africa, there was a widespread belief that the African possessed an unusually large penis' (ibid.: 22). Thus the myth of black male hypersexuality existed before the peak of colonial expansion.

By the mid-eighteenth century, it was a commonly held view that sub-Saharan Africans were a different species to white Europeans, rather than a variety of the same species. This distinction was significant since if a racial group was designated as belonging to a separate species, then it would be assumed that sexual union between black and white people would be highly undesirable and result in infertile children. By the end of the eighteenth century, black people were frequently characterized as representing sexual deviancy: furthermore, theories of natural selection were appropriated and used to validate the belief that the superior white group would be detrimentally transformed by mixing with other 'inferior' groups, particularly black people.

Thus it can be seen that there was a set of myths and fantasies in place regarding black inferiority, the undesirability of 'mixing races', and black hypersexuality which led to the pathologization of interracial relationships. As Walvin notes:

> This belief [in black sexual prowess] shared by both white men and women, became something of an institution in the course of the eighteenth century and was used to explain or deride mixed unions. The strength of, and widespread support for this myth was perhaps one of the most powerful factors in moulding the racial attitudes between the two sides.
>
> (Walvin, 1973: 53)

Two comments from Edward Long – written in the late eighteenth century – indicate the depth of feeling engendered by interracial sexual relationships and the interaction between class, gender and racial difference: 'The lower order of [white] women are remarkably fond of the blacks for reasons too brutal to mention' (Walvin, 1973: 52-55) and – referring to the issue of 'miscegenation' – he too invokes the pathological model in his comment that it is: 'a venomous and dangerous ulcer that threatens to disperse its malignancy far and wide, until every family catches infection from it' (quoted in Walvin, 1973: 52). Long had no more favourable remarks to make regarding black women of whom he said: 'Ludicrous as it may seem I do not think that an oran-outang husband would be any dishonour to an Hottentot female' (quoted in Walvin, 1973: 169). Buffon, a French naturalist linked black women to simians when he claimed that they were prone to such uncontrollable lust that they frequently had sex with gorillas, and this association of animal imagery with black people is persistent and a recurring feature of scientific racism (Gilman, 1985: 83).[11]

Important in the context of this study is the nature of the psychic conflict occasioned by the encounter between white male and black female which is in evidence in a number of texts of the late imperial phase of British history as is argued in chapter 3. During slavery, African women were dehumanized and deprived of any privileges which accrued to gender. The middle class European woman was idealized and symbolic of the planters' control – control of self, of sex, of Others – and her femininity was made distinctive from that of the African woman and the white women of the 'lower' social orders. Both of these groups of women – black and lower class white women (especially prostitutes) – were seen as pathologized but they were also a source of illicit sexual pleasure for many white men (Hyam: 1991). This transgressive sexual activity was denied to white women who, burdened with the responsibility for reproducing the 'race' were supposed to adhere to a certain moral standard which precluded lesbian relationships and interracial sex. To indulge in either was to be ranked alongside the insane (Gilman, 1985).

However, in spite of the publicly stated hatred of interracial sexual relations, sexual unions between white men and their black female slaves were numerous, although many of the black women were not willing partners in these associations. Due to the way that life was organized on plantations, relations between white and black, male and female, were institutionalized and backed by law and social interdictions.

Neither the white female field hand nor the planter's wife were able to link their subjugation under the economic system and patriarchy to the oppression of the black female through slavery for a number of complex, inter-related reasons. The former was encouraged to see the relationship between herself and her fellow exploited black woman worker as one of superiority and inferiority, encouraged by racist ideologies (Beckles, 1989).

Laws applied to the control of slaves placed great emphasis on sexual behaviour and sexual contact between black and white was strictly regulated. In public, the notion that only women with low morals were attracted to black men was pervasive: that a white woman of high morals and 'good breeding' should want to have sexual relations with black men was deemed unthinkable and the regulation of European women's sexual activity in regard to black men was part of the exercise of white male control which set the limits for her sexual freedom. The white women whose husbands sexually used and abused their black slaves, would often avenge themselves on their human property with brutality (Beckles, 1989). Thus the potential for an alliance between women oppressed through 'race', class and patriarchy was subverted by racist ideologies and the social and sexual hierarchies instituted on the plantation.

Although for the ruling male elite, sexual relations with black women were a right, for labourers and servants such liaisons were considered as an abuse of their racial heritage and privilege and white male servants were often forbidden to develop sexual relations with African women. Furthermore, in order to ensure that no children of interracial relationships would ever be in a position to inherit their white father's property, specific legislation was passed and children born of slave mothers were born into slavery whatever the status of their father (Beckles, 1989). The ideological infra-structure for the support of such policies was already in place through the systematic inferiorization of black people.

The 'primitive' had long been associated with uninhibited sexuality and promiscuity and belief in these alleged characteristics combined with fears about interracial mixing and served to make the major cause of anxiety about black people a sexual one. Politically, this anxiety – fuelled by economic determinations – manifested itself in the institutionalized compulsion to monitor and control black sexuality and fertility, and to police sexual activity with white people. Having structured these differences into the Other, sexual 'intermixing' becomes un-representable, other than as an act of violation.[12] Expressions of fears for the future purity and superiority of the white 'race' relating to 'miscegenation' and 'race-mixing' were bound to the notion that blood varies from 'race' to 'race' and that the mixing of those bloods is undesirable. These beliefs under-pinned the anxiety and fear surrounding interracial sexual relationships that many white people had.

THE RIGHT TO LOOK

If one of the most arresting features of the eighteenth century in terms of early empirical scientific enquiry was the compulsion to order and to construct taxonomies, it should also be noted that the development of scientific empiricism privileged the status of ocular proof and consolidated the power of the investigative colonialist eye. Structured into this assumption of the right to look is the power to define and categorize and this is crucial in determining who may or may not initiate or return the look. A key historical instance of the assumption of the right to look and to investigate can again be traced to the end of the eighteenth and the beginning of the nineteenth centuries as scientific and medical investigations of the human body became more common.

In the nineteenth century European popular imagination, the sexual prowess of African men and the dimensions of their genitalia were 'known' to be excessive and black men's sexual organs were frequently objects of study. During this period however, the anatomy of black females also held a fascination for members of the medical establishment and examinations of their bodies were a pervasive practice.[13] The focal points for these scientific investigations were black women's genitalia, seen as the external signs of a deviant excessive sexuality.

During the late eighteenth and early nineteenth century there was a generalized view of female genitalia as deviant: connections were made between what were alleged to be the overdeveloped genitalia and secondary sexual characteristics of African women and the sexual 'excesses' of lesbians and prostitutes (Gilman, 1985: 76ff.). The perversity or abnormality was located in what was perceived as physical overdevelopment – 'large' buttocks, 'extended' genitalia and 'pendulous' breasts. Thus, in relation to black women, differentiated anatomy constituted the external stigmata of a primitive sexuality which pathologized African women's sexuality and marked them as a potential sexual threat.

The search for and location of these external signs of sexual anomaly as an indication of a generalized and emblematic inferiority, suggests the complexity of black women as sign or symbol. Black women were located at the intersection of racial, class and sexual difference in scientific discourse. It was as if the ultimate signifier of difference from the 'norm' of the investigator was the one which least resembled him, according to his own criteria: that embodiment of difference stood as representative of all difference. This perception of female anatomy indicates the difficulties involved in trying to unravel some of the issues raised by the interaction of the construction of racial and gender identities: what were perceived as physiological anomalies in the structure of the African female's genitalia were seen as evidence of anomalies in *all* women, whilst retaining the specificity of their racial identification.

As the human body became the focus and object of analysis so, towards the end of the nineteenth century, visual imagery was implicated when photography emerged as a form of documentation (Green, 1984; Green, 1986; Gilman, 1987; Tagg, 1989). Photographs were used to illustrate evolutionary explanations of human development, and became a key factor because they were considered to be objective representations of reality, presenting the viewer with a transparent window on to a previously unknown world. Photographic evidence was called upon to explain inequality in terms of hereditary factors as marked on the physical character of the body (Gilman, 1985: 95ff.).

Given the inscription of Otherness on the black body established through colonial and imperial anthropological, medical, literary and photographic discourses, it seems it was inevitable that the cinema would become instrumental in the attempted demystification and control of black people.

The important roles which photographic and cinematic imagery played in the construction of difference is connected to the privileging of the visual in western culture. Visual images have provided: '[a] primary route to scientific knowledge. We speak of "knowledge as illumination, knowing as seeing, truth as light"; throughout Western thought, the illumination that vision gives has been associated with the highest faculty of mental reasoning' (Martin, 1990: 69). Thus seeing is not only linked to 'believing' but also to 'knowing'. This is important because through this, the film camera – when it is used as an extension of the imperial/anthropological eye – may be characterized as an instrument of the power and control of the Other.

EUGENICS AND THE HEALTH OF THE NATION

The need to impose a moral and physical order on colonial subjects was seen as the duty of the Christian, civilized nation: various scientific explanations regarding the inferiority of black people formed the rationale for carrying out this mission.

Towards the end of the nineteenth century it became accepted that the health of the British nation was bound up with what were considered to be the proper forms of sexuality and sexual behaviour became one of the key sites specified in socio-medical health programmes. Expressions of sexuality were seen as inherently dirty, and aberrant behaviour such as incest, promiscuity and prostitution amongst the working class was identified as evidence of their inherent moral degeneracy. Notably, female sexual depravity was alleged to be one of the gravest threats to the moral rectitude of the decent, deserving poor in the working classes (Bland, 1984).

Eugenics is the science of selective breeding for the health of the 'race' and was one of the founding ideologies of Nazism. It was introduced towards the end of the nineteenth century by Charles Darwin's cousin, Sir Francis Galton. Galton claimed that a number of groups – notably black and working class people – were intellectually inferior and congenitally defective. For eugenicists, intellectual, physical and moral qualities were innate. Those designated deviant, dysfunctional or criminal were not socially constructed but members of naturally occurring categories which should be eliminated through the process of selective breeding (Gould, 1981; Barker, 1981; Searle, 1981, Bland, 1984).

Any hint of 'invasion' from outside of Britain was seen as a threat to the health of the nation and characterized as a disease and this is evidenced in the metaphors relating to the healthy and the sick body. The use of such terminology as 'infection', 'scourge', 'diseased', 'plague' and so on with reference to 'alien' others and to sexually 'deviant' women and men is extensive. These categories of healthy and sick, operated in terms of class, gender, 'race', sexuality, and mental ability. For example, Africans were identified through skin colour and that was not only associated with a number of negative attributes and conditions, it was also – through the early part of the nineteenth century – marked as being the result of congenital leprosy (Gilman, 1985). Subsequently, in the late nineteenth century, it was possible to read that syphilis – which is, of course, a sexually transmitted disease – was a strain of leprosy brought to England from Africa. Through this link of the pathological and the sexual, black African women in particular, came to stand for both excessive sexuality and corruption and agents of racial decay.

Eugenics was important because it became influential amongst a diverse range of people and because its terms became accepted into the mainstream of British political life. In 1910, public bodies were established for the physical and moral regeneration of the white English 'race' and intellectuals, feminists, liberals and Fabians subscribed to eugenicist ideologies: H. G. Wells, Julian Huxley, George Bernard Shaw and Marie Stopes were just a few of the prominent thinkers to support eugenics. The extent to which this set of ideas permeated popular consciousness and maintained a powerful hold in setting agendas for social attitudes, is indicated in chapter 4 where I discuss publicly expressed twentieth century attitudes to interracial sexual relations.[14]

For many – particularly those who, during the mid- to late nineteenth century, belonged to the increasing numbers of administrative, technical and scientific local government functionaries –

eugenics provided the scientific legitimation of the desire and willingness to rule others, to prescribe the behaviour and determine the future of those not born to rule. These new bureaucrats and health professionals justified what they did and the way they did it – controlling, monitoring, administering – because of their 'genetic' destiny.

The importance of 'race' is that it is seen as providing:

> the objective correlative of crisis – the arena in which complex fears, tensions and anxieties, generated by the impact of the totality of the crisis as a whole on the whole society, can be most conveniently and explicitly projected and, as the euphemistic phrase runs, 'worked through'.
>
> (Hall *et al.*, 1986: 333)

This can be seen in the case of eugenics, so that, for example, as Philip Abrams has argued:

> Eugenicists . . . were caught up in the general ideological crisis of the late century. Seeking to account for the facts of economic and social disorder on the basis of specifically biological training, they brought the principles of genetics to bear on contemporary vital statistics and discovered, as a more or less imminent danger, the prospect of race degeneration.
>
> (Abrams, 1968: 123)

Abrams sees this crisis as linked to the crisis in capitalism brought about by the surplus of labour.

The pathologization of particular groups has served as a means of drawing a differentiating line between those who are acceptable, and those who are not: the act of delineation serving to avert crises of confidence, guilt and loss of control.

WHITENESS, BLACKNESS AND GENDER

For white men, white women are both self and other: they have a floating status. They can re-inforce a sense of self through common racial identity or threaten and disturb that sense through their sexual Otherness. It is still predominantly white middle class men who have privileged access to the right to look in regard to the cinema, and black women are most often 'punished' for their stimulation of sexual anxiety and the castration complex by their continued struc-tured absence and low status in films. In terms of representation, black and white women may be linked by their common sexual unknowability, but white femininity is both foregrounded and privileged in relation to black women.

In this system of domination and subordination, white people have seized the right to define and determine the status of the Other. The stability of white identity is dependent on the notion of its normality and supremacy (Pajaczkowska and Young, 1992). The constant effacement and naturalization of whiteness from discussions about racial and sexual difference serves to maintain its hegemony. Historically, black people and women were literally and metaphorically dissected by white males constantly seeking reaffirmation of their superiority: later, cinematic discourses on the Other further consolidated the power relations embedded in looking.

As will be discussed in chapter 6, initially many black filmmakers consciously set out to construct images which countered what they saw as misrepresentations of black people and experiences but beyond that, it is difficult to generalize a position for black film-makers.

CONCLUSION

Anxieties about power, control, virility and dependence may be identified whereby, protected by his power to define, to look, to control and to demystify through continual and intimate examination, the white middle class male characterized the troubling, confusing and unruly elements of his unconscious, as black, as working class or as female (Pajaczkowska and Young, 1992). The black woman may then be punished, literally and metaphorically for tempting white men to participate in the degeneration of their 'race' and for being agents in the reproduction of the black 'race'.[15]

On a connotative level, black is aligned to 'dirtiness': sex is also considered 'dirty' and the two combine in notions of black sexuality. In film, 'dirty' or transgressive sexuality may be displaced onto the racial Other, so that perverse sexuality may be embodied in, for example, in the black prostitute in *Mona Lisa* (1986) or the young black woman who invites Kathie to participate in troillism in *Flame in the Streets* (1961).[16]

Images are ideological, a discursive practice: in racist societies, no image is neutral or innocent of the past whether or not that past is acknowledged. Slavery and colonialism have been and continue to be profoundly traumatic events, the traces of which are to be found in many contemporary cultural forms.

Chapter 3 is concerned with literary texts of the late nineteenth century, and films of the 1930s, and covers the period of British colonial and imperial expansion in order to illustrate the points made in this chapter. Although most interesting cinematic texts on 'race' and sex occur later, once more black people arrived in Britain in the 1940s and 1950s, it is also instructive to examine some earlier works which engage with themes of Otherness. It is these films of the 1930s and 1940s which are the concern of chapter 3.

Chapter 3

Imperial culture: the primitive, the savage and white civilization[1]

In the previous chapter, I argued that white Europeans thought that they had full and complete knowledge about Africa and Africans, although this 'knowledge' was gained through the representations and stereotypes constructed by, and sustained in, myths, ancient travellers' narratives, and later in literature and popular fiction, anthropology, photography and cinema.

In this chapter I will examine how racialized discourses manifested themselves in texts, in terms of ideologies of superiority and inferiority and where they connected with beliefs about femininity and masculinity, and sexuality. Critical analyses of orientalist, colonialist and primitivist discourses will be considered in terms of their applicability to imperialist texts. I will analyse specific representations of Otherness in some literary instances of the late nineteenth century, suggesting how these images were subsequently consolidated and constituted in the cinema.

This chapter marks the beginning of the analysis of specific films which are of interest because of the ways in which they engage with racial and sexual issues. I am not concerned here with films that have an aggressive imperialist vision since in many respects these tend to be less interesting in terms of tensions and contradictions within the text. The British archetype of this kind of jingoistic, compulsively xenophobic film is probably *Sanders of the River* (1935). Films such as *The Song of Freedom* (1936) and *Men of Two Worlds* (1946) are more engrossing as they slide between an aggressive objectification of black African subjects, marking them as an ignorant, 'primitive' undifferentiated mass, and an acknowledgement that specific individuals can be redeemed by being properly schooled in the moral and cultural values of western Europe. Another point of interest is that both *The Song of Freedom* and *Men of Two Worlds* show the black protagonists living and working in England at some stage and it is possible to see their interaction with white English people in terms of class as well as 'race'. In *Sanders of the River* (1935), *Rhodes of Africa* (1936) and other similar dramas, all the 'natives' are safely contained in Africa and the virtues of colonialism unequivocally extolled. Another reason for including *The Song of Freedom* and for devoting a chapter to imperialism and British cinema is that doing so provides a context for the discussions in later chapters about the kinds of representations against which black film-makers in particular have reacted.

NOTES ON IMPERIALISM

On an economic level, it has been suggested that the imperial expansion which started from roughly 1875 and carried on until World War I, was due, at least in part, to capitalist overproduction coupled with an under-consumption in the home-market which led to the search for markets overseas.[2] For the African colonial subject, colonization meant that the organization of whole populations was destabilized, and the right to administer and derive benefits from those societies seized from black Africans by invading Europeans. Ideologically, nineteenth century British colonialism was justified as a moral duty, a benevolent effort to spread Christianity and civilization across the continents of Africa, Asia and America.

Discernible in both the literature of the late nineteenth century and the films of the 1930s referred to here is the pervasive belief that Britain was responsible for the economic, moral and social welfare of its colonial subjects (Smyth, 1983). Economics, science and religion were pivotal since they provided the financial, intellectual and moral justification for creating and constructing a resource of subordinated peoples who were available to serve European needs.[3]

ANALYSING COLONIAL DISCOURSE

There have been a number of critiques of the discourses of Orientalism, primitivism and colonialism which have been helpful in identifying the role of ideology and discourse in the constitution of the colonized Other. A persistent critic of the way in which 'knowledge' and western European supremacist ideologies have constructed the Other and informed European culture, has been Edward Said (Said, 1985 and 1993). Although specifically referring to the way in which the notion of the Orient is a product of the western European imperial imagination, Said's theses in *Orientalism* can be usefully extended to a discussion of the way in which other cultures have been figured, although it is also necessary to bear in mind the specificities of the particular examples being discussed (Said, 1985). Said analyses Orientalism as an attempt to contain and control the Otherness of the Orient.

Said refers to a discourse of Orientalism, a set of terms, ideas and ways of constructing and thinking about the subject. Orientalism may be seen as preparing the way for colonialism discursively, ideologically and rhetorically. Both Orientalism and colonialism denied subject peoples' human agency and resistance and constructed explanatory models to account for the alterity of those subjects.

Similarly, much literary production during the late nineteenth century is replete with examples of 'knowledge' about the character of Africans based on white supremacist attitudes towards 'race'. In particular the notion of atavism – the belief that the 'primitive' people of Africa constituted an earlier stage of human development – often recurs: all the references to primeval swamps, to primitive rituals, the colonial subjects' perceived deficiency of language, intellect and culture attest to this belief. The texts are saturated with metaphors of 'darkness' infused with the presupposition of the positive associations of whiteness, light and so on, and negative attributes of blackness, dirtiness, ignorance, evil and so on.[4] The cultural (Christian) mission was, then, to introduce 'civilization' to the 'primitive' Other. Similar tropes are evident in the films of the 1930s such as *Sanders of the River* (1935), *The Song of Freedom* (1936), *King Solomon's Mines* (1937), *The Drum* (1938) and *The Four Feathers* (1939), and indeed, later in *Men of Two Worlds* (1947) and *Simba* (1955).

Marianna Torgovnick uses the idea of primitivism to identify and explicate a primitivist discourse in which the judgements of white Europeans about the intelligence, rationality and sexual practices of those deemed Other, are not acknowledged to be ideologically formed but are taken as categorical statements about the 'primitive' world (Torgovnick, 1990: 8).[5] Such convictions are abundant in the literature and cinema of imperialism. The necessity for Europeans of defining the primitive, Torgovnick argues, may be considered as an attempt to define the qualities and boundaries of white identity; an exploration of the self without problematizing the normalization of whiteness and its equation with civilization.

In specific instances, such as in the case of women, and in the case of the masses – frequently characterized as a teeming, primeval horde – some white people are attributed the qualities of 'primitiveness' thus becoming an internal Other. There are a number of instances when white women are positioned in ways analogous to the way in which black people – and working class people – are positioned albeit with variations in the woman's relative hierarchical status, and depending on her class and the degree of her heterosexual attraction. Torgovnick acknowledges this when she observes:

> gender issues always inhabit Western versions of the primitive. Sooner or later those familiar tropes for primitives become the tropes conventionally used for women. Global politics, the dance of colonizer and colonized, becomes sexual politics, the dance of male and female.
>
> (Torgovnick, 1990: 17)

Torgovnick's analysis conceptualizes these two issues – of primitivist discourse and patriarchal discourse – as parallel, linear developments and this does not allow for an analysis of the intersections and discontinuities. I argue that these discourses sometimes converge, and sometimes overlap in the cinematic examples which follow. Furthermore, in Torgovnick's examples there is little sense of the historical role of scientific and historiographical discourses in providing the 'objective proof' for the development of ideas about the relative statuses of black/white and male/female which I argue is crucial to an understanding of the potency and persistence of ideologies of racial and gender difference, and sexuality. [6]

As has been discussed in chapter 1 and above, both Homi Bhabha and Edward Said in their accounts of colonialist and Orientalist discourses see the construction of stereotypes as crucial to the imperialist hegemonic project. Elaborating on Said's critique of the European 'archive' of knowledge, Bhabha asserts that colonial discourse is:

> a form of knowledge and identification that vacillates between what is always 'in place', already known, and something that must be anxiously repeated . . . as if the essential duplicity of the Asiatic or the bestial sexual licence of the African that needs no proof, can never really, in discourse, be proved.
>
> (Bhabha, 1983: 18)

The necessity for vacillation is occasioned because the discourse attempts to fix and stabilise that which is not static. The desire for scientism, exemplified in the valorization of systematic categorization based on empiricism, inevitably produces some instances which refuse to be contained by the conceptual boundaries established. In these cases either the lines of demarcation have to be re-ordered or the exceptions denied, and this is why stereotypes are protean, rather than stable.

Although a good deal of what is expressed with regard to racial differences is contradictory there is 'a rigorous subconscious logic' which:

> defines the relations between the covert and overt policies and between the material and discursive practices of colonialism. The ideological functions of colonialist fiction ... must be understood ... in terms of the exigencies of domestic – that is, European and colonialist – politics and culture; and the function of racial difference, of the fixation on and fetishization of native savagery and evil, must be mapped in terms of these exigencies and ideological imperatives.
>
> (JanMohamed, 1985: 62–63)

For this fetishization and demonization to cohere and 'make sense', there had to be in place a systematic oppositional differentiation in *all* spheres, made between colonizer and colonized: that such a dichotomous relationship existed was not often challenged by the middle of the nineteenth century, even amongst those who had opposed slavery. Once such notions enter the popular domain and hence discourse and ideology, then they are, to all intents and purposes, 'reality', since

> The work of ideology is to present the position of the subject as fixed and unchangeable, an element in a given system of differences which is human nature and the world of human experience, and to show possible action as an endless repetition of "normal", familiar action.
>
> (Belsey, 1980: 90)

The conventional practices of colonial/imperial cinematic realist representations attributed fixed, inferior characteristics to black people, basing such characterizations on an archive of 'knowledge' about the African character, and, arguably, the cumulative effect of such images was to limit informed public debate and to justify policies regarding colonial rule. It is important to remember that the beginnings of cinema coincided with the peak of colonial expansion towards the end of the nineteenth and the first decades of the twentieth centuries. Imperialist growth and policies had to be sustained and the emergent mass medium of the cinema offered the opportunity to promote and consolidate colonial policy overseas. It should also be noted, as Ella Shohat points out, that:

> Western cinema not only inherited and disseminated colonial discourse, but also created a system of domination through monopolistic control of film distribution and exhibition in much of Asia, Africa, and Latin America.
>
> (Shohat, 1991: 45)

MASCULINE, FEMININE

During the peak period of colonial expansion, a number of fictional works emerged that were fantasized depictions of Africa and its people which served as an exotic background against which white men could act out and test the prescribed masculine qualities such as courage, tenacity and self-control. These narratives are characterized by their vision of a robust, bourgeois, homosocial masculinity.

Newspapers, popular entertainment, postcards and comics in the first decade of the twentieth century constantly reinforced the idea of war as glamorous, character-building and fascinating: an activity which occurred in far-off exotic places, away from what was seen as the stifling confinement of domesticity. These images and fantasies were inextricably linked to conceptualizations of masculinity, and the idea of what constitutes masculinity was a key site for confrontations springing from racial conflict, since in racially stratified societies, the notion of masculinity is not only determined by its being in opposition to femininity but by its racial specificity.

Ideas about masculinity, as is the case with other socially constructed categories, are in a continual state of flux and specific to historical time and place, although this is not always recognized to be the case. Particular ideas about what constitutes 'manliness' in terms of physical and athletic prowess became dominant in the late nineteenth century through public concern about British men's physical weakness at a time of expanding imperial conquests and the demand for the defence of existing colonies (Bristow, 1991; Roper and Tosh, 1991: 19).

There was also a crisis of masculinity which arose because of the success of the bourgeois vision of domestic life. Crucial to this lifestyle was the man's duty to provide moral and religious support, and the adoption of an ideology of hard work and thrift. In the bourgeois household, the home was the domain of the economically dependent wife whilst the rough world of industrial capitalism and work was the province of the male. The home was thus associated with the feminine since that was where the woman could exercise what power she did have. The bourgeois feminine world was that of domesticity, physical weakness, emotional displays, and masculinity was the antithesis of these characteristics.

White women – both middle and working class – and black people are again both implicated here as both were characterized as being dependent on others, and as being defined only through their oppositional relationship to white middle class men.[7] Although during the nineteenth century black and working class women were expected to carry out arduous physical labour, white middle class women were assigned a position of physical delicacy and fragility and were placed on a pedestal of sexual unattainability. The idealization of white female sexual purity and the valorization of 'masculine' attributes such as courage, autonomous action and independence served to privilege the celebration of essentialized characteristics of masculinity and femininity. Whilst it is the case that white middle class women were used and abused, they also colluded in shoring up the structures of supremacy and domination, supporting both class and racial stratification, as was demonstrated in chapter 2 in regard to plantocratic hierarchy.

The desire to look on and control the female body had limited acceptability in regard to white women: with the institutionalization of black people's inferior status, no such inhibitions existed in regard to the bodies of African women. As demonstrated in chapter 2, during the late eighteenth and nineteenth centuries, the black female body was subjected to rigorous scientific examination and her naked body placed on public display, the vast majority of such investigatory work being carried out, of course, by white male doctors and scientists. However, even into the twentieth century, the story was different when it came to white women who wished to exercise their privileged racial status through the right to look as is made clear in the following passage from a popular magazine, *Titbits*, 21 July, 1917:

Some years ago we used to have large bodies of natives sent from Africa on military service or in some travelling show, and it was a revelation of horror and disgust to behold the manner in which English women would flock to see these men, whilst to watch them fawning upon these black creatures and fondling them and embracing them, as I have seen dozens of times, was a scandal and a disgrace to English womanhood. How then is it possible to maintain as the one stern creed in the policy of the Empire the eternal supremacy of white over black?

(quoted in Henriques, 1974: 141)

Here the links between bestiality and sexuality, the gendering of the criteria by which sexual impropriety is judged, femininity, and the putative effects of transgressive sexual relations on the imperial project and white supremacy are decisively articulated. The passage is also reminiscent of earlier diatribes against interracial sexual relations cited in chapter 2. Historically, then, the right to define and to look has been monopolized by white middle class men and as far as film-making is concerned, this is still the case.

BLACK FEMININITY

In chapter 2, I discussed how the cumulative effect of the eighteenth century concern for categorization, as manifested in the construction of racial hierarchies, was to facilitate the development of the conditions for the generation of racialized discourses. An analysis of representations of black femininity in the genre of colonial and imperial literary adventures and their cinematic successors needs to take account of the African women's metaphoric status which has arisen from the intersection of these discourses on gender, 'race' and sexuality.[8] The literary texts are of note, not just because of the recurring metaphors and themes, but because several important films of the 1930s such as *King Solomon's Mines* (1937), *The Four Feathers* (1939) and *Sanders of the River* (1935) were based on these novels.

In imperial literature regarding the terrain, there is much talk of 'penetration', 'conquering the interior' and so on. Africa is characterized as feminine with all the contradictory connotations of passivity, uncontrollability, desire and danger and indicating the extent to which colonial metaphors are gendered. An indicator of the elision of African landscapes and the (forbidden) desire for (black) and be effected through Africa is indicative of the anxieties being displaced onto the land and onto black women. If white men's fear of white women is based on the 'uncontrollable' sexual arousal instigated by them, then since African women have been frequently described as hypersexual and are phenotypically marked as inherently and immutably different, the anxieties instigated by sexual difference are exacerbated. In the case of both females and males, the contention that blacks are oversexed is historically linked to and 'proven' by alleged anatomical excesses in one form or another. Whether or not there was or is any empirical evidence to support or deny such beliefs is irrelevant: it is the fact that such notions were, and still are, considered meaningful, are still perpetuated either directly or indirectly, and are still the subject of many ribald jokes, that is the significant issue.

At the same time as functioning as a contrast through which the white European male could conceive of himself as fearless, active, independent, in control, virile and so on, the African woman also represented a double negation of that heroic self, being not-male, not-white. Freud's epistemology, as Shohat argues: 'assumes the (white) male as the bearer of knowledge, who can penetrate woman and text, while she, as a remote region, will let herself be explored until truth is uncovered' (Shohat, 1991: 58). The question is, the truth about whom? Through the sexualization of the feminized African landscape, lying passively on its (her) back displaying naked splendour and availability (for penetration and conquest), the white male unconscious can indulge itself in fantasizing about his assault on, his merging with the forbidden object of fascination and desire. But there is fear embedded in that desire, hence the necessity for denial.

Although black women were seen as 'not-male', neither were they seen as women in the same sense that white women were. Since slavery, African females had been seen as at once women – inasmuch as they were sexualized, reproductive and subordinate – and not-women, that is not pure, not feminine, not fragile but strong and sexually knowing and available. Thus an implicit contrast was established between white (middle class) and black women and this generated the complex set of relations under colonialism as described in chapter 2.

This in itself posed a number of problems for white men in their actual and fictional imperial adventures. Given the firmly established ideas about the inferiority of black people, it was femininity is embedded in Freud's use of the term, dark continent'.

> The seduction and conquest of the African woman became a
> metaphor for the conquest of Africa itself. A powerful erotic
> symbolism linked a woman's femininity so strongly to the
> attraction of the land that they became one single idea, and to
> both were attributed the same irresistible, deadly charm.
>
> (Nicholas Monti, quoted in Doane, 1991: 213)

The feminization of the landscape points to a fascination with, and
desire for, African women which cannot be made explicit or elaborated due to its transgressive nature: thus the desire may only be
articulated through displacement. A prime example of this figurative
displacement occurs in H. Rider Haggard's novel, *King Solomon's
Mines* (1885). From the perspective of the imperial 'I/eye' of his
hero, Alan Quatermain, Haggard gives a detailed description of the
African landscape which likens the mountainous panorama to a
woman's breasts:

> . . . I attempt to describe that extraordinary grandeur and beauty
> of that sight, language seems to fail me. I am impotent even at its
> memory. Before us rose two enormous mountains . . . These
> mountains . . . are shaped after the fashion of a woman's breasts,
> and at times the mists and shadows beneath them take the form of
> a recumbent woman veiled mysteriously in sleep. Their bases
> swell gently from the plain, looking at that distance perfectly
> round and smooth; and on top of each is a vast hillock covered
> with snow, exactly corresponding to the nipple on the female
> breast.
>
> (Haggard, 1979: 56–57)

Significantly, Quatermain, white hero and narrator of the novel, on
recalling the beauty of the sight of that landscape admits to being
cast back into the pre-symbolic realm without language, rendered
speechless and impotent 'even at its memory' (Bristow, 1991: 127).
The loss of the accoutrements of civilization and culture is figured
through sexual impotence: these fears are the continual fears of the
oppressor. Those African 'breasts' recall the dependency of infant
on mother and as a consequence, the anger experienced at being
separated from her, the primary love-object, and it is the enforced
recognition of difference which produces 'impotence'.

  That the sight of these 'breasts', the female's visible signifiers of
sexual difference and maternity, should generate such powerlessness

unacceptable for white men on their travels across Africa to admit openly to engaging in interracial sexual activity. Referring to Edgar Wallace's eponymous hero, from the novel, *Sanders of the River*, Jeffrey Richards notes:

> Not surprisingly he [Sanders] is unshakeably opposed to misce-genation. When a succession of young officers become enamoured of the beautiful M'Lino he sends them home declaring: 'Monkey tricks of that sort are good enough for the Belgian Congo and for Togoland but they aren't good enough for this little strip of wilderness.'
>
> (Richards, 1973: 31)

Again, there is the linking of simian imagery with black people and sexual activity, and the often repeated assertion that the colonialism practised by other European powers was immoral and brutal as opposed to Britain's 'benign', paternalistic version. [9]

The European, as JanMohamed argues, has a choice when confronted with what she or he imagines as an unfathomable, alien Otherness. Hypothetically, she or he:

> has the option of responding to the Other in terms of identity or difference. If he assumes that he and the Other are essentially identical, then he would tend to ignore the significant divergences and to judge the Other according to his own cultural values. If, on the other hand, he assumes the Other is irremediably different, then he would have little incentive to adopt the viewpoint of that alterity: he would again turn to the security of his own perspective. Genuine and thorough comprehension of Otherness is possible only if the self can somehow negate or at least severely bracket the values, assumptions, and ideology of his culture.
>
> (JanMohamed, 1985: 64–65)

First though, white people have to recognize the 'values, assumptions and ideology' and to acknowledge the extent to which Otherness is a construction arising from those assumptions and beliefs. JanMohamed's argument is here locked into its own binarism, as he posits two alternatives and imputes a stability and cohesion in colonial and primitivist discourses which is illusory as has been argued by Homi Bhabha. Neither is it clear just what constitutes a significant difference or how singular a cultural perspective might be. Nonetheless, such an analysis recognizes the contradictions inherent in the colonialists' hazardous psychic positioning. Violation of the Other, whether literally, metaphorically, or representationally, must of necessity also be an act of cultural masochism since the Other is necessarily a part of the self constructed in and through difference.

> This establishment of the other *as* other is promoted by the initial drive to establish self-identity by identifying *with* the other. Negating others, *denigrating* them, becomes in part, thus, also self-negation and self-effacement.
>
> (Goldberg, 1993: 60)

This assertion regarding self-effacement should not be understood as a relinquishing of power, rather it comes as a result of possessing and naturalizing relations of power.

As the embodiment of an 'archive' of fantasies, 'primitives', 'orientals' and colonized black people have been expected to behave in particular ways and obliged to occupy particular positions in films. The power to define the Other – a power derived from economic and political dominance – is clearly demonstrated in the construction of the colonial subject represented in the literature and cinema of Empire: African men were at once feared and admired, being the objects of feelings of repulsion and veneration. White masculine cultural superiority is signified through the comparisons of weaponry (the 'savage' with the spear versus the gentleman with the revolver being a contest of phallic symbols), intelligence and courage. In these texts white masculinity is constantly revered, femininity excluded and derided and racism is naturalized.

The ambivalence that was structured into the consciousness of so many fictional adventurer heroes in Africa during that period finds expression in the recognition of the Africans' 'beauty' and the incongruity of their 'evil'. Rarely are Africans portrayed as individuated human beings. The primitive, homogenous mass is emblematic of the Manichean confrontation between Self and Other; a scene often re-enacted in the cinema and literature of Empire. [10]

The testing of white masculinity was explicitly represented through combat with the savage Other: more covertly (though there are exceptions to which I will refer later) white masculinity was concerned with establishing white male virility within a heterosexual context, and the feminine metaphors used to describe Africa, including the controlling trope of the 'dark continent' itself indicate the repression of the feminine. Part of the explanation for the repression of the sexual element lies with the fact that:

the whole genre bears the distinct imprint of the public school. The virtues and characteristics of the Imperial archetype are the virtues and characteristics bred into him by his public school. The male camaraderie and the subordinate role of women reflects the all-male environment of the public schools.

(Richards, 1973: 220)

It would seem that the flight from the feminine and the domestic must be absolute: and with white women absent, homosexuality unspeakable and interracial heterosexual relations unthinkable, what is the white male hero to do in terms of sexual expression but circumscribe the field of sexual activity and sublimate sexual thoughts?

THE CINEMA OF EMPIRE

During the late 1920s, Britain's Colonial Office decided to exploit the propaganda qualities of film as it set out to explore how best to capitalize on cinema's potential for disseminating imperial ideology. By the 1920s North American cinema was already dominant. There was concern that some of the images of white people could be interpreted as deriding European or British culture and that steps should be taken to counter this. For example, the films of Charlie Chaplin were immensely popular but much of his work involved the humiliation of respectable male figures, men of authority and propriety such as clergymen and policemen, and eventually such texts were censored for screenings in the colonies (Smyth, 1983: 129–143). In the USA during the 1920s the Hays Office codes ensured sexual propriety by establishing a code of conduct for film-makers which severely limited, in particular, the sexual content of films. The North American Production Code of the Motion Picture Producers and Directors of America, Inc. (1930–1934) made its policy on the representation of interracial sex explicit: 'Miscegenation (sex relation between the white and black races) is forbidden' (quoted in Shohat, 1991: 66). Also subject to censorship were any representations of white women behaving seductively (Smyth, 1983). In Kenya and Rhodesia (now Zimbabwe) where there were substantial white populations, viewing was racially segregated and censorship practised until at least the late 1940s according to whether the black population or white people were the intended audience. [11]

Although there were significant numbers of black people in

Britain during the early part of the twentieth century, in the 1930s Otherness was almost always located 'out there' geographically, in adventure films such as *King Solomon's Mines* (1937), *The Drum* (1938) and *The Four Feathers* (1939). Africa was still conceptualized as belonging to prehistory, its peoples supposedly uncivilized.

In colonialist adventure films and literature, it is often the case that Africa's primeval existence is figured through the lush vegetative landscape, and edenic vistas. The strange animals and the strange people are seen as one entity, one powerful evocation of an exoticism impossible to find within the confines of Europe. However, although the primitive and the exotic were depicted as being in a location far removed from Britain, the texts in the imperial adventure genre served to confirm white European notions of cultural superiority and are thus, essentially parochial and introspective, telling us about how whiteness imagined itself rather than about these Other cultures.

An illustration of this 'speaking of self' in the guise of discussing the Other occurred when European men encountered tribal kinship structures based on polyandry and polygyny: they viewed these familial practices as expressions of an allegedly excessive black sexuality which was to be both tamed and exploited.

That such polygamous practices exemplified a supposed black male sexual potency which was both feared and envied is still evidenced in *Sanders of the River* (1935), where 'Sandy the strong, Sandy the wise' (Leslie Banks) dissuades ten young 'African' women who all wish to marry Bosambo (Paul Robeson in a revealing animal print loincloth) by proclaiming that Bosambo is already married to five older women, stronger than any of them. In fact Bosambo is not married to anyone but Sanders' role at this point is to actively control the potential reproduction of his favourite 'native' – an ex-convict – by introducing him to the concept of a monogamous heterosexual relationship.

Sander L. Gilman has asserted that the 'white *man's* burden' was actually his sexuality and its control (Gilman, 1985: 112). This is particularly pertinent to the lone figure of the British District Officer or Commissioner such as Sanders, who ruled over 'thousands of tribesmen like a beneficent father, with only a handful of native troops at his back and no other white man within three weeks' march' (Richards, 1973: 114).

Again, the hierarchy established between the master and servant is one derived from the public school system according to Jeffrey

Richards:

> Most significant of all, all the relationships in the Imperial structure, between masters and servants, officers and men, Imperial administrators and native subjects, can be paraphrased into an identical headmaster-pupil relationship along the lines of the public school.
>
> (Richards, 1973: 220)

However, the difference between the 'headmaster-pupil' relationship and that of the 'Imperial administrators-native subjects' is that although at that moment the headteacher has more power and authority than the child, the child may one day attain similar or even superior status. This could not be the case in the administrator-'native' relation since within colonial discourse, whatever else might fluctuate – and however successfully the 'native' might revolt against her/his subjugation – the relation of domination and subordination is psychically fixed.

In a 1950s critique of colonialist cinema production in Britain and the USA, Jimmy Vaughn argues that the colonialist and imperialist film genre's representations do a disservice to Africa, as the primary motive in constructing these narratives is to 'extol the virtues of her [Africa's] colonisers, police officers, District Commissioners, and settlers' (Vaughn, 1959: 10). Vaughn relates the nineteenth century imperial fictions of H. Rider Haggard to the fiction of Graham Greene, John Buchan and Somerset Maugham and notes how much of that material has been transferred to the screen. Although, in the light of more recent debates about realism and representation, it is possible to take issue with Vaughn's emphasis on the lack of correspondence between the reality of Africa and its representation in British and North American popular cinema, this short article marks an important, if largely unnoticed, critical intervention during a period when most film criticism did not engage with such issues.

The imperialist position explicated by Vaughn – both in regard to its representation on screen and its ideological imperatives – is neatly summed up by Jeffrey Richards as follows:

> Again and again in both the literature and the cinema of Empire an axiomatic truth has been stated: that the natives are children and, for their own good, need to be ruled by the British. Rhodes, Sanders, Bill Crawford, William Scott and all the other gods and heroes of the Empire see themselves as just but firm father-

figures ... The British do not exploit the native. They stand between him and exploitation.

(Richards, 1973: 200)

This position represents an inversion of the actual circumstances of colonial rule, which is frequently found in colonialist discourse: it is not the British who are at fault in their colonial policies, but other forms of colonialism such as those practised by the French and the Belgians which are deemed exploitative and brutal. Even though British rule disrupted and undermined local agricultural production and social and political organization, and deprived the continent of some of its most able inhabitants, it was claimed that Africans would not progress without benevolent British intervention (Rodney, 1988).

DIFFERENT WORLDS

It would be misleading to suggest that Britain's hegemonic colonial practices met with or maintained uniform success or to assume that all black African opposition was located in Africa. Although the black population of Britain was still relatively small during the 1930s, there were a number of politically active people who saw the issue of black equality in this country as inextricable from questions of colonial policy. This activity led to the establishment of a number of organizations opposed to colonialism and racism. Pan-African sentiment grew whilst white people's participation in these political struggles was increasingly felt to be unacceptable: building on the connections between people of the African diaspora was considered to be the most effective way of organizing campaigns against oppression. Barbara Bush has noted that:

> In their efforts to improve race relations white liberals worked from a middle-class perspective, and thus to them "racial equality" usually implied equality for cultured, Europeanized blacks such as Paul Robeson and Harold Moody.
>
> (Bush, 1981: 47)[12]

Paul Robeson is a complex figure in terms of what he signified for both black and white audiences, and he did what he could to challenge supremacist ideologies in the film industry and wider society. He had the advantages of being both articulate and clever, and conforming to the conventional role of black male as performer and sporting personality, and – in the British context – of being from the USA.[13] African–American actors have often been preferred over British-based black people in a number of British films, a practice which still goes on today and which signals a degree of exoticism attributed to the black Other from 'elsewhere' which accrues in a limited way to the black Other within.[14]

Paul Robeson starred in *The Song of Freedom* (1936) with Elizabeth Welch, another African–American singer who lived in Britain. The film's opening sequence, beginning as it does with a mass of running, clamouring, African 'natives' – whose threatening, uncivilized demeanour is diminished by the angle of the shot which sees them running away from the camera – immediately draws the audience into the perspective of the explorer seeking to discover the Otherness of Africa. The legend, 'AFRICA' appears as the scene dissolves into a classic mountain/sea/landscape shot of a tropical island. Again, a caption appears in order to anchor the meaning of the visuals: 'The island of Casanga, off the west coast – in the year 1700 AD. The island had not yet attracted the attention of the slave traders on the mainland' we are told but 'its people suffered as fierce an oppression under their hereditary Queen Zinga – tyrant, despot, mistress of cruelty.' This last phrase may be indicative of a disaffection with female heads of state and matrilinearity and is significant if only because so few of the films set in Africa feature autonomous women. However to claim Queen Zinga as a powerful woman is to ignore the derisory treatment her character is given and the sadistic overtones of her 'mistress of cruelty' label.

Queen Zinga is played as a woman with a face fixed in a grimace, matted hair and an oiled body indicating a perpetual sweatiness. Zinga – wearing animal pelts, shells and beads – is flanked by further representations of primitiveness: tribal iconography consisting of archetypal primitive 'African' statues and two men whose bodies merge with the statues. In the face of the violent irrational matriarch, the men are reduced to ciphers. Zinga's men are passive male bodies, echoing the stance of the statues through both their physical positions and the way that they hold their shields. The interplay here between sexual and racial difference is marked. There is an appeal to white patriarchy: note that women who rule are insane megalomaniacs and to wield power is unnatural for them. Power strips women of their femininity – Zinga's gender is initially ambiguous – and men under matriarchy lack dignity, losing their ability to act autonomously.

This early sequence introduces us to a mad, cruel primitive African woman who is the opposite of most cinematic images of white femininity. In relation to her physical appearance and demeanour, the white male audience is interpellated as superior through their rationality, their intellect and the physical attraction of 'their' women. The primitivization of Zinga does not invite white women to identify with her or to be identified with her.

The process of cinematic identification of viewing subjects with characters and situations in the film is, however, a complex one and it should be acknowledged that identity may be characterized as fragmented with only an illusory coherence (Ellis, 1988: 43). It is not possible to assert that black people always or exclusively identify with black characters, although one can posit that black audiences viewing this type of film may experience a range of feelings which might vary according to context.

Fanon felt that, through representation:

> The Negro is a toy in the white man's hands . . . I cannot go to a film without seeing myself. I wait for me. In the interval, just before the film starts, I wait for me. The people in the theater are watching me, examining me, waiting for me.
>
> (Fanon, 1986: 140)

He then painfully reconstructs the sense of embarrassment and internalized self hatred which may entrap the black viewer of such texts: a viewer fixed by the gaze of the film-maker and white members of the audience. Fanon is explicit about the different effects that films such as *Tarzan* may have on black people, depending on the viewing context:

> In the Antilles, the young Negro identifies himself *de facto* with Tarzan against the Negroes. This is much more difficult for him in a European theater, for the rest of the audience, which is white, automatically identifies him with the savages on the screen.
>
> (Fanon, 1986: 152–153)

Paul Robeson is close to the 'noble savage' archetype in *The Song of Freedom*. His popularity as a singer is extensively brought into play in the film. His ability to sing is naturalized, reiterating the notion that all black people are able to sing spontaneously, without training: this 'natural' ability is then used as a crucial marker for his racially defined and differentiated subjectivity. John Zinga/Paul Robeson is a both a 'natural' singer and a natural worker – he is, in this narrative, after all, of royal descent and thus not so feckless and unreliable as the average black male. Perhaps this royal lineage is intended to account for his resilience, as, in spite of being conceived during the Middle Passage, into slavery – which according to the film was not an unpleasant experience – Zinga manages to make his way to England.

Zinga's naturalness is contrasted with the white upper class people who disembark from the ship in the docks where he is employed: they are remote from the world of physical labour which is going on around them. One of these passengers is an opera director, Gabriel Donozetti; his status as a foreign Other, albeit 'white' is established through his feminization: that is to say that arm and hand movements associated with 'feminine' gestures are deployed to signify both his exoticism and his distance from the experience of manual labour. Donozetti is a purveyor of opera, the exemplary cultural form of the privileged classes.

Part of what is interesting about this film is the fact that John Zinga's class allegiance is to the dockers with whom he works. The narrative posits a somewhat utopian vision of racial harmony in England where racism is clearly not an issue but where divisions based on social class are immutable and natural. 'Race' does, however, intrude on this cosy scenario on an unconscious level. For example, Zinga's nobility and royal lineage serve to make him only on a par with white workers, rather than according him the privileges of upper middle class English society. His entrée into the upper echelons of English society is made possible by his voice rather than by his birth, and is strictly limited.

African–American film historian Donald Bogle describes John and Ruth Zinga as living 'a rather arch domestic life. . .who together are almost too wholesome and bourgeois to be true' (Bogle, 1988: 197). In her gingham dress the character of Ruth certainly looks as though she is designed to fit in with the minimum of visual disruption but their social status is rather that of the respectable, socially aspirant working class rather than the middle class.

John Zinga yearns to travel to Africa, even though he has no idea of his ancestry and it is posited that such a yearning is inbred. Richard Dyer suggests that this aspect of Robeson's characterization which surfaces in his other films too, may be an unconscious expression of the problematic relationship between African–Americans and Africa.[15] I think it has as much to do with white people's (sometimes unconscious) desire to see Africans returned to their 'natural' habitat; that is, Africa. The fact of black people being out of place here is emphasized by their isolation and the focus on their discomfiture in white English society.

Bogle's short commentary on *The Song of Freedom* is not able to be developed due to the encyclopedic nature of his book: it is beyond the scope of his work to attempt to account for some of the more interesting and contradictory aspects of the text. For example in the first domestic scene we see, John Zinga looks longingly at a poster depicting an 'African' landscape. This poster is in a pivotal location, above the fireplace and the association here between home–hearth–heart is made clear as it becomes the focus of the audience's gaze, of Ruth's gaze and, of course, of Zinga's gaze. The caption on the poster encourages the reader to 'Go where there's sunshine! Christmas and New Year tours to South Africa': standing in front of this image is the ubiquitous archetypal African statue. The juxtaposition of these divergent representations of Africanness potentially establish a tension between the Zingas' English working-class lifestyle and what are held to be their cultural and racial origins. Ruth mildly castigates John for his desire to be in Africa by interrupting his fantasies with 'you're happy here: the people are kind' to which John responds with 'oh they're grand people . . . somewhere down there are *our* people Ruth and I've got a feeling they're grand people too. The people we belong to. Funny . . . that [white] fellow didn't want to go . . . natural – he's leaving his people to go out among strangers: he'll be out of place – lonely maybe. However hard I try, I always feel the same here.' Thus John Zinga makes explicit the 'unnaturalness' of black people in England whilst pointing to the reluctance of the white traveller as confirmation of the notion that people should remain with 'their own people'. It does not appear to matter how friendly or decent the host society is, these attempts at crossing the racial divide are bound to fail. Why Zinga should aspire to travel to South Africa is not established. It seems that the poster might be appropriate in a white working class home where South Africa would represent an opportunity to improve their social standing, and perhaps it is there in order to indicate the extent of Zinga's assimilation. It may perhaps also indicate that South Africa was considered an appropriate political system under which black people should work: clearly delineated statuses for black and white, systematic and inflexible ordering and categorization and supporting legislation were already in place by the 1930s.

STANDING BY THE MALE

No rationale is offered for Ruth's presence in England which is not in itself problematic: it is anomalous though, because we are given such a highly elaborated account of John's background. The character of Ruth is that of the necessary female support for a major male role, a textual emphasis of his masculinity: she also serves to reduce the threat of black male sexuality by containing it in their heterosexual monogamous relationship. Her reproductive function remains unrealized and with it the possibility – and white people's fears – of producing black children.

John Zinga sings the spiritual-orientated 'Down the River of Dreams', a suggestive title not only because of its allusion to the manifestation of the unconscious at work in dreams and fantasy but because of its aquatic imagery indicating a return to the motherland and to the womb: the narrative logic for his singing is that a child is crying and needs calming. As Zinga sings, a sequence shows a blonde woman looking adoringly at her baby in a crib, cutting to a black couple gazing on their three children asleep in one bed. There are two points to note here. First is that here again we see the white contrasted with the black: the indication of excessive black fertility emphasized by the squeezing of three children in a too small single bed. Second, the black family may be seen as offering a merest hint of a black community in the dockland neighbourhood. This is surprising because it is not until the sixties – and not with any degree of consistency even then – that black people are represented as having a community to whom to relate, by white film-makers. Apart from during his stage performance, it is not until the Zingas go to Africa that other black people appear with them, and then it is in the position of inferiority to the Europeanized blacks.

When Zinga is cast in the title role of an operetta, *The Black Emperor*, Ruth assumes the clothing appropriate to the wife of a man of substance.[16] At the premiere she wears a flowing, white dress with wing-like appendages. The whiteness of her dress acts as an aesthetic foil to her skin colour – even though she is lighter skinned than Robeson, the contrast is there – and emphasizes her status as a 'good' black woman rather than the hypersexual, wild exotic.[17] Ruth stands as a pivotal point between acceptable notions of white femininity – very much under-elaborated in *The Song of Freedom* – and both the unacceptable but quintessentially black, femininity as exemplified by Queen Zinga at the beginning of the film, and the 'primitively' dressed 'native' women in the 'real Africa' and in the staging of *The Black Emperor*. Later, in Africa, Ruth wears a 'native' cloth, carefully wrapped around her body: this is self-consciously modest and indicates only a little loosening or loss of western cultural values and attitudes towards female modesty.

Although Ruth attempts to fit in through this change in her dress, she contravenes a major taboo by looking on that which is forbidden and here the emblematic figure of the witch doctor, a metaphor for Africa's atavism and savagery, enters the scenario. Mandingo the witch doctor – his primitive mores and superstitions emphasising the prehistoric character of the continent – performs secret rituals not available to the female gaze. Thus it is the woman who is in the position of having betrayed patriarchal traditions and she must be punished. It is interesting that it should be the forbidden look which is implicated here, since to seize the right to look is to attempt to seize power. The referent for this incident might be the biblical story of the curse of Ham whose gaze upon his naked father in a drunken stupor caused God to curse his successors with blackness thereafter. Significantly, Ruth's punishment is to be thrown into the snake pit with all its phallic symbolism: here again, John is unable to articulate a plea for her to be saved or act physically to rescue her. Instead, he wins over the 'natives' who are calling for her death by singing the song which has been passed down through the ages to those of Casanga's royal lineage: music that 'soothes the savage breast' of both child – as seen earlier on – and 'native'.

CULTURAL AND CLASS MOBILITY

When John Zinga sings, Donozetti says to him 'With me you have a great future' and offers Zinga the opportunity to train with him; to become rich and famous. Here, the assumption is that despite his 'natural' talents, Zinga still needs the refinement of European training. It is significant that he is not offered the opportunity to sing his popular folksongs or spirituals: he has to be totally Europeanized to become fully cultured and thus acceptable. The implication is that he cannot rightfully take up his regal position until he has undergone a process of acculturation. This strategy has some success in creating an African who serves as an agent of imperialism: this is Zinga's trajectory in the narrative.

When Ruth and John go with Donozetti to his hotel to rehearse, they wear the 'wrong' clothes and John calls the man on the door, 'sir'. Ruth and John are, at this moment, both class and racial migrants traversing clearly established boundaries, marked as different by their demeanour and dispositions. Donozetti begins his attempt to transform Zinga into what he wants, just as a benevolent slave master might have taught his recalcitrant slaves or Professor Henry Higgins worked on Eliza Dolittle in Bernard Shaw's *Pygmalion*. Zinga, however, initially rejects the accoutrements of Europeanization by discarding the stiff, constricting clothes he is given to wear and proclaiming 'I can't sing with all this stuff on'. Ruth, as is so often the case with women, is characterized both as a calming influence and an upwardly aspirant, culturally conservative force who tries to persuade John to acquiesce.

The down-to-earth spontaneity of John Zinga's singing is frequently contrasted with the artificiality of the European operatic tradition. The necessity for white Europeans of having to train, to rehearse and constantly to refine their vocal technique is foregrounded and contrasted not only with the African John Zinga's natural ability but also the spontaneity of working class culture. The recreational pursuits of the working class community consist of going to public houses and watching dance bands, activities which point to the gulf which exists between bourgeois and working class cultures. The sense of working class community and solidarity is exemplified by the communal singing led by Zinga in the public house where again his songs speak of travel and arduous journeys.

Later on, we see how John Zinga ascends the ladder of entertainment success as he sings 'Stepping stones help me cross the river/To that other shore'. Through yet another aquatic metaphor the musical motif voices the desire to 'return' to Africa, though at this stage he is still unaware of his royal birthright. The lyrics also suggest that he has succeeded in crossing class and racial boundaries to be accepted by the bourgeoisie across Europe.

John Zinga, playing the eponymous Emperor dies in the final act of the opera and it is as if this echoes the death of John Zinga, working class black man and his rebirth as a participant in white bourgeois culture and man of royal lineage. Zinga's working class friends attend the performance and behave inappropriately by shouting out 'Well done John!' and conversing with each other during the performance. Again, we are offered a vision of an unchanging natural order of things which fixes social and cultural differences into an ossified hierarchical structure in which no matter what you do or learn, your destiny is pre-determined by your biological heritage. This ideology is precisely the terrain of eugenicist discourse as discussed in chapter 2.

When John Zinga says to his friends that he cannot make a speech, we know that despite the training and refinement he has undergone, he is still, at base, an inarticulate black man whose lowly status is only redeemed by his ability to sing in a culturally privileged idiom. He is able to sing about freedom but not once does he articulate a spoken acknowledgement of black struggles for autonomy and liberation. Loss of speech is equated with a lack of intellect and powerlessness, since speech is privileged as the point of access to the workings of the mind: the inability to speak suggests a poverty of thought and an inferior subjectivity, and was one of the key textual strategies for representing the 'primitive' nature of Africans in imperialist literature of the nineteenth century.

John Zinga's family and cultural background are located for him by a white anthropologist, Sir James Currie, who is in the audience. His recognition of the song Zinga sings as an encore, and the medallion that he wears is based on rational knowledge and empirical evidence in contrast to Zinga's intuitive knowledge about where he belongs. This again emphasizes the perceived differences between the sophisticated intellect and rationality of the white male academic and the instinctual behaviour and feelings of the primitive black male. The binary logic of a split between mind and body may also be discerned here as the elderly, frail looking anthropologist is seated passively watching and listening to the theatrical display before him, whilst the physically robust Zinga acts out his role.

From this man then, the white paternal figure of authority, Zinga learns of the state of his country: it is uncivilized, backward and superstitious, and the people are stricken by disease and poverty, stuck in a timelessness emphasized by the visual discourse at the start of the film. The notion of existing in the continuous present is identified by Edward Said as a consistent feature of Orientalism (Said, 1985: 72). This sense of always being in the present implies no history and thus no background or context need be given to elaborate on the condition or motivation of the 'native' or the 'primitive'. It relates to the idea that the colonies existed in a static condition until they were 'discovered' by white Europeans. The 'fact' of this frozen condition then allowed the colonizer to claim that their uninvited occupation of those countries was of benefit to the population since it was through the white invader that hospitals, schools and 'civilization' were established.

To reinforce the sense of timelessness, the unchanging atavistic nature of Africa, we are introduced to Casanga – through John's and Ruth's approach to the island – by means of the same scene depicted at the beginning of the film. Talking drums announce the arrival of John and Ruth who arrive dressed in classic colonial safari suits and topees. John Zinga is superior amongst his people because of his royal lineage and this relationship of power and status is reinforced by his being significantly taller and of a more sturdy physique than the rest of his tribe: this is one of a number of visual references to Zinga/Robeson's physical presence, particularly about how big he is.[18] Unable to exist without help, John and Ruth have taken with them a black servant played by Robert Adams, whose antics as this character belong firmly in the comic coon tradition.[19]

To John, everything is primitive but Ruth encourages him to help the people – that is his role and destiny. They are his 'race' and his 'blood' and 'the worse things are, the more you can help them', evidencing a change of attitude on Ruth's part. As Bogle points out, Zinga is merely an agent of colonialism in approach and attitude (Bogle, 1988: 197). John is eventually recognized as the true king and Mandingo's despotic rule is curtailed: even primitive people can recognise hereditary authority when they see it. John and Ruth return to Europe for a farewell concert, in order to raise funds to build hospitals and so on to help his subjects.

Unfortunately, despite the film's attempt to posit a harmonious integration of black and white working class conviviality, it cannot help drifting into sentimental set pieces and offers no political perspective on racial or gender oppression. *The Song of Freedom* in spite of its liberatory title posits class and racial divisions as fixed and immutable since Zinga must return to 'his' people: it is the destiny of his blood lineage and thus the text supports rather than undermines the notion of racial fixity and the dynastic principle.

PEOPLE FROM DIFFERENT WORLDS

Men of Two Worlds does not have the presence of a star persona such as Paul Robeson but ten years after *The Song of Freedom*, it is still foregrounding similar issues and themes. Interestingly, the title *Men of Two Worlds* resonates with more recent descriptions of young black people in Britain as being 'trapped between two cultures' and this will be discussed in chapter 6.

This time the black male protagonist is named Kisenga – which sounds similar to Casanga, the island in *The Song of Freedom* – and he is a concert pianist rather than an opera singer but still firmly located within the realms of high rather than the emergent popular culture. Kisenga's music is a hybrid of traditional 'African' and classical European music, signifying that Kisenga is Europeanized but retains, as he puts it, 'the thousand years of Africa in his blood.' He decides to go to Africa to help 'his' people plagued by the tsetse fly which causes sleeping sickness.

Again the ignorance and primitivism of the 'African native' is embodied in the figure of the manipulative witch doctor who will not allow his fellow villagers to take the medicine prescribed by Doctor Munroe (Phyllis Calvert), the white female doctor. As is the case in *The Song of Freedom*, the principal evil of the witch doctor's rule is seen as his rejection of European values and his abhorrence of white people's presence in Africa.

A rationale for refusing to move away from the infestation is not attributed to this 'primitive' tribal community: they merely act, they do not think. This reinforces white European assumptions about rational motivation being absent amongst 'primitive' people. In contrast to the childlike Africans, the archetypal figure of the District Commissioner, Randall (Eric Portman), is the voice of European masculine reason, trying to get the Litu – Kisenga's people – to move to a place which is not infested with tsetse flies. When the community, influenced by the 'witch doctor' reject European medicine it is seen as evidence of their irrationality and they thus forfeit any claim to be thought of as autonomous human beings. This is a similar justification for domination to that proposed during the eighteenth and nineteenth centuries as argued in chapter 2.

Another point to note is how, just as in the earlier imperial literature described above, 'natives' are depicted as a primeval, undifferentiated horde. This colonialist tendency is identified by Albert Memmi as a strategy of depersonalization named by him as 'the mark of the plural.' Memmi, talking in general terms, notes: 'The colonized is never characterized in an individual manner; he is entitled only to drown in an anonymous collectivity ("They are this." "They are all the same.") (Memmi, 1990: 151). In *Sanders of the River* (1935), *The Song of Freedom* (1936), *Men of Two Worlds* (1947) and *Simba* (1955), only the quiescent or Europeanized Africans are allowed the privilege of individual subjectivity and the limits of this autonomy are strictly defined.

Men of Two Worlds has the characteristics of a film which was a tired attempt to revitalize and sustain the myth of benevolent British paternal colonial rule when it was already clear that the British Empire had little life left in it. However, there is a point of interest to which I would draw attention: Phyllis Calvert's performance as the doctor. Her disgust at the sight and proximity of the black people in the film is almost palpable. Her whole body seems to be infused with a nervous tension that manifests itself in the way she speaks, moves and relates to the other actors. She refuses to engage in eye contact with Kisenga and on occasion acts as though he does not exist, talking and looking through or past him. She barely acknowledges his presence and ensures that their bodies are never close enough to make contact even when they pass each other in narrow spaces. The extent to which Calvert's demeanour is intended to be a trait of her character is not clear. It could be that this hypertense performance is attributable to the repression of sexuality which informs the film and the taboos regarding interracial relationships between black men and white women which were even more marked then than they are today.

Made in 1955 *Simba*, represents yet another reworking of these themes of the black African male who is educated and has taken on in some clearly signalled sense western European culture. Here though, British fear regarding the increasingly vociferous demands for autonomy, and colonial subjects' rebellion against the experience of subordination is manifested in what Dyer calls 'the rigid binarism, with white standing for modernity, reason, order, stability, and black standing for backwardness, irrationality, chaos and violence' (Dyer, 1988: 49). The role of the bad Other is displaced from the witch doctor and intensified in relation to the Mau-Mau in *Simba*. This text is a late entry into the colonial adventure canon, coming as it did towards the end of British colonial rule in Africa. It does not engage with the black presence in England and may be seen as representing the terror of the imminent end of Empire and the assumption of white supremacy.

CONCLUSION

It was necessary to conceptualize and depict the colonial Other as an infantile, sexually licentious savage in order to justify continued economic exploitation, surveillance and the ruthless wielding of power. Bhabha sees the attribution of such qualities as perverse contradictions:

The black is both savage (cannibal) and yet the most obedient and dignified of servants (the bearer of food); he is the embodiment of rampant sexuality and yet innocent as a child; he is mystical, primitive, simple-minded and yet the most worldly and accomplished liar, and manipulator of social forces. In each case what is being dramatised is a separation – *between* races, cultures, histories, within *histories* – a separation between *before* and *after* that repeats obsessively the mythical moment of disjunction.

(Bhabha, 1983: 34)

Attributing cannibalism to savage Others serves at once as justification for taming those savages, as a confirmation of white European supremacy and as a screen onto which to project guilty repression of the knowledge that it is the white oppressor who behaves in a cannibalistic manner. The act of cannibalism also functions as a useful metaphor for colonial exploitation. This is examined further in the discussion of *Leo the Last* (1969) in chapter 5. There is also in evidence in these anxious repetitions of colonial tropes, the fear of being re-absorbed in to the dark, articulated as a fear of the dark or being swallowed, or ingested by the Other. In order to exercise 'mastery' over that 'darkness', to pre-empt the retaliation that they guiltily fear will be enacted against them, acts of violation are perpetrated, such as rapine penetration, and genocide.

The notion of British colonialism as a global civilizing mission is explicit in *Sanders of the River* (1935), *The Song of Freedom* (1936), and *Men of Two Worlds* (1946), and reflects the narcissism embedded in colonial and neo-colonial fantasies. The central character of the white male is represented as whole, unified and coherent, a perception constantly in danger of disruption through the mirror-image of the black Other. Embedded in the psyche is the 'knowledge' that difference – specifically racial and sexual difference – subverts and disrupts the notion of cohesion and order and this anxiety needs to be constantly mollified. These films served as comforting narratives for a nation which, used to assuming spiritual, cultural and political superiority, was traumatised by the Indian 'mutiny' and the subsequent fear of further destabilizing uprisings and acts of resistance. Through cinema – and literature – the old self-assurance could be re-asserted with the likes of 'Sandy the strong, Sandy the wise' able to rule over devoted black subjects, in spite of being vastly outnumbered.

Five years before *Simba* was made, Basil Dearden's *Pool of*

London was released. This film indicates a significant break with the colonial adventure genre since no direct link is made between the black male character and Africa. Although he works on a ship which necessitates him spending long periods away from London, his presence is not specifically marked as unnatural or out of place. However, attempts to date a white woman are thwarted in order to avoid any controversy.

Significant numbers of black settlers from Africa, South Asia and the Caribbean came to Britain after the Second World War and it is to these groups that film-makers who wished to explore racial difference turned in the latter part of the 1950s. Exoticism and Otherness no longer had to be sought 'out there' – indeed, could not now be with the imminent demise of this phase of colonialism – since the Other was actually 'here'. This marks the moment where the *numbers* of black people became imbued with more significance than they had been before. Although represented as living in Britain, in *The Song of Freedom* (1936), *The Proud Valley* (1939) and *Men of Two Worlds* (1946), black people posed little threat because one way or another they did not settle in or reproduce in Britain. The numbers of black people involved outside of well-established communities in Cardiff, Bristol and Liverpool were perceived as insignificant. The narratives dealt with such problems as did arise by removing the source – in these three examples the African men – through death or repatriation. Vast numbers of Africans in Africa were not so problematic since one efficient District Commissioner could control them all with the assistance of a compliant 'native' chief.

The term 'racial problem' – previously associated with the racial traumas of South Africa and the USA – took on a whole new dimension in the 1950s when black people started to settle across Britain and themes relating to sexuality which had previously been studiously avoided became issues demanding attention. In the chapter which follows, films from the late 1950s and early 1960s will be analysed and considered with reference to the social context of their production and consumption.

Chapter 4

'Miscegenation' and the perils of 'passing'
Films from the 1950s and 1960s[1]

In chapter 2, I argued that 'race' and sex need to be considered in conjunction with each other since many of the anxieties that white people have about black people have been of a sexual nature. Chapter 3 was concerned with charting how this anxiety – which has been a distinctive feature of British society since the first encounters between merchant adventurers and Africans – was manifested in a range of texts from the late nineteenth to the mid-twentieth centuries.

This chapter focuses on interracial sexual relations as depicted in two films: *Sapphire* (1959), and *Flame in the Streets* (1961) and draws on the theories of narrative and realism discussed in chapter 1. The chapter is concerned with close textual analyses of *Sapphire* and *Flame in the Streets*, concluding with a critical overview and comparison of the themes of these films. The history outlined in chapter 2 is referred to in order to indicate the extent to which long-established ideologies of 'race' resurface in the texts under consideration.

Sapphire explored social issues, used 'authentic' non-studio locations and conscientiously introduced a few regional accents, although it was still mainly dependent on the strained tones of Received Standard Pronunciation. It was intended as an entertainment with serious treatment of the 'real' social issues. As has been noted by John Hill the 'reality' of cinema of this period was 'always conventional, a discursive construction rather than an unmediated reflection' (Hill, 1986: 127) although whether the latter is ever achievable is arguable.

Before I analyse these films, I discuss the ways in which interracial sexual relations have generated anxious commentary from a variety of sources, from the early part of the twentieth century to the

1960s. In particular, the perceived threat of black 'infiltration' of the self-contained, 'pure' white family is considered. In relation to this and with specific reference to *Sapphire*, the notion of 'racial passing' is analysed as a sign of duplicity which threatens to undermine the stability of racial categorization.

THE SOCIAL CONTEXT

Britain's major conurbations from the mid-1950s onwards underwent a steady demographic transformation.[2] Despite Britain's long history of systematically inferiorizing black people, there was a complacency about 'race relations' and the presumed level of tolerance amongst white people. This complacency was shattered when in 1958 a number of violent racist assaults were carried out against black settlers in Nottingham and Notting Hill: these attacks were characterized as 'race riots' in the press. Although not the first manifestations of organized racist aggression, the attacks were used as supporting evidence for the claims of the anti-immigration lobby. Opinion was mobilized around the paradoxical notion that it was black people that represented a threat to the rule of law. Local and national press coverage of the so-called racial problems – housing conditions, employment issues, crime and so on – became more frequent (Rich: 1986).

In the year following the 'race' riots, racial issues were especially topical which is indicated by the fact that Ted Willis' play *Hot Summer Night* was produced as a stage play, a television play and the film *Flame in the Streets*.

'RACE' AND BRITISH CINEMA

From the 1930s to the early 1950s, since film became a major component of popular culture, the anxieties and fears – and also the pleasures – associated with black people and their alleged characteristics have emerged in British cinema almost surreptitiously, in a non-systematic, erratic manner. As Jim Pines has pointed out: 'There isn't a substantial body of films which reflect an ongoing or developing concern with race-related themes, but rather sporadic "moments" in which particular motifs have featured prominently' (Pines, 1981: 3). There are a number of 'racial moments' which have arisen due to the convergence of particular circumstances: the 1950s and 1960s was one period which generated several representations of racial difference. The themes and preoccupations of these texts, made by white film-makers, articulate the tensions regarding inter-racial relations and black people's contradictory status and presence here.[3] Again, manifestations of a specifically sexual problematic are evident in films such as *Sapphire* (1959) which is an investigation into both the murder and the sexual activities of a 'light-skinned black woman' and *Flame in the Streets* (1961), a narrative concerned with interracial marriage. In each of these films, 'misce-genation' and fertility are seen as key problems.

The perception of the inevitability of 'race' always being a problem is evident in most films that feature black people in signif-icant roles during this period, such as *Sapphire*, *Flame in the Streets*, and *A Taste of Honey* (1961). Although the last example is different, as the presence of the sole black character, Jimmy (Paul Danquah) does not provoke an explicit discussion of 'race' and sex, even though his action in getting her pregnant precipitates a potential crisis for Jo (Rita Tushingham).

Although black people, especially women, are by and large absent in any significant roles from much of British cinema of the late 1950s and 1960s, there are occasional references to racial difference and imperialism. For example in *Look Back in Anger* (1959), Jimmy Porter, bitter and misogynist though he undoubtedly is, is not consciously racist. He befriends Kapoor, an Indian stall holder who sells cheap shirts and who is victimized by other stall holders. Also, during one of his verbal attacks on his upper middle class wife, Porter refers to her family as the 'master race' due to their privileged position in India. This comment is linked to his visit to the cinema where he is disgusted by a film depicting the slaughter of fleeing Indians by the rampaging British. Porter is a jazz fan and declares that those who don't like jazz are not 'real' people thus encapsu-lating the qualities attributed to the 'good' stereotype of black people which are envied by whites. Jazz is the medium, he claims through which people can 'connect', thereby linking, music, sexuality and blackness.

Intruding black male characters are often dispatched during the course of a narrative, particularly when they have been linked to white women in the text. This occurs in *A Taste of Honey* (1961), when the young sailor returns to the sea after getting a young white woman pregnant, and in *Flame in the Streets* (1961), when the black workers complain that they are sexually incapacitated by the cold climate thereby indicating they lack the adaptability necessary to thrive in local conditions and rendering them sexually safe. In many British films, black people make brief appearances and have an enigmatic status: just what are the meanings which may be read off the character of the black vicar brought in by Peter Sellers' dissident clergyman in the Boulting Brothers comedy, *Heavens Above* (1963)? In this text the African vicar is chased from the English country village where he has been posted. Within these films, the intractability of the problem of 'race' is not there to be discussed: it is taken as given.

RACIAL DIFFERENCE AND SEXUAL RELATIONS

The alleged threat to Britain's standards of sexual propriety posed by the presence of black settlers was repeatedly invoked, particularly by the national and local press, at particular moments during the period covered by this chapter (Rich, 1986: 180). In particular, the monitoring of the sexual activity of black men has been a consistent political manifestation of the tension engendered by the reactions of white Britain to the presence of black people in their midst.[4] This preoccupation contained within it expressions of fears for the purity and superiority of the white 'race' which, as they relate to terms such as 'miscegenation' and 'race-mixing' are evocative of earlier scientific racist discourses. All language related to the conjunction of sexual and racial difference is problematic: miscegenation, mulatto, half-caste, mixed race, interracial and so on all carry with them the stigma of racist discourses, suggesting as they do an acceptance of the precepts of separate, biologically determined racial groups.[5]

It should be noted that the eugenicist argument still had currency in the 1950s and it was claimed that black immigration, 'ran counter to a great developing pattern of human evolution' based on an 'array of variants': underlying this was the argument that black immigrants had 'measurable and largely inheritable, physical attributes below the average for the United Kingdom.' (Bertram, 1958: 21).

BLACK SEXUALITY/MORAL PANIC

During the first two decades of the twentieth century, a major focus of white people's disquiet was the presence of black seamen in British ports and their sexual liaisons with white women: embedded in this anxiety was the spectre of racial decay and degeneracy. In January 1929 the *Daily Herald* – utilizing the language of eugenics

– reported that 'Hundreds of half-caste children with vicious tendencies' were growing up in Cardiff as a result of 'black men mating with white women' while 'numerous dockland cafes run by coloured men of a debased and degenerate type are rendezvous for immoral purposes' (quoted in Rich, 1986: 189). It was believed that interracial sexual activity would lead to social, moral and physiological decay. In 1927, public expression of fears regarding interracial sexual relationships reached a nadir when the Cardiff Chief Constable, James Wilson, argued for legislation to prohibit interracial sexual intercourse similar to the recently enacted Immorality Act in South Africa. Wilson spoke of how white Englishmen were able to resist the temptations of black female sexuality both in the colonies and in Britain (this was, of course, a fantasy since there is ample evidence to suggest that the opposite was true) due to the fear of being socially ostracized (Hyam, 1990). Wilson noted:

> strangely, that feeling does not dominate a certain class of women in the British isles . . . . The day may come when public opinion will awake to the fact that our race has become leavened with colour strain to such an extent that calls for action.
>
> (quoted in Rich, 1986: 128)

The rationale for establishing the right to increase police powers of control and monitoring of black and working class sexuality is here expressed in quasi-eugenicist terms and serves to pathologize black men and white working class women whilst exempting white middle class men from any implication in or responsibility for 'racial degeneration'. It should be noted that black people were not the sole targets of this habitualized 'race-thinking': Chinese, Maltese and sometimes Jewish people were regarded in a similar manner. The difference lies in the emphasis which is placed on the sexual and genital attributes of black women and men and the specific histories of the different oppressions.

During World War II, the presence of black North American soldiers precipitated another moral panic about miscegenation and British regional police headquarters were asked to monitor their behaviour and interaction on three levels, two of which concerned sex:

> friction between white and black American troops . . . breaches of the peace caused by the fraternization of American troops (black

and white) with British girls, and lastly the particular association of black Americans with British women.

(Smith, 1987: 177)

Troops from the USA were supposedly policed by their own personnel but in the areas where there was a concentration of black troops, the local police were required to make reports to Home Intelligence, the Foreign Office's North American department, and the Ministry of Information about their sexual activities.

After the Second World War there was an acute shortage of suitable labour to rebuild Britain and the decision was taken to encourage peoples from the Caribbean, Africa and South Asia to come and work in Britain. These settlements of visibly 'different' strangers precipitated a number of studies in the popular press as to the nature of the 'problem' being imported. The ignorance and fear surrounding the settlement of numbers of black people of African descent was, by that time, embedded in the collective British psyche.

The attitude that it was necessary to monitor and control sexual relations between black men and white women was foregrounded again in the 1950s, and in much of the sociological material written about black immigrants from the late 1940s up until the mid 1960s, there is an obligatory section dealing with the controversial issue of interracial sexual relationships (Little, 1948; Patterson, 1963; Hill, 1965).

It was also during this period that an atmosphere of moral panic was apparent due to the alleged decline in standards of sexual behaviour, particularly amongst young people (Cohen, 1972). Given the eugenicist sub-text of much of the concerns expressed about the threatening fecundity of the working classes, the increasing opportunities and quest for independence of young women, the gathering momentum of demands for autonomy in the colonies, and the dangers posed to the health of the 'race' by interracial sex, the conjuncture of a moral panic about sex and with the arrival of black settlers was almost inevitable.

This set of apprehensions – regarding gender and racial difference, sexuality and class – intersect on the level of the alleged attraction that black men held for women of the lower classes, a popularly held belief that dates back many years. The perception of the threat of vast numbers of black people detrimentally transforming British society was, of course, strongly allied to fears about black male sexuality. Clifford Hill wrote in his sociological survey of attitudes to racial difference: 'The subject of intermarriage is undoubtedly the most controversial in the whole field of white and coloured relationships' (Hill, 1965: 37–38).[6] According to *The Times* of 3 September 1958, black people 'are charged with all kinds of misbehaviour, especially sexual'. In general terms, white people's ignorance about black people was rife in the 1950s. Questions asked of black settlers here included: did you live in a mud hut?; did you live in the jungle?; do you eat cat food?; do you eat people? At least two of my contemporaries' mothers on giving birth were asked where their newborn babies' tails were. The durability of these images was assisted by the contents of the popular press, by the popularity of 'jungle' and imperial/colonial adventures such as the Tarzan cycle (the films of which started in 1918), *King Solomon's Mines* (1937), *The Song of Freedom* (1936), *Men of Two Worlds* (1946) and *Simba* (1955), and by popular fiction such as the James Bond series of novels. The interaction of constantly circulating racial stereotypes – established through popular British and North American films, generally xenophobic and imperialist literature and comics, and newspaper articles and reports – together with the resurgence of racist political organizations and intense debates in Parliament, ensured that common sense attitudes towards 'race' focused on blacks as problems, needing control.

These and other habitualized forms of 'race-thinking' were further compounded in the 1950s by social and economic factors which served to keep blacks and whites within largely separate spheres of existence, each with their own sets of social networks and spaces. Crossing the colour line was not merely a matter of breaking the boundaries of colour-based social divisions in a figurative sense; it was also often a matter of literally transgressing the geographical boundaries of the 'ghetto', often with violent consequences (Gilroy, 1987).

Films of this period that make use of racial issues in their narratives seem to promote a set of ideas which assume a consistent and uniform set of social expectations and practices in relation to beliefs about racial and sexual difference.

Of especial interest is the way in which fears about the conjunction of 'race' and sex were articulated through interrogations of white female sexuality and this will be discussed in relation to both *Sapphire* and *Flame in the Streets*.[7] In terms of expressions of racism both white women and working class youths are perceived as prone to prejudice. A conformity to social expectations and an adherence to the violations of socio-sexual taboos is presupposed in these films, even though compliance in regard to these interdictions cannot be taken for granted and has never been true for all people. The texts often involve narratives constructed in such a way that if such interdictions are broken and the boundaries of racial propriety transgressed, then the perpetrators are 'punished' or threatened with punishment. Thus the racially ambiguous Sapphire is murdered after consummating her relationship with her white fiancé; in *A Taste of Honey*, Jimmy is dispatched once he has had sexual relations with Jo, never to be seen again; the narrative in *Flame in the Streets* sees to it that Gaby Gomez is badly burned although in this same film, Peter Lincoln manages to escape any specified 'punishment' other than a humiliating first encounter with his white fiancée's father, Jacko.

Fears about black immigration and the moral decline of British youth focused on sexuality and popularized notions of biological determinism and human behaviour. Delinquent white youths were described as 'uncivilized' and 'barbarians' with all the attendant primitivist, colonialist connotations. They adopted unacceptable modes of dress, and listened to degenerate popular music influenced by black performers from the USA. They 'savagely' attacked innocent victims, engaged in 'orgies' of violence and were responsible for participating in a steady decline in sexual mores. Colonialist metaphors were used to pathologize white male working class youths and deployed to align their behaviour with that of the primitive Other, blacks and the threat of Americanization. Popular musical forms and dance styles were seen as contributors to the process of moral degradation.[8] In both *Sapphire* and *Flame in the Streets*, it is the Teddy boy types, the young working class men who are seen as being violently aggressive towards black people and, significantly, alluding to black men's alleged sexual superiority. Interestingly these youths are not portrayed as demonstrably sexually active, suggestive, perhaps, of repressed sexuality being sublimated in violence.

INFILTRATING THE WHITE FAMILY

The idealized white family was represented in the films discussed here, as being under threat. I want to draw attention to some of the reasons why the stability of the family was seen as so significant and to suggest its relationship to British colonialism. The Empire itself was a metaphorical family, with Britain represented as both benevolent paternal influence and welcoming motherland; indeed familial metaphors and figures abound in colonial and nationalist discourses.

In regard to the period during which *Sapphire* and *Flame in the Streets* were made, the stoical English family, consolidated during World War II, was seemingly under attack by the 1950s. Thus the figure of the family may be seen as analogous with the predicament of a Britain without the 'Great': a country which was losing its identity as the custodian of its colonial subjects/children as they struggled for independence from oppressive/parental rule.

Like the body, the family may be characterized as a 'bounded system' and as with the body, it is: 'a system the boundaries of which are formed by skin at once porous but perceived as inviolable and impenetrable' (Goldberg, 1993: 54). Likewise, the nation is an attempt to create and maintain a 'bounded system' and – perhaps this sense is particularly heightened in the case of an island such as Britain – it is feasible to see that system as a permeable but protected structure. Crucial to a sense of group identification in this schema is the process by which:

> the body comes to stand for the body politic, to symbolize society, to incorporate a vision of power. Porous and permeable though the boundaried 'skin' of the body politic may in fact be, it is constituted always in terms of the bordered criteria of inclusion and exclusion, identities and separateness, (potential) members and inevitable non-members.
>
> (Goldberg, 1993: 54)

One of the reasons that may be posited for the intense emotional responses to interracial relationships is that of a fear of dissolution of the self represented by fusion with the Other. That fusion destabilizes the Manichean dichotomy which has been so meticulously constructed and crafted over centuries. In *Flame in the Streets*, Nell's violent reaction to her daughter's choice of a black husband may be founded on such a fear, of the loss of self. This dissolution is linked metonymically to the boundedness of the self and the invasion through 'swamping', 'flooding' and 'inundating' by 'waves', 'tides' and 'floods' of immigrants: these oceanic images signify the ultimate dissolution of the self through remerging with the point of origin – the return to the womb when the dichotomy between self and other had no meaning. Thus the 'infection' that is interracial sexual relations is an invasion of the individual family in the first instance, then of the national body/family and is constituted as a rape/violation of that nexus. Within such texts I argue that the black subject is the interloper, the alien intruder who threatens disruption of accepted racial positions.[9]

'PASSING' AND *SAPPHIRE*

Interracial sexual relations have been perceived as problematic by black as well as white intellectuals and writers. Black people in mixed relationships are seen as participating in a form of racial suicide.[10] Fanon sees the 'mulatta' woman as particularly problematic in this respect. Referring to the reactions of 'the woman of colour' – divided into 'the Negress and the mulatto' – to white European men, Fanon writes:

> The first has only one possibility and concern: to turn white. The second wants not only to turn white but also to avoid slipping back. What indeed could be more illogical than a mulatto woman's acceptance of a Negro husband? For it must be understood once and for all that it is a question of saving the race.
>
> (Fanon, 1986: 54)

Another difficult situation brought about by 'mixed' relations is the predicament of someone who 'passes' for white – that is, a person with black antecedents who lives as a 'white' person. 'Passing' is a complex term, overlaid with various meanings depending on the context from which it emerges: it is a recurring motif in North American literature, drama and film and occasionally in British cultural forms as well. *Sapphire* is possibly the only film to engage with 'passing' in a British context.

Mary Helen Washington pinpoints some of the ambivalent emotions which cluster around the notion of 'passing' by referring to an African-American literary classic, Nella Larsen's novel, *Passing*:

> 'Passing' becomes, in Larsen's terms, a metaphor for the risk-taking experience, the life lived without the support other black women cling to in order to survive in a white and male-dominated society. But *passing* is a word that can also connote death . . . . She [Clare, the woman who passes] does in fact die as a result of passing for white.
>
> (Washington, 1987:163)

Many fictional accounts of 'passing' for white refer to women and the major films which are concerned with 'passing' have been about women caught in the trap of racial duality, one exception being *Lost Boundaries* (1949) – in whose very title is embedded the anxiety about loss of identity – which focuses on a heterosexual couple's racial ambiguity and duplicity.[11] 'Passing' requires the denial of temporal continuities: the past, the present and the future represent danger and have to be disavowed and constantly reconstructed. For Sapphire her past life as a 'black' woman, her old friends, memories and so on have to be more or less discarded in order to live out her new identity as 'white'. Her denial of the present involves the anxiety of being 'revealed' as a racial impostor. The fear of the future is particularly acute for the 'passing' woman. As the locus for reproduction of the 'race', anxiety about the future is represented by the possibility of bearing a dark-skinned child. Thus the 'passing' subject can never settle: there is never a moment in the past, present or future which she may safely inhabit.

The female 'passing' subject is a figure which represents the embodiment of racial liminality, occupying the interstices between the codification of racial difference located in the terms black and white, Negro and Caucasian, Other and self. The faith in identifying racial groups by selected phenotypical characteristics is shattered by what may be seen as the fallibility of ocular proof and visual knowledge.

The act of 'passing', whilst undermining absolutist notions of racial categorization is ultimately based on a skewed essentialism within that racial taxonomy. A person who has both black and white antecedents is most frequently designated black. There is at least some justification for this when the person concerned has the skin colouring and features associated with the archetypal phenotypical characteristics of black people. However, if that person's character-istics indicate 'whiteness' in spite of having black ancestors, why then are they still perceived of as 'black people passing for white'? In North America this notion that 'one drop of black blood' means that 'whiteness' is obliterated was institutionalized in the form of detailed legislative measures designed to prevent 'miscegenation': although in this country in 1959 no such legal processes existed, it seems that with *Sapphire*, the principle was nonetheless accepted.

In the Hollywood 'passing' film, the tragic 'mixed race' protago-nists were played by actors 'known' to be white. At the core of such casting was the belief that white audiences would not be able to identify with black actors in these leading roles and that the 'tragedy' of 'passing' was that basically good, honest people had their lives blighted by the taint of 'negro' blood. The white audience was encouraged to feel these characters were literally no different from themselves and thus should not have to endure the intolerance of racism (Bogle, 1991). In *Sapphire* the problem of casting is neatly avoided by allowing Sapphire to exist only as a photographic still, since from the start of the film, she is already a corpse.

In her chapter on the 'dark continent' trope, Mary Ann Doane claims that the use of white actors to portray black characters in the North American film, *The Birth of a Nation* (1915), 'directly confronts the issue of visibility and its relation to racial politics by transforming the visible aspects of racial identity – blackness and whiteness – into signs whose theatricality is marked' (Doane, 1991: 216). Although this casting strategy was based pragmatically on the unacceptability of black actors playing important roles and scenes with white women, it would seem to point to the discardability of one of the main signifiers of racial difference. Doane implies that the Douglas Sirk melodrama, *Imitation of Life* (1959), holds a vision of skin colour in which it is indicated that blackness is a coating which can be shed and that thus the notion of 'passing' may be seen as a potentially non-essentialist approach to 'race'. However, this theoretical position can only be sustained if the material strategies and effects of racism are denied, since the success of the 'mixed race' woman who passes is based on her expectation of reaping the benefits which accrue to white women. Such advantages do exist – in the economic, educational and social spheres – and are based on established racial privilege. The casting of white people in these roles actually confirms the notion of racial superiority both in terms of the obvious – the part does not go to a black person – and the less apparent – the assumption that 'whiteness' provides the 'base' for portraying the complexities of human subjectivity.[12]

SAPPHIRE

The narrative of *Sapphire* is concerned with the investigation of her murder. Although Sapphire looked 'white' it is eventually revealed that her mother was a black singer, and her father a white doctor. Initially, Sapphire's fiancé David (Paul Massie) is a suspect as it is discovered that she was pregnant which would have spoilt his plans to study architecture in Italy. Her obviously black brother Dr Robbins (Earl Cameron) informs the police officers Superintendent

Hazard (Nigel Patrick) and Inspector Learoyd (Michael Craig) that Sapphire had led a double life. Various contacts are pursued and eventually Mildred (Yvonne Mitchell) – David's sister – confesses to her hatred of Sapphire and her murder.

Before she discovered that she could take on whiteness by 'passing', Sapphire dated only black men. The text assumes that a woman 'known' to be 'black' would not necessarily have the option of dating a white man: when she is able to choose her sexual partner due to her assumed racial privilege, Sapphire rejects black men as serious contenders, and opts for the pleasures of whiteness. Inferred here is that marriage to an English man would consolidate her class privilege and allow her to detach herself from the stigma of blackness. Is this instance of a black woman's rejection of black men an acknowledgement of the power associated with whiteness, or are these textual denials a narcissistic assumption on the part of white men that black women see white men as more sexually attractive? Whatever the answer, it seems that Sapphire never fully relinquished her past 'blackness', choosing instead to oscillate between racial positions, sometimes acknowledging her racial origins.

Sapphire's 'passing' is only fully revealed when her brother enters the narrative – the first black person to appear in the text – and he is immediately identifiable as black: he is also linked musically to the revelation of Sapphire's dual identity by a similar musical chord to that used when her petticoat – a signifier of her double life – is freed from her drawer by Superintendent Hazard. Significantly, at the same time as her brother reveals that she is 'mixed race', the autopsy reveals that Sapphire was pregnant. Typically, given her racial heritage, Sapphire's deviant behaviour manifested itself as sexual licentiousness. Inspector Learoyd remarks that it is not now possible to be sure who the father of the child might be since she is now established both as *black* – read, essentially promiscuous – and, worse still, a racial impostor. Thus the racial essentialization of Sapphire's cultural identity is the pivot of the film and her sexuality is investigated as an integral constituent of her racial ambiguity.

'Passing' as white is not necessarily to be perceived solely as a desire not to be black: it is as much to do with the desire to have access to the privilege invested in whiteness by white people. It is the case that white people deny their racial specificity all the time, refusing to acknowledge their ethnicity by naturalizing it, by universalizing it, by rendering it invisible and by refusing to reflect upon it. By assuming whiteness, the passing subject disrupts the normalization of whiteness.

THE LOOK AND RACIAL AUTHENTICITY

The liberal aim of *Sapphire* as stated by Basil Dearden the director was to 'show this (colour) prejudice as the stupid and illogical thing it is' (quoted in Tarr, 1985: 53). Tellingly, in both *Sapphire* and *Flame in the Streets*, the most overtly racist characters in the texts are sexually frustrated white women and white working class male youth. In *Sapphire* although Inspector Learoyd starts out as a racist, his powers of reason predominate and he realizes the error of his ways: once again the white bourgeois man is foregrounded as a rational subject. As the film is structured as a murder investigation, *Sapphire* is a perfect vehicle for a demonstration of superior (masculine) powers of logic and deduction. It also provides a legitimate excuse for the investigators to satisfy their curiosity about black life in London and their desire to observe and pry into the sexual life of the Other.

Whilst Sapphire spent her time enjoying the delights of the Tulips Club, Mildred and her twin girls live a quiet life with her parents and brother David, in a neat, modest terraced house somewhere in London. The twins' room is decorated all in pale blue, as is the hall and the kitchen: even Mildred's cardigan is the same muted, ice-blue. The suggestion of coldness and frigidity surrounds Mildred at home as it does in the grocery store where she works. Perhaps Sapphire's vivaciousness and animation, were they to be realized on screen, would have provided too much of an overwhelming contrast with Mildred's sexually frustrated, tense and cold persona. Even their respective names resonate with oppositional connotations: the 'exotic' Sapphire representing the antithesis of the 'plain' Mildred. The name 'Sapphire' in North American culture is one given to African–American women who are characterized as 'loud, obstinate, domineering, emasculating and generally immoral' (Ferguson, 1973: 590). The use of that name in a British film and the use of the trope of 'passing' seem to indicate a North American influence although the expressions of racism and the lower middle class social milieu created in the film are distinctively English.

Regarding those who may be of mixed racial heritage, Learoyd states that he can 'tell them a mile away', a point he makes several times and one which is echoed by Sapphire's former landlady: 'Nice enough girl considering she was coloured . . . I guess you can always tell . . . too eager to please, laughed too much, noisy with her gramophone . . . I didn't mind . . . so long as they don't look it.'

Reflecting, perhaps, on her economic relationship with Sapphire, the landlady comments 'Passing for white . . . would you be pleased with a brass sovereign?'. It is worth noting how the economic exchange is constructed as analogous with the notion of racial authenticity.

What of David, Sapphire's last sexual partner? Surely in that most intimate of relationships, Sapphire's 'racial essence' must have been revealed? David's mother asks him 'What made you get mixed up with a coloured girl?' to which David replies 'I didn't know' perhaps indicating that had he known, he might not have been so keen to pursue the relationship. However, later on, he admits to knowing although it is not claimed as an intuitive knowledge such as that claimed by Inspector Learoyd. Both Learoyd and the landlady lay claim to a knowledge which cannot be reliably verified by visual signification but in case visual evidence fails there are a number of ways of fixing someone's racial ancestry: the important concern is that such an identification be made.

As previously suggested, the fallibility of the look is structured into the narrative in *Sapphire* as in *Imitation of Life* and other 'passing' films: this implicitly undermines western European culture's valorization of 'seeing is believing'. Looking is subverted as a reliable means of recognising who is and who is not a member of 'our' group. Thus the ascription of 'blackness' to Sapphire has to fall back on a biological definition of 'race' as being about genealogy and heritage rather than that of phenotypical features or political and cultural construction.[13] This is especially highlighted in the scene at Tulips nightclub where seeing is emphatically not believing.

The two policemen, Hazard and Learoyd, replicate the colonizer's entry into the unknown 'interior' – in this instance, the Tulips Club – where the 'natives' perform their alien rituals: the 'dark continent' in the middle of London. A number of apparently white women are in the club, some are dancing, some sitting down. One in particular is questioned by the two officers, a young blonde woman sitting at the bar. The club owner, a suave black man, identifies her as a 'lilyskin' and proclaims that although she may look white, she is 'really' 'black': such women are given away by the fact that when the bongos start to play, they cannot resist tapping their feet. Such essentialist notions having been previously denied by Hazard, this confirmation from a black man of what Learoyd already 'knew' serves to undermine the liberal discourse of the text. To underline the point, the music becomes more frenzied, the pace of the cutting speeds up and the camera angle is lowered, so that the audience is offered close-ups of swirling skirts, whirling legs and glimpses of underwear. The audience has already been told that in spite of being a student at the Royal College of Music, Sapphire could not help but return to Tulips to be moved by the rhythm of the bongos: she was only ever temporarily able to sublimate her desire for 'savage' music – symbolic of the potential of her wild, 'black' side – by studying civilized 'white' classical music.

The women in the Tulips Club, all of whom 'look' white, dance with men, all of whom are unambiguously black, and are subjected to Learoyd's fascinated gaze. The voyeuristic look up the skirts of the women in the Tulips Club is legitimated through the law and functions both as a monitor of black male sexual behaviour, and an investigation of the sexualized bodies of the women who may be black or may be white and working class: their racial indeterminacy, the question mark hanging over their racial essence seems to problematize their sexual availability for the police officer. This results in Learoyd being mesmerized by the spectacle before him. The Inspector's curious but controlling look is emphasized by the camera angles, the framing and focus which attempt to suture the viewer into his look and assume his bewildered perspective.[14]

If Sapphire's physical appearance undermined notions of racial essentialism and the certitude of ocular proof, then these 'racially ambiguous' women – 'the lilyskins' – observed dancing in Tulips are interesting because of the way in which their sexuality and their racial uncertainty is foregrounded. This physically active female sexuality is perceived as latent in all women perhaps: here it is figured through the women's codification as – possibly – 'black'. This may be seen as a partial acknowledgement of white femininities' dependency on the oppositionality of black women's sexuality for a definition of their own. It may also be an extension or another kind of 'passing', this time of a sexual nature, whereby the ostensibly controlled and controllable white woman may escape the confines of the repressive demands of bourgeois white patriarchy when she 'hears the sound of the bongos'. In this case, 'passing' is a figure for female sexual duplicity and ambiguity, and for freedom, as well as being concerned with racial anxiety. Again, the two elements – that of racial and sexual difference – manifest themselves most potently through the 'black' woman. The fear is of 'slipping' from white to black: a potentially downward trajectory from pure to debased sexuality, from rationality and civilization to illogical emotion and primitiveness. And who is it that dances with these women and beats out the rhythm that can unlock their sexual pleasure and power? The black man, not the white: the 'civilized' white men can only stand and observe.

Carrie Tarr has examined *Sapphire* in terms of the centrality of (white) women's sexuality and she claims that the racial element is subordinated to the sexual, not considering the extent to which sexuality and gender are racialized in a society where racial and sexual difference have been so thoroughly intertwined historically (Tarr, 1985). I would argue that the two elements are inextricable here, and that the element of racial difference is essential to the playing out of the sexual concerns. Mildred's sexuality stands contrasted both to Sapphire's and to the 'lilyskins' at the Tulips Club: Mildred is the 'racially pure' white woman contrasted with the 'racially tainted' Other. The distinction is being made between competing types of femininity: the images of white women are exemplified by Mildred's frigidity, her mother's non-sexualized maternal role, the suggestively 'butch' police woman and the huskily voiced female proprietor of a shop selling exotic underwear; all are implicitly compared to the image of the heterosexualized liminal Other's sexual identity as primitive, wild and excessive.[15]

WHITENESS/BLACKNESS: A MATTER OF DEATH AND LIFE

For Sapphire, to take on whiteness is to literalize Richard Dyer's contention regarding the series of *Living Dead* films directed by George Romero:

> If blacks have more 'life' than whites, then it must follow that whites have more 'death' than blacks. . . . All the dead in *Night* [of the Living Dead (1969)] are whites. In a number of places, the film shows that living whites are like, or can be mistaken for, the dead. . . . Living and dead whites are indistinguishable.
>
> (Dyer, 1988: 59)

Mildred's life is dull and loveless. When she was living as a black woman, Sapphire led an exciting life, but her 'white' life is marked by its speedy demise.

Sapphire is seen by the audience only as a dead inanimate being – only available for viewing as a corpse or in photographs, thus our sense of to which racial group she might belong is never really put to the test. This 'deadness' is in contrast to the descriptions of her vivaciousness offered by her doctor brother and Mildred. Instead of directly witnessing her behaviour, the audience has to rely on the testimonies of the people who 'knew' her: friends, relatives, former and current lovers.

Wherever she went, it is apparent that Sapphire bore the threat of disorder, culminating in rousing David's sister to such a frenzy of passion that she murders her. Sapphire has already disrupted the surface calm which existed beforehand within the previously united, hard-working respectable white family, through becoming pregnant by David. Mildred's murder of Sapphire is also the murder of her unborn child and any others which might follow.

Sapphire's potential as a black, reproductive female is indicated by her pregnancy but ultimately denied through death. Mildred's sexual tension and implied frigidity is in marked contrast to the looseness of the women dancing at the Tulips Club. Mildred awaits her husband who never returns. Her surrogate husband – brother David – having had sexual relations with a 'mixed race' woman, has betrayed the family's racial heritage and upset her re-constituted family: thus the annihilation of Sapphire is necessary in order to attempt to reconstruct Mildred's family. As with Nella Larsen's heroine Clare, Sapphire 'does in fact die as a result of passing for white'.

RACIAL FIREWORKS AND *FLAME IN THE STREETS*

Flame in the Streets (1961) was originally a stage play by Ted Willis, *Hot Summer Night*. The drama emerged during the period of turbulent 'race relations' culminating in 'race riots' in Notting Hill and other urban areas. The indication of heat and the association with passion is maintained in the film's title through the invocation of fire. The film is concerned with the relationship between Kathie (Sylvia Sims) who is a very blonde, white woman, and the daughter of a trades union activist, Jacko (John Mills) and his neglected wife Nell (Brenda de Banzie). Kathie decides to marry Peter (Johnny Sekka), a black teacher originating from the Caribbean. Jacko argues for worker solidarity across racial boundaries and his union involvement leads him to neglect his lonely, anxious wife, Nell (Brenda de Banzie). Although distressed by the thought of her daughter marrying a black man, Nell is eventually persuaded to meet and discuss the future with the couple. Unlike *Sapphire* where the text exhibits a high degree of narrative closure, the ending of *Flame in the Streets* is unresolved, and the audience is left with Kathie's mother and father on one side of a room and Peter and Kathie on the other: the space between them indicating the distance between their attitudes.

Fanon, in response to the familiar question asked of white parents, 'would you let your daughter marry a black man?' responds with: 'In what way, taken as an absolute, does a black son-in-law differ from a white son-in-law?'. Fanon quotes Octave Mannoni as claiming that the initial question regarding interracial marriage demonstrates the use of racism as a defence mechanism against the guilt aroused by incestuous feelings between father and daughter. Fanon responds to Mannoni's explanation thus: 'Why not, for instance, conclude that the father revolts because in his opinion the Negro will introduce his daughter into a sexual universe for which the father does not have the key, the weapons or the attributes?' (Fanon, 1986: 165). Fanon's answer might be equally applicable to all possible suitors were it not for the mythologies surrounding black male sexuality. He pinpoints here white male anxiety over masculine sexual potential, sexual potency being a central locus of anxieties about black men. Fanon attributes to white women sexual frustration as the principal determinant of anxiety about black people. This is problematic since white women are then implicitly marked as inherently prone to sexual neurosis, and racism is seen as an effect of sexual frustration. Both of these issues, the fear of interracial sexual relations and white women's sexual frustration and neurosis are contained in *Flame in the Streets*.

Physically violent racist acts are committed by white youths in the film, but the most memorable and in some ways, most telling account of racist fears comes from Nell. Her vividly insinuating description of the sexual horrors which await her daughter has its echo in Clifford Hill's later, controversial sociological study, *How Colour Prejudiced is Britain*. Noting how the issue of interracial sexual relations 'generates more heat and rouses deeper passions than any other aspect of the race/colour situation in Britain' (Hill, 1965: 209), Hill goes on to comment: 'The very idea of actual intimate physical contact with a coloured person is repugnant to

most white people' (ibid.: 209).[16] Nell's account of what she feels
will be her daughter's experience stands testimony to those sentiments.

FEAR OF NUMBERS

Flame in the Streets makes references to some of the major concerns
of white Britons at the time, expressing hopes and fears which do not
solely refer to sexuality but also relate to economic, employment
and housing issues. Although it clearly intends to articulate a non-
racist viewpoint, as with *Sapphire*, *Flame in the Streets* consistently
calls upon a reservoir of attitudes and approaches to racial difference
which render the black people within the text as powerless and, to a
large extent, subordinate to white people.

White people's concerns about black settlers were constantly
articulated in terms of numbers, and fears of being overrun and
contaminated by black people with their alleged hypersexuality, the
threatening potential of their fecundity, and their aberrant familial
structures. Such anxieties were frequently expressed in the
newspapers and journals of the time: Paul B. Rich notes how:
'Pathological terminology describing black immigration became
increasingly prevalent in the press by the late 1950s' (Rich, 1990:
189).[17] Imagery relating to 'floods', 'tides' and 'waves' of
immigrants and references to crime 'breeding' in areas 'teeming'
with black people became commonplace. The use of this aquatic
imagery in conjunction with the bestial is consistent with many
expressions of racialist thought as has been previously argued.[18]

The increased black presence in the 1960s precipitated a fierce
political debate. Pressure groups, political organizations and other
extra-Parliamentary activists vociferously expressed enough anxiety
over the potential transformation of British society and culture to
make it an issue within Parliament: the political argument culmi-
nated in the Commonwealth Immigrants Bill becoming an Act of
Parliament in 1962.

Paul B. Rich has argued that:

apparent during this period is the bewilderment and confusion of
many sections of the liberal intelligentsia in grappling with the
immigration issue at the same time as they had difficulties in
understanding the new elements of youth culture brought on by
the emergence of what was in popular parlance being termed an

'affluent society'.

(Rich, 1986: 189)

The sense of white supremacy did not fall away in the interests of working class solidarity since this supremacist attitude is:

> complexly interwoven with the experience of competition between the metropolitan working class and the 'cheap labour' of the peripheral economies . . . . This experience of competition was of course intensified by the partial *internalisation* of the periphery's 'cheap labour' during capitalism and its dependence on immigrant labour.

(Hall, *et al.*, 1978: 147)[19]

The left's response to black immigration failed to recognize that there were common interests of both black and white workers as they, like the rest of the country, demonstrated their susceptibility to accepting racist arguments for curbing the numbers of black settlers.[20]

FERTILITY AND SEXUALITY IN *FLAME IN THE STREETS*

The action of *Flame in the Streets* starts at the entrance to the school on the morning of the 5th November – an apocalyptic date as will also be shown in *Leo the Last* (1969) – and finishes, literally explosively, the same evening during the Guy Fawkes celebrations.

The children with whom Kathie enters the school grounds are all white – perhaps pointing to the 'pure white' offspring she will never have – while the girls which Kathie actually teaches are black and white. It is beside a black girl that Kathie stops, to place a friendly hand on her shoulder and encourage her in her work – there has been no dialogue so far, only a musical soundtrack up to this point in the narrative. The film then cuts to Peter's all boy class who are also hard at work and it is his approach to observing a pupil eating an apple in class to which our attention is drawn. The child is not admonished; Peter, a wise, reasonable, symbolic father, chooses to note with amusement but not to reprimand him. The audience is encouraged to witness both the teachers' professionalism and in particular, asked to feel sympathetic towards Peter.

Peter's acceptability – though that is limited – is predicated on his attitude and his social position. His character is reminiscent of

Sydney Poitier in *To Sir with Love* (1966): the more or less
Europeanized black male character who has no political statement to
make. Due to the casting and playing of Peter, the extent to which he
may be characterized as sexually threatening is minimal.
Importantly, he is a teacher in a primary school, a section of the
teaching profession where women are in the majority. It is a job with
lower pay and lower status than those associated with teaching in
secondary schools or higher education. That, in conjunction with his
gentle, non-predatory manner tends to feminize him and thus
diminish his sexual threat to Kathie. Peter takes on a paternal role in
the classroom and the absence of sexual spark between the two
players suggests a fatherly role in Kathie's life too; a compensation
for her own absent father. As is common with films constructed by
white film-makers, the amount of information given about Peter's
family background is minimal and nothing is shown to suggest that
he has a social and cultural life beyond his work and his insipid
relationship.

Outside a factory bearing the legend, 'Visser and Crane Furniture
for the Homes of Britain', two white boys ask for pennies for the
guy. This guy is a grotesque 'nigger minstrel' style guy whose head
falls ominously onto its chest as if the possessor had been lynched
and hung, signalling the difficulties which black men in the text will
encounter.

Inside the factory, there are a number of black men employed
whom we see working, and singing calypso, traditionally a vehicle
for strident political commentary. The calypso presented to the
audience here is not of that kind, of course: it is the bland depoliti-
cized version, the version associated with 'gossip' as popularized by
personalities of the time. The association of popular music derived
from black culture with the explicit and dangerous sexuality of black
men is immediately made here through the invitation of one of the
black labourers to a passing blonde female office worker: 'hey baby,
do you want to sing with us?' The woman acknowledges them
looking at her, and their comments, not, apparently, displeased by
what has occurred. The sexualization of the black men is further
emphasized in this short sequence by the comment from one of them
that, 'the terrible thing is, I am unable to give the chicks my full
attention in this weather' and 'the weather is turning my blood to
ice'. These remarks also serve to reassure the audience – who are
assumed to be white, given the pleas for tolerance towards blacks –
that these working class black men represent little threat to the purity

of white womanhood in this narrative. The scene also serves to vindicate the sentiments of those who saw black settlers as having come to take the jobs that were seen as properly belonging to white people and to indulge their sexual preference for white women: work is apparently low on their priorities. In contrast to Peter's professionalism, these men do not appear to be interested in their work. Like Paul Robeson's character of John Zinga in *The Song of Freedom* (1936) referred to in chapter 3, Peter is the exceptional black man, set up as a contrast with his less diligent peers. Already married to a white woman who is heavily pregnant, Gaby Gomez (Earl Cameron) castigates his fellow black workers in a scene which is also reminiscent of the incident involving Zinga's reprimand of the sleeping black docker in *The Song of Freedom*.

Of interest here is the colour casting. Peter is the darkest in skin colour and his colour serves as the visual antithesis to Kathie's whiteness. This whiteness is accentuated by her blonde hair and in fact, the four most significant white women in the film are blonde: the significance of blondeness in representations of white femininity is an area worth investigating. The colour casting is of note because of the status attached to lighter skinned black people in both black and white societies. It seems to be the case that gender differences operate within this colour scheme: light skinned black women – especially those who can 'pass' for white are often sexually troublesome as has been suggested earlier, whereas men of that colour are often 'good negroes'. The use of skin colour as a sexual and social marker is another area which warrants further investigation.

If Peter may be crudely characterized as a modern 'noble savage' then Gomez is something of an 'Uncle Tom' whose desire for acceptance is manifested in his marriage to a white woman, his bid for promotion, and his willingness to make jokes at his own expense. To the young white men who work in the factory though, no matter how compliant a black man is, he is first and foremost a 'spade'. Attractive women are referred to as 'skirts', 'bits of muslin' and 'Janets'. The main protagonist amongst the racist young men, a blond youth, comments 'you know they say, they reckon that spades are special with the Janets; that's why they go for them' and this statement is greeted with raucous laughter from his fellow white workmates. Blacks are spades, women are 'skirts' and 'Janets', neither are individuated human beings. This homogenizing naming suggests an attempt to control what is essentially uncontrollable:

those who stimulate anxiety. The power to name is as crucial to power as the power to look and because of their gender and their 'race' the men are able to do both to those whom they see as subordinate to them. These men – as working class youths – do not, of course, have real power but the illusion of control is important for those who are oppressed but unable to recognise that.

This inability to recognize the source of oppression is echoed in the character of Jubilee, the black slum landlord who is seen as exploiting fellow black people and whites by charging high rents for inferior accommodation. He wears expensive, flashy clothing and drives a new car: Judy Gomez, Gaby's blonde wife, refers to Jubilee as a pimp suggesting his involvement in sexual exploitation as well as social. Whether or not he is actually controlling prostitutes is immaterial: it is the connection that is being made that is important here.

MATERNITY AND AMBIVALENCE

The house in which the Gomez couple live – one amongst many similarly decrepit properties owned by Jubilee in the vicinity – is full of the signs of sexual activity. There are often several children to be seen playing on the stairs, in the hallways and running along the landing and there is Judy Gomez in the later stages of pregnancy. Judy informs Gaby that 'I feel as though I'm carrying an elephant': it is as though she has been impregnated by the 'jungle'. She makes this remark shortly before she accuses Gomez of 'behaving like an animal' for having torn off a piece of bread rather than cutting it. In later scenes we are shown a black family crowded into one room with a man playing a calypso on a double bass. Towards the end of the film, we see a black man and a black woman in bed together, who invite Kathie to join them. This short scene represents a surplus moment inasmuch as it does not further the narrative, merely reiterates the point that the house is overcrowded and there is an excess of transgressive sexual activity taking place. It is the woman who poses the question, thereby locating her as the source of perverse sexuality. This vignette occurs after a telling moment in the narrative, when Kathie has tried to persuade her mother that marrying a black man is not the disaster she anticipates.

In the scene between Kathie and her mother, Nell, the issue of sexual relations between black men and white women is brought out into the open. It is clear that Nell has a considerable emotional investment in her only child, and she advises Kathie that 'black and white don't mix . . . you'll be neither one thing or the other.' The latter phrase 'neither one thing nor the other' is one often used to described what is perceived as the plight of those of 'mixed-race' heritage and clearly there is a hint here of the stereotype of the 'tragic mulatta' doomed by her embodiment of racial/sexual trans-gression to live in confusion and fear. What is significant here is that this is being applied to a *white* woman: the implication is that she will cease to be 'white' when she marries a black man. She will be 'dirtied' by association.

Neither will Kathie be 'the Other' since she will still appear to be white: in effect, she will be indulging in a kind of 'passing'. Kathie's fate will be to become an outcast, living with people who are alien to the British way of life. 'They're not like us Kathie', asserts Nell, 'I don't just mean the skin . . . other things are different . . . ways, habits, everything.' Nell's distress about black people's 'ways' and 'habits' reaches peak intensity with the dreaded realization 'you'll have children, black children!' This last comment comes after an apparently horrific imagined scenario involving her daughter in bed with her black fiancé.

This outburst makes a link between Nell's feeling of lack in regard to her own relationship with Kathie's father, Jacko, who is too engaged in the public world of trade union negotiations to pay attention to her emotional and physical needs. All Nell ever wanted, she tells Jacko, was a house with a bathroom – which, given her disgust at the thought of black sexuality and the association of blackness and dirtiness, seems an appropriate symbol of her desire – and emotional satisfaction from her husband. The implication here is that this white woman with bourgeois aspirations, through being denied sexual satisfaction, is susceptible to irrational forms of thought and behaviour in the form of racial prejudice. Note that in *Sapphire*, it is also a socially aspirant, sexually frustrated white woman – Mildred – who becomes so embittered and bigoted that she kills Sapphire.

Judy – whose name is rather close to Judas, the betrayer – offers only gloom and discouragement when Kathie seeks her advice on her decision to marry Peter. For Judy to be dissatisfied with her pregnancy is not unexpected in British films of the late 1950s and early 1960s: *Room at the Top* (1959), *Look Back in Anger* (1959), *The L-Shaped Room* (1962), *A Taste of Honey* (1961) and *Sapphire* (1959) all emphasize the difficulties associated with fertility and child-bearing. Pregnancy is a curse, a form of punishment for sexually active women and indicates some of the anxieties which were accruing to the idea of women's emancipation and its implications for the family. Repeatedly, the family is invoked as a fragile structure, liable to disruption externally and internally. As previously indicated, the death of Britain's imperial family heritage was reworked in the representation of the demise of the family itself (Hill, 1986: 16ff.).

Manifestations of sexuality are – in contrast to other issues such as economic exploitation – given plenty of space in which to be articulated. References to sexual relations, the visually strong presence of an abundance of children – from the initial scene at the school to the house where Gomez lives, and to the pregnancy of Judy Gomez – abound.

TEXTUAL/RACIAL STRATEGIES

A major flaw of the liberal discourse of social realism of this period is the attempt to explain away racism by locating it in individuals who are often already pathologized Others, such as working class youth or sexually frustrated women. The individual act, thought and attitude are emphasized, whilst institutional and state endorsement of racial inequality is ignored. Such texts seem incapable of analysing or explicating social inequality as being a consequence of government policy, and are unable to place trade union, working class and anti-racist struggle in a wider political and historical context. This lack of contextualization or elaboration of political struggles is a feature of many films of this period, and here it works as a particularly potent device for disavowal of racial guilt and responsibility, since the white spectator is invited to dissociate her or himself from the racist individual.

It is also apparent that the fantasy of white male middle class identity as liberal and tolerant remains intact as he is rarely depicted as holding racist views. This relates to the equation of racism with irrationality and, amongst whites, it is women and the working classes who are most likely to be depicted as the source of illogical, emotional, non-rational, 'primitive' thought. Black women, in this scenario are seen as responsible for eliciting the violence they receive.

Flame in the Streets does at least attempt to approach the question of both individual and (working class) collective responsibility, and the struggle against racism. However it cannot adequately deal with either issue without stepping out of its self-imposed framework which sees prejudice as the unenlightened, deviant behaviour of individuals. This tension is resolved by coming back from the brink of recognition of the politics of divide and rule at a macro level and instead binding the issue to the micro-politics of individualized self interest.

There exists a tension in both *Sapphire* and *Flame in the Streets* between the verbally expressed liberal sentiments and the privileging of the visual discourse. For example, although the liberal intention of *Flame in the Streets* may be to examine the issues raised by interracial sexual relationships in an 'objective' and tolerant manner, the visual evidence offered consistently undermines such intentions. A good illustration of this is when Nell, in her attempt to dissuade Kathie from pursuing this relationship, claims: 'you don't know how they live ... like animals. Have you seen them? Six, eight, ten to a room. Is that how you want to end up? In one room with a horde of black children?' These are precisely the views of black people's living conditions seen earlier in the narrative and the suggestion is that it is black hypersexuality and overbreeding, combined with black economic exploitation that is the cause of the problem: and the problem is so deep that even a nice middle class black man like Peter, and a respectable working class black man like Gomez are forced to share similar circumstances.

Both Peter and Gomez are characters who point to black men's alleged predilection for white women – particularly blondes: the only black couple shown represent the sexually perverse with their attempt to corrupt Kathie. These images do not, of course, operate in isolation; they interact with other texts both fictional and non-fictional. In particular, newspaper accounts of similar conditions would combine to confirm for many white spectators that housing, crime and unemployment plus the ever-present though frequently unspoken sexual issues are inextricably bound up with the presence of black people in this country.

When he is trying to persuade Nell to concede and meet Peter, Jacko argues that if she does not compromise then their daughter will be lost to them forever, thereby appealing to her emotions and self-interest rather than what is fair. Kathie, we are reminded, is all Nell has got. Thus Jacko absolves himself of any familial and emotional responsibility whilst evading the issue of what is morally or ideologically correct. The politics of 'race relations' are not addressed and cannot, therefore, be interrogated.

READING 'RACE' IN *SAPPHIRE* AND *FLAME IN THE STREETS*

There are always problems in reading off meanings from historical material. Stuart Hall asserts in a discussion of issues raised by the analysis of photographic images of black post war settlement:

> It is difficult, if not by now impossible to recapture the earlier meanings [of photographs]. In any event, the search for their essential truth – an original, founding moment of meaning – is an illusion . . . . No such previously natural moment of true meaning, untouched by the codes and social relations of production and reading, and transcending historical time, exists.
>
> (Hall, 1992: 106)

However it is necessary to undertake this historical work in order to try and understand contemporary predicaments. Of interest – and this is raised by Hall in his essay too – is the bearing that the formal constraints of realism had on narratives of 'race' and the 'real'. One of the points about social realism is that it has a particular power to encourage belief in its constructions of reality and this clearly has political implications.

What both *Sapphire* and *Flame in the Streets* have in common are their attempts to be liberal and tolerant in regard to their depiction of black people. Solutions to the problem of prejudice are inferred, usually from a 'more knowledge equals less prejudice' perspective: a classic liberal position. The point is that the texts are not organized so as to be critical of the systems and institutions within which racism and prejudice flourish. This inability to articulate certain kinds of problems is located, in part, in the formal conventions as John Hill notes:

> the ideas and attitudes expressed by the social problem film . . . do not derive simply from the focus of their subject-matter but also from their deployment of certain types of conventions . . . which, then, inevitably structure and constrain the way in which that subject-matter is presented in the first place.
>
> (Hill, 1986: 56)

Despite its containment in liberal discourse and social realism, inevitably, repressed racial anxiety seeps out from the edges of these texts, returning to defy its enclosure and that is where the contradictions arise.

CONCLUSION

White women are frequently seen as agents in the narrative disruption which black people initiate: it is the 'skirts' whose sexuality is – in one form or another – out of control or misplaced. Thus in *A Taste of Honey*, it is suggested that all Jo really needs is an adequate amount of love from a properly caring mother; instead she is forced to seek the transitory solace of a passing black sailor, a man portrayed as little more than a child himself who cooks and tends her like a mother might be expected to.[21] Mildred, Sapphire's murderer, clearly misses male sexual attention, fantasizing as she does that her absent husband's return is imminent. Her sexual frustration and jealousy lead her to destroy the hedonistic, deceitful Sapphire who otherwise would have become her sister-in-law and produced a child. Nell makes explicit her feelings of rejection by Jacko who is too involved in union work to spend time with her.

Both Nell and Mildred indicate that the pleasures of marriage and domesticity are located in children, domestic artifacts and physical environment. Both are largely confined to the home and neglected by their husbands. In other films too, sustenance from men as fathers is simply not available; they are either literally absent as in *Sapphire* (1959), *A Taste of Honey* (1961) and *The L-Shaped Room* (1962), or there in body but emotionally absent in, for example, *Room at the Top* (1959) and *Flame in the Streets* (1961). Therefore it should not be surprising that:

> With physical pleasure apparently so divorced from marriage and domesticity, it is inevitable that those films which rely on marriage as a means of conclusion tend to imply less a positive endorsement than an emphasis on compromise and acceptance of constraint, the eschewal of fantasy already noted.
>
> (Hill, 1986: 111)

In regard to the function of 'race' in these texts, Jim Pines argues that the racial interaction functions as 'a catalyst for white characters' anxieties which in themselves are not wholly rooted in 'race' as such, but which nevertheless become the major preoccupation in the narrative' (Pines, 1991: 4). There is a sense in which neither *Sapphire* nor *Flame in the Streets* are about 'race' as such but – particularly with the introduction of black characters – they become narratives of racial difference and sexual anxiety. Repression in the texts focuses on sex and sexuality because:

in English culture the preferred forms of discipline are all *internalised*: they are forms of *self*-discipline, *self*-control. They depend on all those institutions and processes which establish the internal self-regulating mechanisms of control: guilt, conscience, obedience and super-ego. The exercise of self-discipline within this perspective has as much to do with *emotional* control (and thus with sexual repression, the taboo on pleasure, the regulation of the feelings) as it does with *social* control (the taking over of the 'morale' of society, the preparation for work and the productive life, the postponement of gratifications in the service of thrift and accumulation).

(Hall, *et al.*, 1978: 144)

The family represents a major site for the establishment and monitoring of sexual mores and behaviour whilst also serving as a metaphor for the nation. Thus a breach of the perceived integrity of the family is also figured as a breach of the cohesion of the nation. In both *Sapphire* and *Flame in the Streets*, the breaching of the bastion of racial purity embedded in notions of the family is attempted by a 'black' alien intruder.

Sapphire, as has been demonstrated, is perceived as a racially liminal subject who represents a dissolution of the line between white self and black Other: this has to be figured through a woman since the white masculine ego-ideal needs to remain intact. The intrusion that this represents must offer guilty recognition because:

In the traditionalist lexicon, the sphere of the *family* is of course where moral–social compulsions and inner controls are generated, as well as the sphere where the primary socialisation of the young is first tellingly and intimately carried through.

(Hall, *et al.*, 1978: 144)

Given that this is the case, where did Sapphire's and Peter's putative in-laws go wrong in the socialisation of their children? Mildred resolves the problem, 'rights the wrong', by preventing further congress between her brother and Sapphire: the ambiguous subject is erased thus eliminating further confusion, and restoring the narrative, if not the family, to some sort of equilibrium.

For Jacko and Nell, their task is more difficult since restoration of the family intact does not look likely. Jacko has to face the fact of blackness, the fact that his daughter is not marrying what he consciously recognizes as a mirror-image of himself, but is engaged to his 'dark shadow-self': he faces this resolution with his intellect whole but his emotions in tatters. The outcome is perfectly consistent with his intellectualized views on brotherly solidarity but at odds with his sense of racial integrity.

Fanon's statement about white women's racism and its alleged link with sexuality strikes me as both reductive and hyperbolic:

> All the Negrophobic women I have known had abnormal sex lives. Their husbands had left them; or they were widows and they were afraid to find substitutes for the dead husband; or they were divorced and they had doubts at the thought of a new object investment.
>
> (Fanon, 1986: 158)

Unfortunately, the women represented as 'negrophobic' in *Sapphire* and *Flame in the Streets* are constructed so as to confirm Fanon's contention. For Nell, Peter is the embodiment of her racial nightmare and – like Mildred – she has not been accorded the masculinized attribute of intellect and rationality to deal with the situation. Perhaps she sees her emotional and sexual estrangement from Jacko as the 'reason' for Kathie's choice of a man phenotypically different from her husband and perhaps – given her fantasies of black fertility and sexuality – she is envious of her daughter's entry into what she perceives as a different sexual plane.

If a narrative is said to progress from one equilibrium to another, with the initial equilibrium being disrupted by a particular event or forces, then in the examples of British cinema that have been examined here, 'race' is frequently the power which motors the disequilibrium.[22] Black people, by their very presence, are seen as a disruptive, damaging force disturbing the previously calm, stable landscape of white cultural supremacy, and familial and sexual complacency.

This view of black people in Britain is rather different from those expressed in the following chapter. *Leo the Last* (1969) is the subject of chapter 5. It is separated from *Flame in Streets* by eight years but a number of significant changes on the political and cultural terrain had taken place by then. In particular, the colonies had become politically if not economically independent and the government had changed from Conservative to Labour.

Chapter 5

Family life

In chapters 1, 2 and 3, I established the extent to which notions about blackness and racial difference have permeated British cultural production. I have also argued that discussing films in terms of whether they portray black characters positively or negatively is understandable but inadequate. The imprint of colonialism may diminish over time but the traces of racist ideologies consolidated over three centuries may still be read in contemporary cinematic texts. Throughout this study I am concerned with demonstrating how sexual themes in particular are explored and what positions are available for black women in these texts. *Leo the Last* (1969) works through a number of the issues I raised in chapter 1: the power of the look, interracial sex, contrasting notions of white and black femininity, and whiteness.

This chapter is solely concerned with *Leo the Last*. The reason for this textual isolation has as much to do with its historical location as with its being of especial interest. As a product of the '1960s', *Leo the Last* does not sit easily with either *Sapphire* (1959) or *Flame in the Streets* (1961). Similarly, although made in the 1960s, it was arguably closer in spirit to 1974 – when *Pressure* was made – than to 1961. However, the cultural interventions of black film-makers and cultural producers, and the demands for equality made by black people in general marks the 1970s as having a different set of sensibilities.

This chapter analyses *Leo the Last* as a film of contradictions which although the narrative progresses from the perspective of a white male's dominant imperial I/eye, nonetheless problematizes whiteness to a considerable degree. The film is not so relentlessly addressed to a complicit white audience as the previous texts discussed since there is a space for non-dominant perspectives on whiteness. This critical space is opened up by the evident loathing of white middle class mores and cultural values.

There is a level on which the social project of white male middle class filmmakers in Britain has frequently been that of the anthropologist. Within the documentary and social realist movements, there is often a sense that: 'riding on the back of "social commitment" to observe "ordinary people", then, emerges as a kind of sexual fascination with "Otherness", the "exotic" sexualities of those it now has a licence to reveal' (Hill, 1986: 136). This fascination with what is perceived as an exotic sexuality is certainly a feature of *Sapphire* (1959) and is part of the subtextual fabric of John Boorman's film, *Leo the Last* (1969).

THE 1960s: LOVE, PEACE AND RACISM

In the early part of the twentieth century, the division of people into racial categories had maintained its credibility through its scientific legitimation but after the slaughter of Jews, Poles and gypsies on racial grounds prior to, and during, the Second World War the academic community challenged the scientific basis of racial categorization (Stepan, 1982). During the 1960s, with the popularization of biology and zoology through people like Desmond Morris and Konrad Lorenz, and psychology through Hans Eysenck and Arthur Jensen, notions of racial and cultural superiority resurfaced and were scientifically legitimated once more (Rex, 1973; Stepan, 1982). The re-emergence of racist scientific theory in the 1960s was particularly pertinent as black peoples' rebellion against their subordinate status manifested itself through urban unrest in the USA, in Britain and in the colonies.

Whilst there are many things to be celebrated about the 1960s, there are also many to be deplored: I am thinking in particular of the racist politics of the mid to late 1960s and beyond, which co-existed with eulogies to love and peace. The political and social infrastructure for the perpetration of overtly racist acts and sentiments goes back hundreds of years as I have demonstrated earlier, but events immediately preceding the 1960s laid the foundations for a pervasive institutionalized racism through the way that 'race' became part of mainstream politics.

In the early 1960s, a policy of integration through assimilation was thought to be the most appropriate way of dealing with the 'problem' of black immigration, and the education system was seen as an obvious place to start this process. 'Assimilation' and 'integration' were problematic terms since it was clear that what was intended was that black settlers should abandon their cultures – which were in any case seen as deficient – and embrace an unproblematized notion of a homogeneous British culture. This policy was pursued through the 1960s and as the numbers of black children increased, so what was perceived as a threat to the British way of life and the national character became greater. In the proposed process of assimilation, black parents were frequently seen as actual or potential inhibitors. Despite hopes to the contrary, the contradictory combination of liberal integrationist principles and increasingly harsh and explicitly discriminatory immigration legislation led to a crisis in 'race relations' yet to be resolved (Walvin, 1984; Solomos, *et al*, 1986; Ben-Tovim and Gabriel, 1987; Gilroy, 1987).

In Britain, about the time that *Leo the Last* was being made, the place of black immigration as a prominent and controversial issue in the media was consolidated. In a number of speeches delivered in 1968, the then Conservative Member of Parliament, Enoch Powell, predicted racial conflict due to a dangerous number of aggressive immigrants who, along with some seditious white supporters were determined to inflame and campaign against their fellow citizens. This campaign, asserted Powell, would leave the white majority without a sense of who they were and what their rightful heritage was (Barker, 1981).

Whilst the reservoir of white racism was being tapped by politicians anxious to gain popular support and maintain their power, black settlers in this country continued their participation in liberation politics, some of which were developed in the USA, others of which had been circulating in India, Africa and the Caribbean.

On British television, it would be an exaggeration to say that there was a proliferation of images of black people, but there was certainly a dramatic increase in programmes which dealt with racial issues from the mid 1960s onwards. This increase in discussion of 'race relations' issues seems to have paradoxically consolidated black people's invisibility: it was white people's views which were sought, their expressions of rage and resentment encouraged. Documentaries in the *This Week*, *Man Alive* and other similar series often dealt with the reactions of white people to black immigration in general, along with specific issues such as – inevitably – 'mixed' marriages, and were specifically concerned with the racial *problems* brought about by black peoples' presence (Pines, 1992: 139).

Speaking of one programme which investigated the numbers of black people who wished to be 'repatriated' due to the racism encountered in Britain and which traced some of these journeys back to the Caribbean, Desmond Wilcox, the producer, is quoted as saying:

> The funny thing . . . was that when we were watching the rushes of them back in the West Indies, all of us wanted to go there with them, because it was obviously a so much happier place. It was a so much nicer place, where people had no sense of prejudice, where there was no intolerance . . . people were returning . . . to a kind of economic disaster, but a happy land where there was no prejudice.
>
> (quoted in Pines, 1992: 140)

This idyllic picture of the Caribbean and black peoples has its resonances in both *Leo the Last*, where the black family under Leo's observation demonstrate their sense of 'community', and *Pressure*, where a nostalgia for 'home' is evidenced.

LEO THE LAST (1969)

Unlike previous films examined here, *Leo the Last* is not a conventionally constructed realist text, inasmuch as the colours, the framing, the acting style, the mise-en-scène and other cinematic devices are deployed in such a way as to give the text a feel of the fantastical, a 'psychedelic' ambience. This is in keeping with the spirit associated with the 'swinging sixties' but it is also as if the kind of problems which are manifested in the film could not be contained within realist conventions, and thus an alternative form was required. Since one of the key motifs of the text is 'looking' – who has the power to initiate looking, to return the look, and the implications of looking as a strategy for avoiding committed involvement – the pain and pleasure of voyeurism and fantasy are foregrounded and emphasized in the film's structure. Although in terms of its cinematic form and narrative, it may seem a long way from *Sapphire* (1959) and *Flame in the Streets* (1961), its narrative progresses in a linear fashion and the text displays some similar preoccupations regarding racial and sexual difference.

The eponymous hero played by Marcello Mastroianni, is a 40 year old East European prince in exile who has come to a rundown area of west London to recover from malaria. The house, which had belonged to his father and to which he has now come to live, is enormous and in resplendent condition. Leo is to share it with his second cousin Margaret (Billie Whitelaw) who is desperate to marry him, David (David de Keyser) a doctor to the rich and Lazlo (Vladek Sheybal) a proto-nationalist ex-patriate zealot. Each of these characters is either economically or emotionally dependent on Leo. From his vantage point of white masculine, upper class privilege, Leo observes the events and experiences which constitute the lives of the black family who are his neighbours. He is particularly intrigued by Salambo Madi (Glenna Forster-Jones), the young daughter of the household, and her boyfriend Roscoe (Calvin Lockhart).[1]

Feeling impotent in the face of their poverty and yet instrumental in causing the death of Salambo's father, Leo decides to hand over his heritage – his family home – to the Madis. After a confrontation with Margaret, David and Lazlo's insurgent cronies, Leo is declared mad, but the working class neighbours rally to his defence and destroy the mansion by setting fire to it with fireworks.

There is much about 'foreignness' in this film. Leo comes to England from abroad suffering from malaria, a disease often associated with the hostility of colonial environments. We are told that Leo was bird-watching during his stay on the Galapagos Islands: an interesting choice of location, since it was here that Charles Darwin developed his ideas for *The Origin of the Species*. It seems clear that Leo was on a quest for his origins and self-identity before journeying to London to seek out his ancestral home. Leo exchanges his ornithology – the observation of the exotic wild birds – for anthropology – the observation of trapped, poverty-stricken but 'exotic' black people – as he sets about observing the movements of his neighbours.

The Madi family play out their lives, unwittingly providing Leo with a vicarious experience of familial contact, warmth and communality although the audience does not hear the family speak. This is one of the most unsatisfactory elements of the film because although it may be argued that white people speak for black and thus this merely symbolically represents an aspect of reality, the opportunity to disrupt that set of relations is not seized. Thus the naturalness of that situation is reinforced.

Leo the Last is rich material for analysis as the intersections of 'race', class and gender oppression and privilege are explored and some of the contradictions and ambivalences made manifest. Made during the period when London was still considered to be the heart of the Commonwealth even though it had lost the Empire, *Leo the Last* is concerned with what happens when a foreign white aristocrat observes, and becomes involved in the lives of his black neighbours. Noteworthy here is that the white middle class characters are not always accorded favourable treatment in the text and that the film attempts a sustained critique of white bourgeois culture, in spite of its implicit naturalization of power relations.

THE IMPERIAL I/EYE OF *LEO THE LAST*

In her critical account of primitivist discourses, Marianna Torgovnick discusses how disillusioned modernists turned their attentions to the notion of the primitive as a route out of the crushing sense of alienation and the identity crises precipitated by the 'success' of industrialization and its aftermath. She posits that these modernists looked to the primitive as the 'last, desperate, remaining endangered model for alternative social organizations, for communities that exert communal power and live amid a sense of wonder that transcends the mundane order of modern urban life.' (Torgovnick, 1990: 192). The problem here for Britain and its troubled colonial history, is that the primitive Other came to inhabit its own space. Torgovnick observes that notions of 'the primitive' 'do not vanish but change into the urban poor, and thus can no longer serve as a locus for our powerful longings precisely because they have entered our own normative conditions of urban life.' (ibid.: 192). Torgovnick typically speaks of an 'us' and an 'our' which is reminiscent of the imperial 'I' ('eye'), and I would contest her assertion that the primitive cannot fulfil its function in the contemporary urban landscape: *Leo the Last* illustrates my point.[2]

Salambo, under almost constant observation by Leo, is also watched and stalked by Kowalski (Kenneth J. Warren), the owner of the junk/pawn shop opposite. Pawn shops are often associated with anti-Semitic perceptions of Jewishness – the fiscal parasite, preying on victims who are down on their luck – and although there is nothing in the text to identify the owner as Jewish, he is identified as 'alien' through his Polish surname. Kowalski makes a number of attempts to seduce Salambo and eventually rapes her whilst Leo looks on. It is when she is returning from shoplifting in the supermarket – when she appears in 'whiteface' because her face is covered with flour – that Kowalski succeeds in his quest to have sex with her, against her will.

All the time as Leo looks on, the audience is encouraged to adopt his scopic position. Leo oscillates between the voyeuristic and the fetishistic gaze. In my use of the terms here, I am following John Ellis's distinction which states that: 'the voyeuristic look is curious, inquiring, demanding to know. The fetishistic gaze is captivated by what it sees, does not wish to inquire further, to see more, to find out' (Ellis, 1988: 47). Also pertinent here are Homi Bhabha's remarks on the controlling look of colonial discourse which is:

> an apparatus that turns on the recognition and disavowal of racial/cultural/historical differences. Its predominant strategic function is the creation of a space for a 'subject peoples' through the production of knowledges in terms of which surveillance is exercised and a complex form of pleasure/unpleasure is incited. It seeks authorization for its strategies by the production of knowledges of coloniser and colonised which are stereotypical but antithetically evaluated.
>
> (Bhabha, 1983: 23)

The scopic drive which underpins the monitoring and surveillance of black people's behaviour – and here I am particularly referring to the observation of sexual behaviour – is heightened in *Leo the Last* but is also evident in *Sapphire* through the law's intervention in constructing a sexual history for Sapphire, and, to a lesser extent in *Flame in the Streets*, where Kathie observes the sexual life of the black people who dwell in the house where she may be about to live.

Through the narrative structure of *Leo the Last*, the audience is encouraged to adopt an observer's position as the Madis' life is exposed through the masque which indicates the parameters of Leo's vision through his telescope. Thus it may be argued that the audience become implicated in acts of voyeurism and fetishistic scopophilia although it would be problematic to assume that all viewers are drawn into the text in this way.

Two of the 'primitives' in *Leo the Last* – the black working class woman and the white male working class immigrant – are connected by their mythic libidinous drives. They perform the primal scene for Leo – a white immigrant also, but *exotic* because of his aristocratic lineage – who chooses not to intervene. In contrast with the other male protagonists, Leo is physically passive. He indulges in observation but not action: he does not try to help Salambo's father when he collapses in the street and he does not attempt to help Salambo when he sees Kowalski attack her. Indeed his ever-present telescope and phallic extension lingers over her ravaged body and all he does is to gasp – an indication of sexual satisfaction perhaps? – and break the window through which he is looking: this vicariously attained climactic explosion suggests that Kowalski functions as a 'shadow self', Leo's active and masculine *alter ego*, where he is actually passive and 'feminine'. Although he appears to disapprove of Kowalski's sexual brutality, he continues to watch. Leo observes the enactment of the sexual drama, having noted the signs that this was an almost inevitable occurrence given Kowalski's persistent stalking of Salambo. He has the choice and refuses to engage directly with the black woman's plight. Roscoe returns and in contrast to Leo's lack of action, finds and beats Kowalski watched by the Madi family and by Leo. Leo watches Roscoe beat Kowalski as if Roscoe is acting on his behalf.

The inability of Leo to confront the issue arises from his subjectivity being formed through the discourses of racial difference – effacing his gender role as protector – which has defined his identity in terms of its binary opposite: thus he is unable to identify with Salambo's predicament, unable to intervene to assist her. This sequence demonstrates the way in which black women are ideologically constructed as being outside of white European notions of femininity, and thus beyond the need for protection from black or white male desire and aggression. Leo's inaction indicates his complicity in an ideology which sees the physical abuse of a black woman as being inconsequential to white onlookers. It is also reminiscent of the imperial 'I/eye' of the gentleman traveller and explorer whose works have been analysed by Mary Louise Pratt:

> The eye 'commands' what falls within its gaze; the mountains 'show themselves' or 'present themselves'; the country 'opens up' before the European newcomer, as does the unclothed indigenous bodyscape. At the same time, this eye seems powerless to act or interact with this landscape. Unheroic, unparticularized, without ego, interest, or desire of its own, it seems able to do nothing but gaze from a periphery of its own creation, like the self-effaced, non-interventionist eye that scans the Other's body.
>
> (Pratt, 1985: 125)

This analogy with the colonial explorer is reinforced by Leo's previous excursion to the Galapagos Islands. The desire embedded within the voyeuristic look undermines his pretensions to innocence and non-authoritativeness and it is only when this is recognized later on in the film, that Leo is able to take action.

FATHERS AND DAUGHTERS

Later on in the film, Salambo takes up prostitution as, with Roscoe in prison for beating Kowalski, and her father dead, there is apparently no other way for a black woman to earn an income and feed the family. Leo buys Salambo from her pimp in order to save her for Roscoe. In attempting to save Salambo, Leo re-enacts the social and sexual divisions and hierarchies of the plantation, exercising his economic power over black men in order to take the black woman for himself. Salambo can only interpret his attempt to 'save' her from prostitution and his subsequent 'kindness' as a prelude to sexual intercourse: through her attempted exchange of sex for care, she completes the circularity of economic exchange within the neighbourhood of which Leo is ignorant but in which he is pivotal. Towards the end of the film, Lazlo apprises Leo of the fact that his wealth is founded on the exploitation of the people he seeks to save, since the rent for the slums in which they live is paid to his estate. Leo's power, both economic and that which allows him to be the sole possessor of the look is ultimately acknowledged, if inadequately challenged.

It is significant that an attempt by the black preacher to cleanse Salambo's soul and reclaim her from the prostitute's life on which she is about to embark, fails. The preacher's ritual involves washing her photographic image and again we should note the significance of this act of male privilege afforded by the church. The black male patriarch, although he subscribes to the religious values of the (white) father, is powerless to effect change in his 'daughter': but it is her image which he is attempting to change, her representation as captured by the eye of the camera/observer. Her corporeal self is beyond his control although not beyond patriarchy, since Salambo is merely to trade one 'father' – preacher – for another – pimp.

It is appropriate that Leo, as an amalgam of anthropologist, colonizer and missionary should also attempt to fulfil a paternal role and to cleanse Salambo through the ritual of a bath in the scene where she enters his house. This washing motif evokes images in Victorian advertisements where black children are washed white (Pieterse, 1992). Not only are there the religious connotations attached to the cleansing process: such actions also induce a feeling that if only black (dirty/heathen) people were white (clean/Christian), then the problem of racism would cease to exist. After the bath, Salambo tries to arouse Leo sexually but he does not intend to have sex with her. She takes this as a rejection, perhaps because of her blackness. This may be seen as Leo being ineffectual again, hesitating to act sexually where other men would not: the denial of her offer of sexual gratification may also be read as yet another instance of the avoidance of depicting interracial sex on screen. The master/slave relation evoked by Kowalski's rape of Salambo was shown but interracial sex in that context is not of the same order of taboo as loving sexual contact: the possibility of sexual contact with an emotional investment across racial and class boundaries cannot be represented.

During the intimate moment afforded by Leo sharing his bed with Salambo, she states 'It's all gone wrong' and relates how 'we were happy in Africa but Dad wanted to come here', after which she cries like a child and lies on Leo's chest. The conflict between generations of black people is lightly touched on here as it is the aspirations of Salambo's father which are seen as precipitating the disastrous turn in the family's fortunes. Salambo's loss is multiple: the loss of her father through death, the loss of respect and support from the community's black preacher because of her prostitution, the loss through imprisonment of her black boyfriend and the loss of the 'security' afforded by her black pimp. The disintegration of her life reinforces the notion of the fragmentation and pathologization of black families, prevalent in 'race relations' discourse of the period: it is significant that the focal point of this loss and disruption is the black female.

The black men in *Leo the Last* are differentially inscribed in this fragmented model. Importantly, they are more vocal than the black women and their sexuality is envied as much as it is despised or feared. Salambo's boyfriend Roscoe is seen as an object of desire by all the women, with even the cool Margaret achieving a momentary outburst of passion for him. Roscoe is a man of action and thus a source of envy for Leo. If the Madi family represent for Leo the yearning for a 'lost' family, community, national and racial identity, then Roscoe is the embodiment of his desire to achieve an active, sexually potent masculinity. The character of Jasper is problematic as a black pimp because of the history of depictions of black men preying on and sexually exploiting white women, a point taken up in the analysis of *Mona Lisa* (1986) which follows in chapter 7. In *Leo the Last*, the linking of the sexual and the economic exemplified in prostitution is worked through Roscoe and Lazlo and, in the end, Jasper identifies his interests as lying with the forces of political reaction – with Lazlo, the insurgent exiles, David the doctor and Margaret. Nonetheless, it is Jasper who makes a telling remark to Leo, when he says: 'you can afford to choose poverty'. Leo's enjoyment of his newly secured liberation from the shackles of material wealth is underscored by the fact that he has always had the privilege of choice.

LEO'S WOMEN

The narrative is not concerned with the emotional or political development of the women in the text. They are not seen as acting autonomously: it is made clear that they cannot survive without the assistance of a man, no matter how disreputable or undesirable he might be. When Mr Madi and Roscoe are eliminated from the narrative – albeit temporarily in the case of Roscoe – Lazlo and Jasper, as capitalist and pimp, act as substitute, degraded versions of father and boyfriend for Salambo.

Salambo's mother's servile gratitude to Leo and Lazlo, and her resigned grief due to her husband's death could be read as her repressed anger as a result of her subordinated role within the family and society as a whole. However, her role relates more to the stereotypes of the strong black woman who suffers, passively and in silence. Problematically, Salambo is silenced for the first half of the film and only speaks when Leo gives her the space to do so: that is, after he has crossed the boundary marked by his house and gone to Mr Madi's funeral. This is indicative of the way in which women in general, and black women in particular, are generally denied a voice within cultural texts.

Salambo and Margaret are eventually pitted against each other as rivals for Leo's affection, although it is clearly signalled to the audience that Salambo is Roscoe's lover and does not intend having a sexual relationship with Leo. This encounter which ends up with Salambo and Margaret engaged in a physical fight, calls to mind the antagonism which results in the murder of Sapphire (see chapter 4). Again, there is the implicit opposition of competing notions of black and white femininities, signified by the exoticism of the name 'Salambo' and the prosaic nature of the name 'Margaret', reminiscent of the Sapphire/Mildred opposition. This difference between black and white females is emphasized visually by the darkness of Salambo's skin colour and the whiteness and blondeness of Margaret. During the course of the fight, Salambo's straight haired wig is pulled off for the first time. This might be seen as indicating that Salambo's 'true' self – represented by her 'natural' short Afro hairstyle – requires a white female agent to release it. It could also be taken to mean that black women can and should fight and win on their own terms without having to adopt a style which is perceived as acceptable to white people.

Use is made of two female blonde stereotypes in *Leo the Last*. There is Margaret, the personification of the cool, self-possessed yet wild-when-aroused blonde woman. There is also the 'cheap' working class blonde used to signify sexual availability in women. This is exemplified in *Leo the Last* by the gaudily dressed and made-up prostitute whose pimp is black. The tawdry lifestyle of the latter is contrasted with the opulence of the former as the film cuts from the view from Leo's window, where he observes the prostitutes promenading, to the scenario in his own house.

Female prostitution is used in the text to demonstrate the necessity of economic exploitation in order to produce and preserve the opulent lifestyles of women like Margaret and men like Leo and to serve as a metaphor for the relations sustained under the economic system. The circulation of capital in the neighbourhood is demonstrated as money passes from one resident to another, passing through the pimp, through Lazlo and eventually back to Leo, although initially, he is unaware of the source of his income. Once this financial system is exposed, Leo can no longer claim innocence or fail to see how he is directly implicated in the maintenance of the existing social order and he is forced to act.

Salambo's economic exploitation is enforced directly, *visibly* by the black pimp Jasper. Her sexual subordination is enforced by Kowalski. The black and the Polish males are both seen as her primary exploiters since that is what is made visible. More difficult to achieve – although I think *Leo the Last* makes an attempt to do so – is making clear how the middle classes are implicated in racism through the less visible inequitable social relations established in British society. Leo's character represents an attempt to situate the property owning middle classes as the locus of racial oppression.

WHITENESS AND OTHERNESS

Leo admires Roscoe and the Madi family as he sees them as embodying certain qualities which civilized whites have 'lost'. The lives and strategies for survival of the black people in the narrative are constantly favourably compared to the mores and lifestyle of the whites. However, this takes place in the context of black poverty and disempowerment and seems to evidence a middle class fascination with the squalor in which they do not have to live: this amounts to a powerful violation of those who are disadvantaged and oppressed. It is also a strategy for avoiding guilt and shame since, the implication is that by leaving behind poverty and disempowerment, and gaining access to privilege – civilization in other words – somehow something more spontaneous, more authentic, is lost, thereby denying the material and other privileges which accrue to those who have power and wealth. To refer back to Torgovnick's argument that the urban poor cannot be the locus of white civilization's longing in the same way that primitives have been, this aspect of the film supports my contention that the (primitive) poverty-stricken Other may indeed have such a symbolic function in modern urban landscapes.

In *Leo the Last* this is shown most graphically in three contrasting sequences. One is where Leo, Margaret, David and Lazlo attend a party where white society women and men indulge their craving for consuming vast quantities of chicken, at which they gnaw greedily. The overconsumption of chicken flesh is a figure for cannibalism, thereby reversing the qualities associated with black and white, the 'savage' and the 'civilized'. It is the white people who behave in an uncivilized manner, in spite of – or rather, because of – the accoutrements of a civilized culture. This is a strong image as we see the 'civilized' whites indulging in gross overconsumption whilst the 'savage' black family Madi have to adopt an ingenious plan to steal food from the local supermarket in order to survive.

This symbolic cannibalism has a twofold function. First, it serves to demonstrate that under capitalism, whether living or dead, flesh is a commodity to be exploited, to be consumed and to be discarded once its usefulness has gone, and second, it suggests the process of introjection – of ingesting Otherness through regressing to the 'primitive' – which is in the first instance, a visual process. By this I mean that Leo's initial attempt at introjection of the Other is effected through his visual consumption of the Madi family.[3]

The party drifts into a sexual orgy to a soundtrack which quotes from T. S. Eliot's poem 'The Love Song of J. Alfred Prufrock', 'Prepare a face to meet the face . . .' together with the sounds of lovemaking and it is significant that during the course of this display of gastronomic and sexual excess, one of the women guests bites the head off of a 'primitive' artifact, a carved statuette or fetish object. Leo looks on in disgust at the exhibition of gluttony in front of him as well he might: his distaste for rich white upper middle class English society is frequently evidenced and suggests a general sense of (self) disgust and hatred regarding the notion of whiteness. This is distinctly located in the discourse of the primitive Other referred to earlier in this chapter, which is at once an exoticization of Otherness and a denunciation of the white self.

It should be remembered that Leo is a *foreign* aristocrat and there is a sense in which he has access to an outsider's vision of bourgeois Englishness – and by extension perhaps, to whiteness – which would not be available to white working class or black people. Leo has access to their society rituals and their deepest fears: about their bodies, their sexuality and their anxiety about maintaining power and privilege. This point is most clear in the second instance of Other-envy and Self-hatred – the swimming pool scene – and it is interesting because of the sense that what is being dealt with here is *whiteness*: it is not an issue of national identity.

At a hot pool, a number of the society doctor, David's rich clients immerse themselves in water and try to 'get in touch' with their inner selves. Leo and Margaret are in this group of women and men, naked in the pool trying desperately to grasp what it means to 'feel'. David orchestrates the group's movements and responses, fully clothed, from the pool side. Leo, using his observer's eye cannot initially relate to these people, and his status as outsider is confirmed by his reluctance to chant the mantra along with the others. Although eventually he comes round it is not because he has become 'in touch with himself' but because he has decided on a course of *action* which demonstrates that he is able to feel for others: the decision is made to take action which is intended to be beneficial to the Madis.

Leo's fascination with a different style of social organization as exemplified by the Madi family is also symptomatic of his avoidance of committing himself to Margaret and the model of stifling middle class domesticity that she represents. Margaret is in pursuit of Leo and is characterized as the epitome of white female narcissism – checking her image in the mirror, always exquisitely made-up, always elegantly dressed with her hair carefully arranged. As is often the case, female narcissism is explicitly represented, but white male narcissism is apparent in *Leo the Last* too, although it is not based on visual representations of excessive self-regard. It manifests itself in the way in which Leo impels the narrative, the audience's encouragement to see events from his perspective, and his pivotal position as overseer of virtually everything that occurs which ensures him a textual centrality denied other characters. Thus, once again, it is necessary for a privileged white male's experience to be at the centre of the text whilst others are confined to the margins.

The first time Leo takes an active role in trying to help the family by giving them food – charity for the deserving black poor – is disastrous since the father apparently dies due to the overly rich meal which Leo has supplied. Leo's masculine potential is subsequently released by Roscoe – again as active male Other – whose decision to lead the local community in routing Lazlo and his nationalist cronies from Leo's mansion generates the energy through which Leo takes direct political action.

The final scenario I want to note briefly here, contrasts the preparations for Leo's impending marriage to Margaret with the funeral of Salambo's father. The marriage ceremony is rehearsed and conducted formally. It falls upon Margaret to domesticate Leo, although this may serve to repress further his 'masculine' vitality by confining him in a monogamous relationship. The marriage itself is intriguing since Margaret and Leo are related; they are cousins. This appears to be a reiteration of the obligation to maintain the institutionalized privilege of the quasi-aristocratic family and the necessity to keep that family – read 'race' – pure. Traditionally, endogamy has been a method of keeping bloodlines intact. By contrast, the funeral is filled with loud, spontaneous outpourings of grief. At this event, Leo is again the envious onlooker, peering through glass at the Madi family's mourning the loss of the patriarch – a loss precipitated by Leo's act of kindness in supplying the family with rich food.

One of the reasons why black women become so dangerous in this situation is that they are frequently fantasized as being able to unlock the repressed desires and passion which will place white civilization in peril. If Salambo were to make love with Leo, what then? White civilization and cultures are unstable conditions liable to regress and the slide into 'savagery' may be caused either by black women, or by white women through an attraction to black men, thereby betraying the 'race', or by the always threatening 'hordes' or 'masses'. The potency accorded to black people in this context may be seen as a recognition of just how precarious a grasp on civilization white people have.

Leo's idealization of black life is based on his desire to achieve an unattainable idealized version of himself – that is, to experience or to regain a sense of spontaneity, to act instinctively, to be naturally sexually uninhibited, to be in touch with spirituality and as such the longing is very much situated in primitivist discourse as outlined in chapter 3. Mary Anne Doane indicates a similar psychic process when she describes how representations of black women have served as a:

> textual echo of the white female protagonists, or at least, an echo of what they have allegedly lost as the price of their middle-classness. The intuitive knowledge or maternal power credited to the black woman acts as a measure of the distance between the white bourgeois woman and the nature or intuition she *ought* to personify.
>
> (Doane, 1991: 240)

I am arguing here that the repressed but desired characteristics and qualities merge with the object of idealization and result in the attempted introjection of the idealized object – the attempted absorption of what are seen as black qualities or characteristics. This signals a sense of lack or absence which is not phallic, except in a metonymic sense, and refers to a lack not in the object but in the looking subject who seeks to compensate for (in this instance) his own inadequacy through the attempted possession of the Other.

THE PATRIARCHAL HOUSEHOLD

The splendour of Leo's house which is located in a controlling position at the end of the street, blocking the road off so that there is no thoroughfare, symbolizes and embodies the detachment and the parasitic nature of the social hierarchy and the glorification of the dynastic principle. Once in the building, it is as though Leo and the other occupants reside in an hermetically sealed unit from which there is no escape and no entry for unauthorized people: a completely self-sufficient bounded system, a concrete embodiment of the idea of 'nation'. At one point in the narrative, Salambo crosses the boundary and enters Leo's house with him which causes Leo's conventional elderly housekeeper to be scandalized.

Ever the observer, when his house is occupied by his enemies, Leo uses his spyglass on those who are now incarcerated in his house: now he is on the outside looking in. The local people's use of fireworks against the machine guns and rifles of the patriots in the mansion is akin to the use of 'native' spears against sophisticated western weaponry and evokes those unequal battles of the past. However, that technological superiority is fallible now as it has been before, and the fireworks ignite the bombs and bullets inside setting the house ablaze. Ultimately the house is wrecked, Margaret's demeanour is wrecked and the patriots have been forced to surrender. Leo's *father's* house was symbolic of the power of patrilinearity and patriarchy power, and its destruction heralds the potential for an overturning of the old social order.

The narrative posits that in order to dismantle hereditary privilege an alliance between the radical elements of the oppressor's class and the oppressed class is necessary and destruction has to be absolute.

As Leo's father's house is destroyed by fire the people take control of the street. This ending is antithetical to the apocalyptic vision of the relationship between black and white as epitomized by Enoch Powell's 1968 speech on 'rivers of blood': the final scene shows the potential for allegiance between progressive forces, even if it is somewhat romanticized.

CONCLUSION

Although *Leo the Last* may be read as a trenchant critique of whiteness, the text does not directly address racial discrimination in the way that *Sapphire* (1959), *Flame in the Streets* (1961), *Pressure* (1974), *Burning an Illusion* (1981) and *Absolute Beginners* (1986) do: yet it does not completely avoid discussing the effects of racism in the same ways that *A Taste of Honey* (1961), *The L-Shaped Room* (1962), *Black Joy* (1977) and *Mona Lisa* (1986) do. *Leo the Last* steers a course somewhere in-between, acknowledging that 'race' is an issue without going into a detailed analysis of how it is sustained through discourse, structures and institutions.

Leo the Last is a clear example of the inadequacy of designating a text and the portrayals within it as being positive, negative or racist. There are a number of constituent features which render such terms irrelevant. In thinking about the way in which relationships of domination and subordination operate within the text, it becomes clear that here too there are no succinct answers or resolutions to the problems posed by the film.

The complex concoction of fantasy and fact, desire and repulsion which characterizes notions of racial and sexual difference are embodied in the formal properties of a film which is never committed to realism or verisimilitude. It does not celebrate white supremacy but rather points to a significant degree of self-loathing which implicitly interrogates whiteness and problematizes the western political and cultural project. However, despite the politically progressive elements, ultimately it is a benevolent form of white paternalism which motors the action. The physical violence which occurs in the film – for example, the brutal attack on Salambo – is not solely about 'race' but is also about the expectations and anxieties associated with gender and heterosexuality. It is the contradictory textual strategies and unanswered and irresolvable questions which make *Leo the Last* such an absorbing text.

If *Leo the Last* works with fantasy, power and the look, and the necessity for direct action, how might black film-makers problematize the look and its significance as an indication of differential access to the power to define? In the chapter which follows, I will assess the extent to which black film-makers prioritised different issues and concerns as a result of their experiences in Britain.

Chapter 6

Representing reality and 'the black experience' in 1970s Britain

All the films previously discussed have been directed by white men and have been mainly concerned with how black people have negotiated their assimilation into an all-white British society. This chapter is primarily concerned with the themes of black female sexuality, gender relations between black women and men, and the role of black political struggle as pursued in a small number of films which focused on black life in Britain during the 1970s and the 1980s.

The first film to be discussed here is *Pressure* (1974) directed by Horace Ove and co-written by Ove and Samuel Selvon. *Pressure* was Horace Ove's first feature length film; it was also the first feature film by a black person in Britain and the first black directed film to be funded by the British Film Institute (BFI). To a significant degree, *Pressure* may be characterized as an attempt by a black film-maker to respond to, and counteract the observations of, white professionals – psychologists, sociologists, anthropologists, film-makers, journalists and television documentarists – through the medium of a fictional realist film.[1] *Pressure* is of note for its explicit acknowledgement of the influence of black North American political struggle in Britain. Horace Ove's interest in diaspora politics is evidenced by his earlier film, *Baldwin's Nigger* (1968) and it is clear that black people had access to, and were aware of, black power ideologies, and their relevance in Britain.[2] Also considered in this chapter is *Black Joy* (1977) which presents a rather different picture of black life in London, distanced from the militant political protest which provides a focus for *Pressure*. *Black Joy* is not a black film inasmuch as the major creative input comes from white personnel but it has black life as its focus and the screenplay was co-written by Jamal Ali.

THE THEORETICAL SPACE FOR CRITIQUES OF BLACK FILM

In chapter 1, and, to a lesser extent in chapter 2, I discussed how realism has been perceived as a reactionary formal strategy and that this led to a dismissal of several black-authored texts. This section traces these theoretical developments and argues that such developments have been problematic in themselves as they relate to black cultural expression. The colonial legacy and dominance of realist photo-journalistic and cinematic practices and the continual construction of black people as curiosities, problems and victims through magazine and newspaper journalism, anthropological photography and television documentaries led to many black film-makers regarding realism as the appropriate means through which to communicate their concerns.[3] As David A. Bailey and Stuart Hall comment with reference to black photography, the use of realist forms in the 1970s and early 1980s:

> has to be seen within a wider political framework – as part of the attempt to reposition the guaranteed centres of knowledge of realism and the classic realist text, the struggle to contest negative images with positive ones.
>
> (Bailey and Hall, 1992: 18)

In the late 1960s and early 1970s, Marxist critics made significant interventions in the arena of cultural criticism and in particular in the development of film theory and realist aesthetics. It was posited by the *Cahiers du Cinéma* editorial group that the camera records nothing but the realm of ideology: they concluded that political struggle in the cinema must inevitably work at the level of form as well as content.[4] Working from the premise that every film is political:

> inasmuch as it is determined by the ideology which produces (or within which it is produced, which stems from the same thing). The cinema is all the more thoroughly and completely determined because unlike other arts or ideological systems its very manufacture mobilizes powerful economic forces in a way that the production of literature . . . does not.
>
> (Comolli and Narboni, 1976: 24–25).

Cahiers du Cinéma and later, others, perhaps most notably Peter Wollen and Colin MacCabe, developed criteria for establishing whether or not a text was politically progressive or worthy of theoretical and critical attention (Wollen, 1982; MacCabe, 1985). Wollen argued for the 'seven virtues' of counter-cinema which were in a formal sense, implacably opposed to the characteristics, or 'seven deadly sins' of mainstream cinema. The popular religious imagery of Wollen's taxonomy was the occasion of a trenchant attack on the pleasures of popular entertainment cinema, in which is embedded elitist notions of high and low culture. The religious analogy is appropriate in view of Wollen's wish to deny the audience the conventional pleasures to be had in watching mainstream films. As I discussed in chapter 1, in this theoretical paradigm, realist cinematic conventions were seen as bearers of a largely unproblematized notion of dominant ideology.

Realism may well privilege the text itself rather than encouraging a look beyond it to the structures of power, but as is asserted by bell hooks, it is important for black people to seize opportunities to 'look' in many different ways:

> Spaces for agency exist for black people, wherein we can both interrogate the gaze of the Other but also look back, at one another, naming what we see. The 'gaze' has been and is a site of resistance for colonized black people globally. Subordinates in relations of power learn experientially that there is a critical gaze, one that 'looks' to document, one that is oppositional. In resistance struggle, the power of the dominated to assert agency by claiming and cultivating 'awareness' politicizes looking relations – one learns to look a certain way in order to resist.
>
> (hooks, 1992: 27)

To accept this is not the same as claiming that any black filmmaker's perspective is preferable to, or more progressive than any white person's perspective. It is also the case that no cinematic form is inherently politically progressive or reactionary. A related point is that black people have produced images and narratives which are inimical to progressive ideas about black people's and women's liberation, or cinematic form, and this should not be surprising unless 'races' and sexes are seen as essential, discrete categories of difference. If it is acknowledged that racial, sexual and gender identities may be experienced and perceived as discontinuous and fragmented, then the sense of order provided by bounded systems of classification such as gender and 'race' is illusory. Diaspora black film and programme makers are a diverse group: it is difficult to maintain the unproblematic use of 'black film' as a generic term as the heterogeneity of the field is reflected in the diversity of the genres, form, content and ideologies of those who make films and videos. This discussion about subjectivity and racial identity is part of a much larger one about black and white perspectives and world-views which will be further addressed in the concluding chapter.

Since realist practices in film and television have been a major component in determining how the 'problem' of blackness is defined and perceived, the demystification of its mechanisms continues to be of importance. The initial imperative in black realist film-making was to counter the dominant (mis)representations of black people and present 'positive' black images which aimed to reflect what was posited as the reality of black people's lives from an 'authentically black' perspective.

PRESSURE: BLACK MASCULINITY, BLACK WOMEN AND REPRESENTATION

Pressure concerns the political and cultural development of a black teenager, Tony, and his family life in London. A number of themes perceived as most significant for black people at that time, are explored by the film: immigration, assimilation into British society, intergenerational conflict and cultural identity. Although Tony does well at school, he is denied employment appropriate to his qualifi-cations because he is black. He gets into trouble through his involvement in petty criminal activity with a group of unemployed young black men. Eventually, he is drawn to radical black politics through his older brother and finds fulfilment in protest and political organization.

In previous chapters, I have pointed out that white men have conceptualized themselves into a position of narrative centrality. Perhaps a question to be asked of black male film-makers is, whether – having apparently seized control of the right to look – their films will replicate the conventional relations of power between women and men. A response to this question involves the consider-ation of a number of issues.

First, the extent to which black political struggles for autonomy and enfranchisement both in the USA and Britain have traditionally been couched in masculinist terms and structured in such a way as to deny black women full participation in, and benefit from, struggles for liberation, is of importance. The language of black liberation struggles was consistently masculinized through the use of terms such as 'castration', 'emasculation' and 'impotence' and served to express what was a predominantly male experience of racism. A consequence of this is that popular consciousness about the period of civil rights and Black Power struggles in the USA, which had a profound effect on black people here too, is very much shaped by the images of Martin Luther King and Malcolm X and other black male leaders: rarely is there an account of that period which foregrounds African–American women's involvement and perspectives.

Another point to be raised is the question of black men's relationship to white patriarchal power in nationalist discourses. An objective of masculinist African–American nationalist discourses has been to participate in the power afforded through patriarchal structures. Such a position served to continue black women's oppression through what would amount to a questioning of racial power relations but entail the maintenance of gender inequalities. The place of black North American women in these structures was not adequately documented or sufficiently problematized in the 1960s and 1970s (Wallace, 1979; Davis, 1981; hooks, 1982, 1984 and 1989). It is even harder to find accounts of British-based black women's struggles during this period although the political activist Claudia Jones – who travelled between the Caribbean, the USA and Britain – was very clear about the implications of neglecting the political needs and struggles of black women (Jones, 1985).[5] The assertion of strident black masculinity was, in part at least, a response to what was characterized as the emasculating properties of racism. From this perspective, black women may be seen as inhibitors of black male ascension to patriarchal rule necessitating their exclusion from structures of power and their denigration.

In *Pressure*, the young black male's experience is seen as representative of 'the black experience' but this gendering of black experience was not new in black-authored cultural texts. Until recently, for example, most of the slave narratives available were written by men. It is interesting to note in the context of this discussion, that there is often a turning point in these narratives when the black male subject achieves a level of consciousness which means that he is no longer able to see himself as a slave, as belonging to a white person. This refusal of the role of uncomplaining victim may be marked by a furious, destructive rage, and is the point at which the slave seizes control of his voice and makes the break – literally and metaphorically – from his white oppressor (Pajaczkowska and Young, 1992). It is this claiming of a distinct sense of (racial) self-identification which is the defining subjective moment in *Pressure*. *Pressure* demonstrates the desire to assert black masculinity in relation to both white racism and importantly, black women.

Black male youth's perceived position as bearing the brunt of racist policies and practices led to a 'certain politics on the black left itself ... beginning to romanticise the youth, separating their struggle from those of their elders – destroying the continuum of the past, the present and the future' (Sivanandan, 1983: 4). The denial of the continuum of political struggle across generations may be seen in *Pressure* through the reactionary conservatism of Tony's mother in particular.

In the popular imagination men who have forceful mothers are deemed weak, emasculated, 'mummy's' boys. The teenage boy, Tony, in *Pressure* whose political development provides the central focus for the narrative, is subject to what is represented as the conservative, reactionary ideological influence of his mother, Bopsie (Lucita Lijertwood) who advocates a complete, unquestioning capitulation to white British cultural and societal values and norms. That such submission and cultural passivity should be particularly located in the mother and to a much lesser degree in the father, is consistent with masculinist notions of women's role in black political activity, although this does not necessarily correspond with black women's accounts.

Bopsie is devoutly Christian, in a religion here regarded as a tool in the subjugation of black people, rather than the liberating theology that many black churches have developed. Characterized as 'another update of the "mammie" symbol', which deploys 'the same currency of signs which have historically worked to limit understanding of our experiences' (Attille and Blackwood, 1987: 206), even her name evokes the derisory black female character Topsy in Harriet Beecher Stowe's *Uncle Tom's Cabin*. Certainly Bopsie is a laughable character, a figure of fun with little political awareness. Her misplaced allegiance to the notion of white English superiority is signified notably by her appearance. She wears a wig which is explicitly attributed to her being ashamed of her 'natural' hair, and yet another black woman (cf. Salambo in *Leo the Last*) has her 'true' self exposed by having her false 'white hair' torn from her head – in this instance by her teenage son. Significantly, Bopsie cooks resolutely 'English' food so that even in the traditional female domestic domain, her skills are inappropriate and she is represented as a traitor to her racial and cultural origins.

The mother's adherence to this particular mode of thinking relates especially to the idea that (black) women are more likely to be socially aspirant than (black) men and that female-dominated households are responsible for the confused state in which black youths find themselves. Another assumption embedded in this emblematic black mother is that older people are politically naive and crave assimilation on any terms whereas, as is usually the case, this issue is much more complex than can be explored within the confines of a strictly linear narrative such as deployed in *Pressure*.

Bopsie's unproblematic assimilation of British culture is not matched by Tony's father (Frank Singuineau), who although depicted as rather conservative to begin with, does develop a political awareness of sorts. This manifests itself in his accusations against his wife that she is a 'middle class shit' and that he never wanted to come to England in the first place. All their troubles are blamed on her for aspiring to what are perceived as inappropriate white middle class values. For Bopsie, her final shame is that her sons are involved in activities which get them into trouble with the law: she blames the young men for being 'bad' and does not question the racism of white authorities as exemplified by the police.

The other main black female character in the film is the political militant, Sister Louise (Sheila Scott-Wilkinson). There is an explicit contrast between the way in which Colin (Oscar James) – Tony's brother – addresses him as a specifically politicized black male subject, and the methods Sister Louise uses to encourage Tony's participation in black political activism. Sister Louise's approach to the teenager is sexualized from their first encounter in the street market. Later, although she gives a stirring speech at a crucial political meeting, her language is more simple and direct than that of the two men who precede her: it is also read rather than delivered from memory like the men's speeches. The camera angles used for her talk are interesting too. Sister Louise is shot from low angles and frequently, from behind. It is only towards the end of her speech that the audience is allowed to see a direct shot of her face which is in marked contrast to the frequent eye contact made with the male orators who precede her on the platform. Later, after the debacle with the police which follows the political gathering, Sister Louise is told by a fellow activist, 'you look sexy with that plaster on your head' thereby consolidating her place within the movement, not as a person making political choices and risking physical pain for it, but as a sexually desirable woman whose every action serves to emphasize her potential for incorporation into the heterosexual order.

Both Bopsie and Sister Louise reject – in varying degrees – the rationalist discourse of black politics as exemplified by Colin and neither engage with men much beyond a servicing/sexual role. Sister Louise although involved in direct political action uses language with sexual innuendo in relation to Tony and is there to direct his sexual maturation as much as his political development. This is stressed when, after having been in bed with Sister Louise, Tony's acquisition of sexual knowledge is linked to his acquisition of phallic power in the shape of a knife taken from Louise's drawer. In fact, through his relationship with Louise, political maturity is associated with an increase in sexual potency, a theme made particularly clear in the dream sequence.

With her 'afro' hairstyle, Sister Louise resonates with 1960s and 1970s images of Angela Davis, who although a folk-hero in her own right, was frequently represented as being involved with black politics through her implication with the events surrounding her male colleagues.[6] Thus black women in *Pressure* are positioned either as apolitical mothers inadequate to the task of raising black men, or sexual predators: in both cases, it is their gender roles that are emphasized. During this period, the term 'youth' became synonymous with young men, and generally speaking, the specificity of young black women's experiences was not addressed (see for example, Pryce, 1979; Garrison, 1980). *Pressure* exemplifies the way in which black women, having been excluded from a feminism which failed to recognize its racial specificity and imperialistic universalism, have also been marginalized by masculinist black cultural discourses.

BLACK YOUTH: IN THE FAMILY, UNDER SIEGE

Media and academic sociological discourses constantly pathologized black sub-cultures and lay the blame for a failure in 'race relations' at the door of rebellious youth who were allegedly torn by intergenerational conflict and a crisis in identity precipitated by their failure to conform to white English cultural proscriptions (see for example, Pryce, 1979; Commission for Racial Equality, 1979).

Problems between the police and black people were highlighted by mainstream media as being the result of black people's predisposition toward criminality and their intransigence in the face of a morally superior culture (see for example, Brown, 1977; Pryce, 1979; Cashmore, 1979). Even self-designated 'radical' white sociologists took to characterizing black male youth as demonstrating the:

> penchant for violence within West Indian culture, possibly stemming from the days of slavery when the only method of retaliation was doing physical damage to the overseer ... black youth do have a certain fascination for violence.
>
> (quoted in Gutzmore, 1983: 26)

No doubt the activities and speeches, and the following of both Malcolm X in the USA and Michael X here in Britain, also contributed to many fears, fantasies (and guilt) about the potency of black men and the retribution they might enact.[7]

The press were noticeably reluctant to give credence to black people's accounts of beatings and murders at the hands of the police, lack of support against racist attacks and continual harassment of black meeting places. A state of heightened tension between the police and judiciary on the one hand, and predominantly black youth on the other, came to be represented as the norm.

As argued in chapter 4, notions about the family have been important in the construction of cultural identities, being seen as the place where the necessity to conform to social conventions should be instilled. If children 'went wrong', then it was because the family was considered to be dysfunctional. Thus:

> fears and panics about the breakdown of social discipline – of which crime is one of the most powerful indices – centre on the indiscipline of "youth", "the young", and on those institutions whose task it is to help them internalise social discipline – the school, but above all, the family.
>
> (Hall *et al.*, 1978: 145)

Pressure's representation of the black family is intended as a counterpoint to the stereotypical dysfunctional, acculturated black family and implicitly struggles with and against the idealized image of the patriarchal white family. However, it converges with white academics' and media 'experts'' notions of the pathologized 'matriarchal' black family through its apparent condemnation of the mother. Bopsie is represented as being at the core of the cultural confusion that leads to Tony's criminalization and rebellion.

Pressure was the first film to articulate the anger and frustration felt by urban young black men in Britain in the 1970s. This anger is given vivid expression in the fantasy sequence which takes place at some unspecified time after Tony first sleeps with Sister Louise. Tony goes to a park and looks at the statues richly symbolic of white supremacist heritage and culture. In his dream/fantasy world, a naked black man in an ornate bed in a country house hacks at a pig, splashing blood everywhere. The direct allusion to the annihilation of white people – previously characterised as devils and pigs – and the apparent call to arms in order to destroy symbols of white privilege clearly resonated with fears about black male youths and lawlessness, particularly after the violent disturbances at Notting Hill Carnival in 1976, and in the midst of the 'moral panics' created regarding 'immigrants' exploiting the state benefit system. Thus, although the film was made in 1974, it did not go on release until 1978. BFI (British Film Institute) ineptitude was cited as being one of the major reasons for the delay, but it was also reported that both Scotland Yard and what was then the Race Relations Board had requested to see the film before its release.[8]

BLACK PEOPLE LOOKING ON WHITENESS

As this is the first chapter to discuss the works of black directors and writers, I want to use comments by Jan Nederveen Pieterse in his study of images of blackness produced by white people to raise some issues regarding black film-makers' representations of whiteness (Pieterse, 1992). The reality of black people's lives in Britain inevitably means some sort of contact with white people. Although white characters in Ove's narrative are marginal in terms of their character development, it is their actions and attitudes which frequently drive the development of the plot, and this is also true of *Burning an Illusion* (1981), which is analysed in chapter 7. In *Black Joy* (1977), white characters are also largely peripheral but the representational status of white women is worth a brief mention here. The white women who appear are either prostitutes or positioned as sexual rivals with black women for black men's sexual attention. However, interracial social relationships are generally absent from the film, the emphasis being on survival within a black community.

For Pieterse, there is a problem in discussing black representations of white people in the same conceptual framework as that used to analyse white images of blackness as he argues:

> Images produced by Africans and blacks of Europeans and whites are ... completely different topics. They require an entirely different treatment, for they concern an altogether different type of historical relationship, which cannot be equated with white–black relations. The images produced by the subordinate party are of a different order from those of the dominant party; they too are stereotypes, but they carry different weight and meaning ... Several hundred years of western hegemony lends western images a range, complexity and historical weight which images stemming from Africa and from blacks do not possess.
>
> (Pieterse, 1992: 10)

Pieterse implies that to consider images by black people of whites in the same way as images by white people of blacks is to equate two opposing and fundamentally unequal sets of relations. Whilst I would agree that because of the power relations involved it is not possible to claim that there is an equivalence, I take issue with his basis for segregating image analyses in the way that he suggests. What is required is to try to develop a way of working which recognizes the inequalities and accounts for them rather than seeking to make a direct comparison which ignores structural and systemic discriminatory practices. Pieterse offers little by way of evidence to support his assumptions. Furthermore, to imply that the cultural practices of black people in both Africa and the West may be viewed as culturally homogeneous and insusceptible to Western or European influences is misleading. Pieterse claims that 'African' images are unable to demonstrate such a wide range of representations as those from the West, although again, there seems to have been very little investigative work carried out in this area to support this contention.

This approach is least satisfactory in its consideration of the efforts of those in the black African diaspora to make images which include representations of whiteness. Historically, there is evidence to suggest that slave cultures continually parodied and 'signified on' white habits and social mores in song, costume and dance, and that such representations were disseminated in the Caribbean and the USA (Gates, 1989). More recently, particularly in film and theatre, black people in the USA and Britain have made significant, if spasmodic, interventions in representing the impact of notions of racial difference. By positing 'an altogether different type of historical relationship' Pieterse denies that black people are absolutely implicated in those historical relations in which the notion of the oppositionality of the colonized was a trope of the colonizer (Pieterse, 1992: 10). Fanon makes the point through his description of internalized self-hatred that subjectivity is not – as is implied by Pieterse – solely determined by the epidermal schema imposed upon black people but is much less fixed than that: it therefore becomes possible for black people to adopt what might – in Pieterse's analytical model – be termed 'white' positions and *vice versa*.

Although I would reject Pieterse's justification for his implicit analytic essentialism, I would, however, point to a certain difficulty in locating the black-centred films I have discussed in the same theoretical paradigm as the white-authored texts. This is due to – as Pieterse avers – historically unequal positioning within the matrix of desire and fascination, anxiety and repulsion that constitutes colonial relations. It is also to do with issues of funding, ownership and control and developing black audiences.

As noted earlier, bell hooks makes a case for the return of the look by black people being an act of defiance which disturbs the power relations between black and white. The possibility of this refusal of subordinate status returns to haunt the white supremacist. Regarding colonial cinema, Homi Bhabha observes:

> In the objectification of the scopic drive there is always the threatened return of the look; in the identification of the Imaginary relation there is always the alienating other (or mirror) which crucially returns its object to the subject; and in that form of substitution and fixation that is fetishism there is always the trace of loss, absence. To put it succinctly, the recognition and disavowal of 'difference' is always disturbed by the question of its re-presentation or construction.
>
> (Bhabha, 1983: 33)

It is important to address the potential power of the colonized subject in this matrix of desire, fantasy and fetishism, and how she or he responds, particularly in regard to being the object of the look. Does returning the look in itself constitute an act of resistance or does this imply an essentialist notion of black subjectivity based on the presumption of a counter-hegemonic gaze which may not be there?

At the beginning of this section, I indicated that white people in

Pressure are marginal in some respects and I will now elaborate on this point. In *Pressure* white people are mainly cyphers: they are deliberately stereotypical and represent the racism of patriarchal institutions such as the police. White women are somewhat more sympathetically portrayed than white men, but it is intimated that black men may be betrayed by the attractions of white women. Contradictory feelings about white people are worked through white women in a number of instances. Tony's brother, Colin whose political stridency dismays Bopsie, is shown to be seeing a white woman, whilst similarly, at one stage Junior (T. Bone Wilson), steeped in militant political rhetoric, says to kill all whites but is shown as having a white girlfriend later. Tony has a young white woman friend, Sheila (June Page) whose landlady is vehemently opposed to his visit to her lodgings. Sheila does at least respond vigorously to the landlady's racist rant but the relationship with Tony ends shortly afterwards. In these black man/white woman vignettes, it is almost as if the text is playing with the notion of enacting revenge on white men by seducing 'their' women. Further ambivalence is demonstrated through the involvement of a number of white people in the political meeting and in the subsequent demonstration aimed at securing the release of those imprisoned after the meeting. At that final rain-sodden demonstration a banner declares 'death to white people' despite their presence on the march.

In the 1970s, focus shifted from the threat that black sexuality allegedly posed to the threat to social order apparently posed by the criminality which was supposedly endemic within black communities. It is possible to see *Pressure* as a response to the accusations levelled against black youth by the media and sections of academia although it should not be seen as primarily addressing the people working in those institutions.[9] The image of black youth as prone to random acts of violence is contextualized and politicized in both *Pressure* and *Burning an Illusion* (1981), and – in a less elaborated manner – in *Black Joy* (1977). In these texts, crime and acts of retaliatory violence are seen as logical and legitimate responses to the oppressive structures of racism.

WHITE CULTURE AND THE BLACK FAMILY

As I suggested earlier in relation to *Pressure*, the black family was a contested site in sociologistic 'race relations' discourse of the 1970s.[10] In the late 1970s, sociologists claimed to have identified a 'culture clash' affecting young black people growing up in Britain. This supposed confusion over cultural allegiance was alleged to be caused by being neither properly integrated into British (white) society nor fully engaged with black culture. As suggested earlier in this chapter, this cultural alienation was seen as being exacerbated by inter-generational conflict caused by the confrontation between older black people's acquiescence to white norms and values and black youths' rebellion against white people's authority. Whilst for academics and 'race relations' pundits, it seemed that black male youth were rootless, for many black people, the youths' reactions were the logical and essential black response to police harassment, racism in the educational system and the countless humiliations experienced on a daily basis.

During the late 1970s and early 1980s, civil disturbances involving substantial numbers of black people took place in Southall, Liverpool, Bristol, Brixton and other areas of Britain: one of the standard 'explanations' for these disturbances put forward in the press, was that West Indian families were unable to provide adequate parenting. An article in the *Financial Times* from July 1981 once again called upon the lexicon of pathological metaphors by explicitly linking the presence of rebellious black youths to an invasive illness: 'Like an epidemic of some alien disease, to which the body politic has no immunity, street riots have erupted in different parts of England during the past ten days' (quoted in Solomos *et al.*, 1986: 31).

Earlier, in 1979, one of the key figures among right-wing thinkers, Alfred Sherman articulated anxieties about black settlers thus:

> The imposition of mass immigration from backward alien cultures is just one symptom of this self-destructive urge reflected in the assault on patriotism, the family – both as a conjugal and economic unit – the Christian religion in public life and schools, traditional morality, in matters of sex, honesty, public display, and respect for the law – in short, all that is English and wholesome.
>
> (quoted in Solomos *et al.*, 1986: 27)

Sherman's definition of 'all that is English and wholesome' is predicated on the assumption of an oppositional and antagonist relationship between 'indigenous' white and 'alien' black people. Clearly, according to such commentators, it is the black population which causes racial problems, contaminating a previously stable and culturally homogeneous landscape. Errol Lawrence notes how 'blacks are pathologized once via their association with the "cultures of deprivation" of the decaying "inner cities" and again as the bearers of specifically *black* cultures' (Lawrence, 1986a: 56).

The characterization of Caribbean societies as dysfunctional and acculturated was promulgated by several sociological accounts of 'West Indians' but runs counter to the manner in which African diaspora peoples have consistently and historically reconstructed their cultures in often difficult circumstances (Lawrence, 1986b). The key modes of resistance to acculturation have been identified as linguistic innovation and the development of distinctive cultural practices which have reconstructed the 'alien social space' within which diaspora Africans have found themselves. This 'reconstruction' has, of necessity, entailed the incorporation and re-articulation of aspects of North American, African, Caribbean and European cultures.[11]

Perhaps because its explicit hybridity undermines notions of pure culture or 'races', Caribbean culture was seen as deficient. Black settlers were thought to be deluding themselves by thinking that they could be assimilated into British society. By way of contrast, there existed the idea in some circles that although they were 'more alien', Asians had, paradoxically, managed to be better integrated into British society. This notion was publicly discussed in the following terms in 1981:

> Their [Asians'] religion and language have stayed different . . . and this, alongside their whole culture, has bound them tightly together both as communities and as families – this family bond being something, incidentally, which many white as well as black parents would envy.
>
> (quoted in Lawrence, 1986b: 97)

As Errol Lawrence suggests, the 'problem' identified by Brook-Shepherd in the above statement, is due in part to the refusal of black people of African–Caribbean descent to admit to their status as 'foreign' and also due to the inherent 'weakness' of their culture: a culture based on a 'weak' family structure which was ill-equipped to give proper support to the community. Brook-Shepherd and others like him, failed to grasp that most Caribbean people in Britain knew full well that they were considered different and could not be assimilated into British society and it is this theme which is explored in *Burning an Illusion* (1981) and, to a lesser extent in *Playing Away* (1986), discussed in chapter 7.

In several texts made by white film-makers – for example, *Pool of London* (1950), *Flame in the Streets* (1961), *Heavens Above!* (1963), *To Sir, With Love* (1966) and *Mona Lisa* (1986) – the small number of individual black characters that are depicted are seen as being isolated from their cultures and their families, although both Franco Rosso's *Babylon* (1980) and John Boorman's *Leo the Last* (1969) represent significant exceptions.

However, in the black-centred films which are discussed in this chapter, the family is not always characterized as pivotal in relation to a conception of cultural identity or sustenance: it is shown to be vulnerable when black people are under attack in a hostile society. Families are shown as problematic, often revealed as being fractured along generational and gender lines. In *Black Joy* (1977), *Burning an Illusion* (1981) and *Playing Away* (1986) it is not family structures which provide a sense of identity and stability: in the case of *Black Joy* and *Playing Away*, male bonding is central to the resolution of problems and tensions, whilst in *Burning an Illusion* as in *Pressure*, organized political activity provides sustenance for the central characters. *Black Joy* (1977) indicates how self-interest and gender difference may fracture both family and the assumed community cohesion.

GHETTO LIFE AS *BLACK JOY*

In 1978, the authors of *Policing the Crisis* provided a sustained critique of the ideological and political underpinning of the construction of the moral panic around black youth and criminality and its reporting in the media (Hall *et al.*, 1978). Commenting on various critical approaches to the analysis of productive and unproductive labour and the relationship to criminal activity, Hall *et al.* write:

> Only through the autonomous struggle in each sector will the 'power of the class' as a whole come to be felt. This line of argument . . . has become the most powerful political tendency within active black groups in Britain. It is predicated on the autonomy and self-activity of black groups in struggle; and it identifies the most significant theme of this struggle as the growing 'refusal to work' of the black unemployed. The high levels of youthful black unemployment are here reinterpreted as part of a conscious political 'refusal to work'. This refusal to

work is crucial, since it strikes at capital.

(Hall et al., 1978: 370)

Although not explicitly articulated as such in the film, it could be argued that the black male world-view as depicted in *Black Joy* constitutes a critique of capitalism through the choice of a strategy of 'refusal to work'. The extent to which this actually constitutes a threat to capitalism as opposed to a consolidation of its ideological hegemony is arguable, since it is posited in this narrative that the rejection of work for wagelessness ends by exploitation of the community by members of that community. It becomes a 'dog eat dog', 'survival of the fittest' course of action which is evocative of capitalist enterprise rather than disruptive of it.

Based on a play by Jamal Ali who co-wrote the screenplay, according to Jim Pines the film bears some resemblances to the popular Hollywood cycle of 'blaxploitation' films of the early to mid 1970s, in that 'its subject-matter, characters and milieu are very much part of the romanticised iconography of the ghetto' (Pines, 1991: 7). This is the terrain of the super-masculine hero who attempts to keep 'his' women subordinate through the exertion of physical and sexual power. As I have argued earlier in this chapter, the criminalization of black youth placed young black men at the centre of media discourses on 'race', and it is not surprising that in 1970s and early 1980s black films, the young black man is seen as emblematic of black experiences in racist British society. In *Black Joy* there is a certain amount of valorization of this position of marginality.

Black Joy begins as Ben (Trevor Thomas) enters Britain with plenty of money but nonetheless a target for a body-search by customs officials on the assumption that as a black man, he may be smuggling drugs. Once released, he makes his way to Brixton and has his money stolen by a street-wise 6 year old, Devon (Paul Medford), who promptly loses the money to his mother's lover David (Norman Beaton). After a number of financially draining but educational encounters with various elements of the black male unemployed sub-culture, Ben learns how to hustle for himself and ends up in a position of dominance in relation to David. In this picaresque film, the innocent young man from the country is thus initiated into the demi-world of hustling street culture in the big city.

FEMININITY AND MASCULINITY IN *BLACK JOY*

The principal female character is Miriam (Floella Benjamin) who sums up David's approach to her as, 'he don't give a fuck, he only wants a fuck'. Miriam runs a cafeteria with no assistance from David and struggles to keep her 6 year old son in check. Women's autonomy, often visualized by white feminism as being bound up with economic independence and the right to work outside of the home, is in conflict with the more (black) masculine defined, 'refusal to work' strategy of resistance to the (racist) system. Although he is financially dependent on her income, David criticises Miriam for being busy working, and thus neglecting the welfare of her son who seems to spend his time roaming the streets on his own. Thus Miriam is seen as the source of the aberrant black family and her inadequacies are located in her refusal to stay at home and look after her truant child, already a hustling, petty criminal.

In David's words, his philosophy of survival hinges on his specialization in 'collecting social welfare cheques, smoking ganja, holing pussy and spreading joy.' Although Miriam presents a verbal and physical challenge to him, she cannot, it seems, live without him. This is significant because when her situation is examined it is clear that she is not economically dependent on him; on the contrary, he takes money from the proceeds of her cafe, for gambling and so on. When she becomes pregnant by David, she acts autonomously and has an abortion. None of this would seem to point to an economic or emotional imperative for her dependence on David. David's character is necessary since he is there to serve as a role model for Miriam's son Devon, even though it is a somewhat dubious one. In representational terms, Miriam's role as mother is important since the problems which have beset black family life and black communities have been located in black 'matriarchy' by both black and white social commentators.[12]

Interestingly, Ben is significantly 'feminized ', in that he is the one man who cooks, cleans, washes up, decorates and makes a home of the small bedsitting room he occasionally shares with David. In a parallel developmental trajectory to that of Tony in *Pressure*, Ben's acquisition of necessary knowledge of street survival runs parallel to his acquisition of sexual knowledge and his passage through the rites of masculinity. He is initially sexually naive, a virgin who does not understand what is being offered to him by the middle aged white female prostitute: he also misrecognizes the flirtatious advances of

Saffra (Dawn Hope) although he clearly has some feeling for her. It is notable that the film ends with Ben's entry into the street as a full member of the black petty criminal fraternity. This development is marked by his acquisition of a car which he is unable to control suggesting that he still has much to learn about using his masculinity and consolidating his street status.

Several of the films referred to previously in this study were noted for their construction of black people as a threat to white societal norms and values who are then viewed as the source of social problems. However, in *Black Joy* the undermining of 'traditional' values of honesty and propriety is not constituted as a social problem – although it may have been viewed as such by many white audiences – rather the 'threat' is contained within this playful version of the black urban ghetto and does not permeate wider society. In this sense, *Black Joy* may be seen as a 'safe' film which does not challenge assumptions about, and stereotypes of, black behaviourial norms in regard to sexuality and criminality.

Black Joy is mainly concerned with the rough world of the urban black male's attempts to survive in a hostile environment, although what it is that makes that world hostile is rarely made explicit. Heroic qualities are not only ascribed to the young in *Black Joy*, as in *Pressure*: *Black Joy* is also concerned with an older generation of Caribbean – mainly male – settlers in Brixton. Both women and men, black and white operate within very narrow characterological confines and the text is clearly marked as a piece of lightweight entertainment cinema. Nonetheless, in a society where racial difference is meaningful, images of blackness and whiteness are endowed with both historical and contemporary significance. In spite of the charmlessness of its characters, *Black Joy* does attempt to depict the ordinariness of a group of working class black people living in London. Although criminality is seen as an inevitable and essential component of the racialized urban landscape in *Black Joy*, it is largely minor and to do with gambling, soft drugs and prostitution. This focus led to the film being described by Akua Rugg, a critic with *Race Today*, as pandering to 'white society's prurient interest in certain aspects of black social life. It provides light entertainment for whites, who after all have their own culture for serious consideration' (Rugg, 1984: 28). Here, Rugg indicates a point which I have made in this chapter and that is the sense that white people are unable to take black peoples' accounts of their experiences seriously. Alongside this runs the reluctance to engage with white racism.

CONCLUSION

Unlike *Pressure*, *Babylon* (1980) and, later, *Burning an Illusion* (1981), in *Black Joy* the systematic abuse of police power against black people is not a significant issue. Similarly, political engagement in an organized sense is largely absent: what is in evidence is an individualistic approach to struggles against the system which belie the capacity for organized political protest or action. I am not arguing that such action ought to be present in the narrative, indeed, it would be surprising if this were the case in what is essentially a 'comedy of manners'. It may be argued that the absence of a figure representing organized politics raises a question about the viability of what began to be institutionalized responses to deprivation and oppression which were the focus of much political activity amongst black activist groups in the 1970s. The drama of particular situations is located in the private, domestic sphere rather than in public. Whereas *Black Joy* encourages its audience to laugh at an amusing story of life in a relatively unthreatening ghetto, and to abandon any kind of political analysis of their position in society, *Burning an Illusion* as will be argued in chapter 7, admonishes such unpoliticized hustlers and unthinking acceptance of black people's subordinated role.

Part of black film-makers' project has been to refuse the positions of libidinous primitive, colonial subject, alien interloper and threat to the nation. I would argue that the look, when it is seized and returned, recasts its parameters and scope of vision: thus the look has the potential to be de-colonized. In *Pressure*, *Black Joy* and *Burning an Illusion* the imperial eye is denied its narcissistic concentration on white subjectivity as the look is not turned on white people but through them. They are not the focal point but a means through which to view both intercultural and intracultural relations.

Chapter 7

British cinema into the 1980s

In preceding chapters, I discussed several films where the main protagonists were black or white males. I have argued that white men have placed themselves at the centre of most narratives and that black men have been positioned as the representatives of black experiences of racism and oppression. The films in this chapter are discussed in the context of developments with regard to 'race relations' in 1980s Britain, and with particular reference to images of black female Otherness.

Pressure (1974) and *Black Joy* (1977) were each more concerned with intracommunity relations than with black/white relations. It is with *Playing Away* (1986) that both black and white relations are examined but even then, two discrete worlds are posited and the oppositionality of those worlds is confirmed by the antagonistic characteristics of their locations in the urban ghetto and the country village. Important to consider here is the shift towards the right in the political climate and this will be discussed in more detail later in this chapter.

As in the case of *Pressure* (1974), so with *Burning an Illusion* (1981) it is once again the necessity for organized political activity which centres the narrative. However, in contrast to both *Pressure* and *Black Joy* (1977), the main protagonist in *Burning an Illusion* is a young black woman. *Playing Away* (1986) betrays its historical location in the peak years of Margaret Thatcher's Conservative government with its implicit rejection of radical political rhetoric, and the confirmation of disjunctive worlds for black and white people. From the experience of political transformation and activism in *Burning an Illusion* and the black male bonding effected through a cricket match in *Playing Away*, I move to a consideration of other films of the mid to late 1980s, with special attention being given to

Mona Lisa (1986). I focus on this film because it is an example of
how racial issues may circulate within a text without being made
explicit: *Mona Lisa* is also noteworthy for its combined use of racial,
class and sexual difference as signifiers of threat and disorder.

IMAGINED COMMUNITIES AND BRITAIN'S IDEOLOGICAL ENEMIES

In Thatcher's Britain of the 1980s, external enemies were clearly
identifiable in the shape of the Argentinians who dared to contest
Britain's 'ownership' of the Falklands/Malvinas: the enemies within
were also recognizable. The miners and trades unions, campaigners
against the proliferation of nuclear weapons and dissident teachers
were amongst those who came under attack from the government.
As well as these familiar targets of conservative ire, there developed
a consensus on the right from which emerged a virulent campaign
against anti-racism in all its manifestations. Press and broadcast
media were efficient assistants to the government in securing the
demonization and demise of anti-racist movements, particularly in
local government and educational institutions. Anti-racist and black
activists were characterized as the problem, it was they who were
'totalitarian' and 'racist' not the 'victimized' 'native' white
population. It was held that British culture was being denigrated, its
imperial achievements belittled and cultural values undermined by
the continuing presence of 'alien' cultures and their supporters.
These cultures were not explicitly labelled 'inferior' but it was held
that separate development was desirable due to natural and inherent
incompatibility.

Several commentators have labelled this cluster of ideas about
culture and ethnicity, the 'new racism' (Barker, 1981), but rather
than representing a break with established patterns of racist thought,
the mutability of racist ideologies is consistent as they adapt to suit
the prevailing circumstances. As John Solomos *et al.* point out: 'it is
important to see that the changes in the *form* of racism during the
seventies were forged in the crucible of the struggles waged by black
people' (Solomos *et al.*, 1986: 35), which suggests the *continual*
shifting of the form of racist discourses according to the context
from which they arise. There is then, both continuity with deeply
entrenched notions of racial difference consolidated during the
eighteenth and nineteenth centuries, and adaptive transformation.[1]

BURNING AN ILLUSION (1981)

Menelik Shabbazz's narrative of a young woman's political awakening was released in 1981 and was only the second feature film directed by a black person to be financed by the BFI (Horace Ove's 1974 film *Pressure* was the first). The narrative concerns a young black woman's transformation from a socially aspirant, anglicized career woman into a radical, Afrocentric black political activist. This shift in Pat's (played by Cassie MacFarlane) sensibilities involves a rejection of white notions of both femininity and feminism, and of the process of embourgeoisement. *Burning an Illusion* is important because it attempts to articulate the convergence of gender, class and 'race' issues in a manner which suggests that relationships are constructed within a racialized social context. The film's approach to black people's experiences of living in twentieth century Britain indicates a greater engagement with the complex nature of that experience than previous narratives had suggested. Related to this is its significance in attempting to give centrality to a black woman's experiences. It is on the issue of Pat's 'conversion' that the following brief analysis will concentrate.

Pat – like Miriam in *Black Joy* – is an economically independent young black woman but unlike Miriam, Pat has no child and at first no boyfriend. She meets Delroy (Victor Romero Evans) whose position may be seen as analogous with David's in *Black Joy*: he is initially in a low waged job, and subsequently financially dependent on Pat. After a confrontation with the police following a brawl at a club, Delroy is beaten, tried and convicted, and ends up in prison. Pat changes from being 'apolitical' to being actively involved in black politics after witnessing the unjust treatment meted out to Delroy. Throughout his prison sentence, Delroy writes to Pat about his political conversion and it is during this period that she undergoes a political and stylistic transformation. Her political awareness is raised further subsequent to being attacked by white racists. In spite of the emphasis on state, institutional and individual racisms, the film manages to end on a positive note with communal singing in political solidarity.

POLITICAL CHOICES

The circumstances of Pat's and Delroy's first date in a restaurant provide the setting for Pat's principal struggle with him: that is, the conflict between the emergence of a generation of black people who subscribe to the norms and values established by white bourgeois society and those attempting to define and assert themselves through a black, working class identity. Pat's bourgeois values and aspirations are signified through her smart clothing, her straightened hairstyle – such a hairstyle having a political significance for black women – and her cultural values.[2] Delroy's attitude is consistently anti-middle class and when he loses his job as a toolmaker, his conflicts with Pat are highlighted further. At this stage, Delroy is not an attractive character as he uses Pat's money to gamble and drink with his friends whilst being critical of her middle class sensibilities. Although he is not politicized in any formal sense, he has ideas about his racial identity and recognizes his subordinate positioning, an awareness not evidenced by Pat.

Given that it is because of Delroy's unjust imprisonment that Pat becomes politicized, it seems that in spite of her supposed autonomy, she still needs a man to facilitate the expression of her 'true' self, to confirm her (heterosexual) femininity and to facilitate her coming to black consciousness. Whilst he is incarcerated Delroy becomes interested in books and black liberatory struggles, thereby mirroring Malcolm X's trajectory of political development. Indeed, to drive the parallel home, Shabbazz has Delroy send a reading list to Pat which includes Malcolm X's writings. Prior to receiving the booklist from Delroy, and before her political conversion, Pat had previously been a reader of Barbara Cartland. This is one of a number of rather crude signifiers of the transformation of Pat's political consciousness.

Through the symbolic use of 'feminine style' the audience is positioned to regard Pat's adoption of proto-nationalist black politics as 'natural'. The signifiers of her acquiescence to dominant western/masculinist notions of aesthetics and beauty are established through her mode of dress and her use of make-up. Her political transformation is marked by her rejection of 'English' dress codes and conceptualizations of female beauty: post-conversion, she wears *dashikis* and no make-up, and ceases to straighten her hair. In one scene Pat memorably underscores her switch to an Afrocentric aesthetic and politics by forcefully wiping off her lipstick. The extent to which her new apparel and politics are also male-defined is a question which is not addressed in the text and signals an analytical problem brought about by an inadequate integration of questions of 'race' and gender. This is especially important since the motivation for her political metamorphosis is impelled by Delroy's experience at the hands of racist police – not as a result of her own experiences or her own political development.

A further problem here is that it seems that in order to depict Pat's political progress in easily assimilable visual terms, the complexities of what induces such a thorough change in outlook are smoothed over. The oversimplified change of perspective cannot accommodate the possibility that it might be possible to be a reader of Barbara Cartland *and* Malcolm X; wear lipstick and straighten hair, *and* actively support black liberation. Another question which was raised earlier in this chapter in relation to Miriam in *Black Joy* is: to what extent is her racial liberation predicated on an economic disempowerment which is antithetical to feminist notions of advancement and equality for women?

A further question raised is what model of freedom for black women is being offered here? What constitutes appropriate behaviour and attitudes for black women is made clear, whilst black men's behaviour and style is relatively under-interrogated. Although both Delroy and Pat undergo political development, Pat's psychological and emotional transformation is more emphatically linked to her outward appearance and behaviour. This suggests a view of women as being concerned with surface appearances and implies that for women, politics is as much a matter of changing your style as your attitudes. It would seem that men change their outlook as a result of their rational choices which results in internal rather than external remodelling.

In *Burning an Illusion*, the question of intergenerational conflict is not emphasized in the way that it is in *Pressure* but nonetheless its presence is inferred. It is the young who carry the mantle of political activism and the audience is given no historical perspective on black peoples' struggles in Britain. Whenever there has been a black presence in Britain there have been black people – and white – denouncing racist policies and practices: similarly black people in Africa, the Caribbean, the United States and Asia, have continually fought against domination, yet, interestingly, no such history is included, or alluded to in *Pressure*, *Babylon* or *Burning an Illusion*. It could be argued that this is a function of the adherence to realist forms which do not allow for such perspectives to be smoothly incorporated into conventional narratives. I would argue that it is not just the result of adherence to particular cinematic conventions, since there are a number of ways in which realist texts may refer to or demonstrate the historical dimensions of the struggles depicted. It seems to relate to a sense of having to deal with the present and with a disappointment about the apparent lack of progress made by previous generations. Whatever the reasons, it means that certain absences established by white cultural practitioners have often been reiterated by black film-makers.

DEBATING *BURNING AN ILLUSION*

Although *Burning an Illusion* has received scant critical attention, a point has been made about the film's cinematic language. The critical essay by Sally Sayer and Laleen Jayamanne observes the use of melodrama and comments: 'We do not mean to say that melodrama is inimical to effective political film-making, but that the film's use of it simplifies complex processes by reducing them to a series of climaxes' (Sayer and Jayamanne, 1987: 88). They go on to say: 'We are registering our disappointment at the taken-for-granted use of white film language.' (ibid.: 88). The meaning of this assertion is not transparent, as their criticism is not adequately clarified. There is clearly though, an assumption that 'white' film language can be differentiated from 'black' film language, although equally clearly, such a distinction is not dependent on whether you are black or white since *Burning an Illusion* was made by a team of black people.

A more cogent and complex theoretical model for the analysis of black film is suggested by Kobena Mercer. His important essay, 'Diaspora Culture and the Dialogic Imagination: the Aesthetics of Black Independent Film in Britain' uses the Bakhtinian concept of dialogics to locate the work of what later came to be seen as the more experimental black film workshops such as Sankofa and the Black Audio Film Collective whose work began in the early 1980s. Mercer further elaborates the problematic issues of form, language and content and characterizes what is at issue as being:

the critical difference between a *monologic* tendency in black film which tends to homogenise and totalise the black experience in Britain and a *dialogic* tendency which is responsive to the diverse and complex qualities of our black Britishness and British blackness – our differentiated specificity as a diaspora people.

(Mercer, 1988: 50)

The development of a black film language is not, he argues, predicated on the concept of an essentialist or absolutist notion of a 'return to origins' and authenticity but the adoption of a critical voice 'that promotes consciousness of the collision of cultures and histories that constitute our very conditions of existence' (ibid.: 51). Mercer bases his broadly anti-realist stance on the assumption that what he terms 'a realist aesthetic' is the product solely of the colonizer. By so doing, the discussion of the various issues arising from the work of such as Menelik Shabbazz is foreclosed by subsuming them under the rubric of 'cultural mimicry which demonstrates a neo-colonized dependency on the codes which valorise film as a commodity of cultural imperialism' (ibid.: 57). Such a statement makes it difficult to accept Mercer's claim that he aims to 'avoid the construction of a monolithic system of evaluative criteria' (Mercer, 1988: 57). The point I wish to make here is that although there may be constraints inherent in certain realist forms of representation, it is by no means the case that all realisms are reactionary or that rejection of such forms results in politically progressive, complex films.

It would be a pity if the more interesting issues raised by *Burning an Illusion*, or any other black films, were to get lost in debates about the appropriateness of particular critical discourses and counter-discourses: the film at least attempts to examine gender conflict in the context of a black community, rather than seeing such an issue as peripheral or too divisive to consider, and this represents a significant break with the treatment of gender issues in *Pressure* and *Black Joy*. Unfortunately, a problem develops in the latter part of the narrative, because when Pat engages with black political activism the gender issues cease to be taken seriously and their narrative centrality diminishes. In this respect, I agree with Sayer's and Jayamanne's contention that:

> Though the conflicts of race and gender undoubtedly intersect in the film, it is only to provide a catalyst for the progress of the narrative. They are left as fairly discrete areas with the gender question more or less disappearing once it catalyses the race issue in the club.
>
> (Sayer and Jayamanne, 1987: 89–90).

This switch in emphasis suggests that ultimately racial politics take primacy over gender issues. *Burning an Illusion* begins to examine difference within black communities even though it does end by suppressing contradictory voices and returning to a more homogeneous conceptualization of black identity.

Burning an Illusion's central characters, Pat and Delroy, reject integrationist approaches to 'race relations', preferring instead to construct a model of politically-informed racial autonomy and solidarity as demonstrated in the last scene which depicts a bus of black radicals singing, on their way to a demonstration. However, although white people have a marginal and emblematic presence, they structure the conditions under which black political action occurs and 'the community' may operate.

PRESSURE, BLACK JOY AND *BURNING AN ILLUSION*: DIFFERENT POINTS OF VIEW

Burning an Illusion posits two separate racialized spheres, and this is emphasized by the separation of black and white worlds, which are seen as incompatible as the Caribbean food and European wine which Pat consumes in the restaurant. This essentialism differs from *Black Joy* and *Pressure*, as in the former the two worlds do not often connect and there is little indication of either solidarity or antagonisms between them. With regard to *Pressure*, there is the suggestion of both hostility (towards, and from, those in authority), and common cause (with politicized white people).

Whilst *Black Joy* has little explicit to say about political organization and action, the narratives of both *Pressure* and *Burning an Illusion* are structured by it, and both of them involve a process of personal development entailing the formation of a distinctively black political consciousness. *Burning an Illusion* is based on coming to a particularized notion of black identity *within* 'the community' and is not concerned, except in terms of racist interactions, with interracial social and political relations. The interrogation of black diaspora identity is not related to notions of national identity or cultural belonging as they relate to the Caribbean, as in *Pressure*, but is concerned with the development of a young woman's awareness of the politics of racism as operated in Britain. As I have indicated in chapter 6 and at the beginning of this chapter, there are some similarities between *Pressure* and *Burning an Illusion* but as Kobena Mercer argues:

> While the linear plot and mode of characterisation are similar to *Pressure* (as the central protagonist is taken to embody a general or 'typical' experience), the shift of emphasis from black/white confrontation to gender politics *within* a black community setting

displaces the binary polarisation in which black identity is reactively politicised by its 'opposition' to white authority alone.
(Mercer, 1986: 10).

Blackness is not explicitly opposed to whiteness in terms of actual characterizations, the contrast is implicit. It is most evident in Pat's initial adherence to 'white' middle class behavioural norms and cultural values and subsequent transformation to an Afrocentric disposition. The film does not set out to 'explain' black community life to white people: rather it represents an intracommunity dialogue.

Jim Pines has noted how in *Black Joy*, 'the hero's anti-establishment individualism takes the place of social and political protest' (Pines, 1991: 8); and that this is a key difference from both *Pressure* and *Burning an Illusion* which are concerned with political awareness. Yet both *Pressure* and *Black Joy* see men as the key protagonists in the struggle to survive and all of them – including *Burning an Illusion* – see women as obstructions in the path of male endeavours to a greater or lesser extent, at some point in the narrative. If the 'anti-establishment individualism' and shunning the world of work in favour of community-based politics is intended as a critique of capitalist social relations, then this point is not adequately clarified in any of the above texts.

The point made earlier about the alleged failure of 'West Indians' to recognize that they could not be assimilated into British culture by adopting British ways and habits is figured through the females in both *Pressure* and *Burning an Illusion*, and arguably through Miriam in *Black Joy*. Miriam's life and character are insufficiently developed to be able to comment on her political beliefs in detail but there is little to indicate anything but acceptance – albeit reluctant – of her position as a black woman. Whereas *Pressure* indicates that there is no prospect of change in the political consciousness of Bopsie (Tony's mother), in *Burning an Illusion*, Pat is eventually able to shake off what are seen as the shackles of adherence to white middle class values.

CHANGING DIRECTIONS IN BLACK FILM

The civil disturbances involving black people which took place in the late 1970s and early 1980s helped to bring about a change in funding policies towards black cultural projects. In particular, the then Greater London Council developed criteria for art and cultural funding in the capital which aimed to redress some of the previous imbalances in the provision of financial support (Owusu, 1986). Black practitioners, who had been subjected to institutionalized discriminatory practices and excluded from cultural debates within avant-garde circles in substantively similar ways to those in which they were excluded from the mainstream of British cinematic debates, did not begin to engage with the politics of form and representation on a significant level until the first generation of film, media and cultural studies students emerged in the mid 1980s.

A major consequence of the shift in arts policy and practice brought about by local government authorities' need to be seen to be taking action was an escalation in the funding of black arts. This occurred at the same time as Channel 4 was established with a remit to cater for 'minorities' and this conjuncture proved to be of crucial importance for black film-makers (Mercer and Julien, 1988: 6). From the mid 1980s the newly emerging cultural practitioners provoked a good deal of controversy amongst black cultural critics and communities, gaining critical acclaim on European 'progressive' film circuits and success and notoriety in the USA. In particular, the work of the Black Audio Film Collective and Sankofa as exemplified in *Handsworth Songs* (1986), *Passion of Remembrance* (1986), and *Looking for Langston* (1989) emerged to establish new interventions in discussions about black identity and subjectivity, and critical traditions (Mercer and Julien, 1988; Cham and Andrade-Watkins, 1988). For those with an investment in the realist mode of representation, the valorization of these more 'experimental' less directly 'accessible' texts were experienced as an undermining of films and practices which did not conform to what appeared to be a new critical orthodoxy being established by black cultural critics such as Stuart Hall, Kobena Mercer and Isaac Julien. This critical position was anti-essentialist and argued for complex analyses of black film incorporating a range of theoretical frameworks.

Although the position which says that black films must be celebrated in recognition of the struggle it takes to get them made is no longer tenable, issues such as the concentration of ownership of the means of producing and distributing films and videos, the financial structure of the film and video industry and, importantly, audiences' attitudes are all relevant factors in considering the potential of a film. Although not every textual analysis can cover every aspect of those issues, their importance needs to be recognised.

THE CRICKET TEST: *PLAYING AWAY* (1986)

Horace Ove's second feature film *Playing Away* was partially funded by Channel Four and departs significantly from *Pressure* in terms of content. Whereas *Pressure* was concerned with black, community-based politics, *Playing Away* is a piece of lightweight entertainment cinema which tries to incorporate a critique of racism in its discourse. In the context of this book it is of interest inasmuch as it comments on racial difference, positing two distinct racial worlds. *Playing Away* is also of note because of the distance between it and *Pressure* which I will discuss towards the end of this section.

It is the only black-authored film included in this book which has a significant number of white characters. Film critic Barry Norman's comment on *Playing Away* was that Ove, 'is black and he knows about black people but he does not know about white people' (Ove, 1988: 57), thereby attempting to set the discursive parameters for black film-makers. Norman denies Ove the right to construct images of whiteness, although it is rarely suggested that white directors may not 'know' black people. There is, however, more to the film than stereotypical white characterizations and a simple depiction of the 'threat' of 'West Indians and the drug culture' (Giles, 1993: 76).

The film is of interest partly because of Ove's involvement and partly because it takes black British people away from the familiarity of an inner-city location and places them in the secluded and exclusive world of the English country village. It is clearly significant that Horace Ove and Caryl Phillips – respectively director and writer - chose to locate a substantial proportion of *Playing Away* in a small 'typically' English village. Although in Britain, black people have traditionally been associated with the rural through the 'jungle' and through plantation imagery, in more recent times people of African descent have been clearly marked as belonging more 'naturally' in urban areas of the over-developed world. Urban dance music, the urban jungle, the ghetto, the inner city, these are the coded terms which are linked to the 'teeming hordes' of 'immigrants' in British cities. In modern times, black people have gravitated towards the cities for economic reasons, and settlers have tended to go to those places where they know there is the probability of supportive networks of friends and relatives to act as a buttress against racial hostility.

In *Playing Away*, the presence of black people in the country landscapes, temporarily incorporated into village life begins to suggest the difficulties in thinking about national identity and Englishness and the relationship to black people. Although the narrative fails to exploit the opportunity to articulate the contradictions of black Britishness through the metaphor of the landscape, it does at least suggest the possibilities of discussing national and cultural identity in somewhat different terms. The film also raises the issue of why so many black people feel alienated and unwelcome in England's rural heartlands. The English countryside may work as a metaphor for tranquillity and freedom for many white people – by no means for all – but it does not necessarily have the same resonances for black people.

Significant also is the choice of sport and in particular cricket as a figure here, due to its specific associations for those from India, Pakistan and the Caribbean islands. During the period of colonial expansion, Britain exported sport to the colonies, the objectives being to distract the colonized subjects with recreational pastimes and to instil in the population deference to rules and to authority. Sport had a political and ideological function, serving as it did to convey values which were intended to assist in the perpetuation of established power relations. However, particularly recently, sport has provided a means by which nations designated 'inferior' or 'underdeveloped' may refuse subordinate status by competing successfully against rich, powerful countries.

Although there is much symbolic potential in using the situation which a cricket match provides, there are two main problems with its use in the film. One arises because of the assumption that black people are 'naturally' good at sports: such assumptions are not challenged by the metadiscourse of the film. The second problem arises because the way in which cricket is used to play out antagonisms between rural white and urban black people ensures that the female characters are peripheral; the women make lunches and confirm the men's heterosexuality. Through the cricket contest, the dynamics of 'race' as played out through competing masculinities are given primacy. This foregrounding of male experience may be seen as a function of the perceived necessity to respond to what are perceived as negative or incomplete images of black masculinity: it also indicates a difficulty with allowing black women to attain a degree of autonomy.

All the women are caricatures, and arguably all the men are too:

however, the black men's experience and attitudes are foregrounded
and elaborated and the black women are even less developed than
their white counterparts. It is as if there is a repertoire of images and
stereotypes of white femininity on which to draw but little which
charts black female subjectivity. This is a continuing problem for
black women as most of the dramas constructed by male film-
makers concerning racial identity and difference are played out in
the arena of robust homosociality.

THE END OF (BLACK) POLITICS?

Burning an Illusion was made seven years after *Pressure*, and the
way in which identity is explored differs in terms of focus, although
it may be argued that in regard to their stylistic and formal
properties, the two films are similar. The focus for *Playing Away* is
quite different, pointing to substantial changes in the social and
political context. *Playing Away* is not concerned with political
organization or sexual politics and even the playing out of racial
conflict is precisely that: a ritualized display of racial prejudice and
sexual banter with little fresh to say about relations between black
and white people or gender relations.

It is interesting to contrast the notion of 'black community' in
Pressure with that portrayed in *Playing Away*. The differences in the
two films serve to highlight the political changes which occurred
between 1974 and 1986. No political demonstrations or communal
action, but men – young and old – gathering in public houses and
parties, pursuing women, drinking alcohol, smoking a little 'ganja',
dancing and resolving disagreements through fighting. The film
seems to be caught between wanting to say something serious about
continued racism and wanting to be 'positive' about the men within
'the black community'. The narrative, which for the most part
progresses in a linear fashion, is unable to give a perspective on the
complexities of the social and sexual relations which occur between
black and white people.

OTHERNESS IN THE LATE 1980s

Much of the longing evidenced in the 1980s wave of nostalgia
seemed to be directed towards a mourning of the loss of 'traditional
values' exemplified in such notions as hard work, strictly defined
moral codes and social stability. Perhaps most importantly, the

period before decolonization was seen as a period when Britain's status as a world power was not in question.[3] Of course these fond memories of the 1940s, 1950s and early 1960s are based on the construction and maintenance of a set of myths and fantasies but they are nonetheless potent for that.

One 1980s film which plays with these fantasies is *Absolute Beginners* (1986) set in 1958. The film re-visits the period of racial unrest as black migrants responded to requests from the British government to live and work in Britain. *Absolute Beginners* – which was neither a critical nor a box-office success – briefly suggests the necessity to have a fresh or different experience which is promised by the fantasies of sexual abundance which adhere to black people and that is why it is briefly mentioned here.

In both *Absolute Beginners* and *Scandal* (1988) – set respectively in 1958 and 1963 – established black singers/performers are used to introduce themes of interracial sexual attraction but this theme is never really elaborated. In the former, Athene Duncan (Sade Adu) is the object of both male and female white desire and in the latter, the white woman's desire (Christine Keeler played by Joanne Whalley-Kilmer) is that of a woman seeking an exotic sexual partner (Johnny, played by Roland Gift).[4]

In another British film made during this period, a black prostitute is momentarily featured in *Personal Services* (1987), perhaps to emphasize the level of sexual transgression and indiscretion. *Personal Services* is a dramatized account of brothel keeper Cynthia Payne's enterprising provision of sexual experiences based on a luncheon voucher system. Like *Mona Lisa* (1986) it was scripted by David Leland.

MONA LISA: REPRESENTING NEGROPHOBIA

There are a number of reasons for examining this particular product of the British film industry. *Mona Lisa* is intriguing because it illustrates the way in which issues of race may be embedded in a text without being made explicit through a strong black presence: one of the absorbing elements of the film is that although it contains a multiplicity of images which refer obliquely to racial difference, it continually refuses to engage with the racial issues raised.

The film's narrative is centred on George (Bob Hoskins), recently released from prison, and his developing relationship with Simone, a black prostitute played by Cathy Tyson. George is hired by

Mortwell (Michael Caine) to deliver pornographic videos and drive Simone to and from her rich clients. Initially, there is much antagonism between the tasteless, sporadically violent George and the aloof, expensively dressed Simone but as the story progresses, George becomes emotionally attached to her and he agrees to search for her drug-addicted young friend Cathy (Kate Hardie), also a prostitute. George locates and then abducts Cathy and subsequently flees with her and Simone to Brighton where he learns that Simone and Cathy are probably lovers. Mortwell pursues the three fugitives. Accompanying Mortwell is the brutal Anderson (Clarke Peters), Simone's former and Cathy's present pimp. Simone shoots Mortwell and Anderson and is about to shoot George when he grabs her hand with the gun pointed at him. The final scene shows George reconciled with his estranged teenage daughter (Zoe Nathenson) and his eccentric friend Thomas (Robbie Coltrane) working together as one contented 'family' unit.

As I indicated in chapter 1, Fanon attempted to explain the psychic processes which foster white experience of black people as phobogenic – arousing fear and revulsion. Believing that 'anxiety derives from a subjective insecurity linked to the absence of the mother' (Fanon, 1986: 154), Fanon points to the endowment of the phobic object with evil intentions, which allows physical contact alone to stimulate (sexual) anxiety. From the beginning, the character of George in *Mona Lisa* displays a phobic reaction to black men. During the opening credits of the film, as George crosses the Thames on his way home, a black man walks towards him, causing him to do a double take. It is interesting that significance is attached to George's reaction so early in the narrative. He has been in prison for seven years. Logically, having lived in a working class district of South London and been in prison, it is highly unlikely that George would be seeing a black person for the first time. However, the instantly recognizable signifier of difference – Fanon's epidermal schema – is mobilized to indicate the threat and disorder to come as George reenacts the shock of white peoples' first encounter with Africans. The grossness of his initial reaction seems to be intended as a contrast with his attitude to Simone as the narrative develops.

In *Mona Lisa*, there is the constant association of the presence of black people and other foreign visitors with the lowering of moral standards, with garbage and with outbreaks of violence and illicit sexual activity. Early in the narrative, just before his arrival at his wife's house, George sits in a park, enjoying the hazy sunshine: it looks more like a countryside idyll than a South London common. In contrast the street where his wife and daughter live, having been 'colonized' by black people is punctuated by overflowing rubbish bins and other signs of decay. Significantly, George's family house is neat with well stocked hanging baskets, whilst the houses of the black neighbours are flanked by bags of garbage.

The perception of the deterioration in the quality of life in London is reflected through George's eyes. Even the tradition and luxury of the Ritz hotel are undermined through their association with the sordid and corrupt activities taking place behind closed doors and the presence of the mainly foreign visitors. London is represented as a place where a sleazy underworld, led by working class villains and fed on by 'foreigners', is in control: a black pimp ensures the loyalty of his fifteen year old prostitutes by beating them and supplying them with hard drugs; the people who stay at the Ritz and use the services that Mortwell runs are mainly rich Japanese and Arab men.

London's depiction in this film has been described as a 'modern-day Dante's inferno'[5]: the scenes in the mythically reconstructed King's Cross with its grotesque population and swirling, constant smoke are clearly meant to signify some kind of nightmare. A popular perception is that London's alleged descent into squalor coincided with the arrival of black settlers from the Caribbean, Africa and Asia. Within the film's fantasy maelstrom of violence, corruption, disorder and transgressive desire, George is a contemporary evocation of the Common Man, signifying a lost, somehow more innocent and omnipotent England from a mythical past.

INTERRACIAL SEXUALITIES

In order to ensure that George's fantasies of romantic love and the sordid reality of Simone's lifestyle do not engage, various narrative and textual devices are deployed: her sexual performances, both in hotels and on videotape are used to inform his ultimate estrangement from her. She is carefully constructed as a non-sexually threatening character in terms of her relationship with George. However, the potential of emotional/sexual relationships between women undermines the heterosexual relationships on which patriarchal society is based. These textual strategies may be seen as further evidence of aversion to depicting overt interracial sexuality in film.[6] The potential danger involved in a sexual union across racial boundaries is averted by suggesting Simone as a lesbian: this also serves to deflect attention from the potential racial antagonisms in the film, since the conflict is then portrayed as springing from George and Simone as male and female, rather than white and black. This also serves to contain Simone's fertility – which constitutes the racists' ultimate fear that black people will reproduce uncontrollably, either with other black people or with white people – since her lesbianism and prostitution mean that her body though useable for sexual gratification is not used for reproductive purposes. Thus her potential as a black woman, symbolic of fecundity and sexual attraction, is invoked but not realized.

CONTROLLING BLACK BODIES

The commodification of Simone's sexuality and its control by Mortwell – a white man – recalls the brutal exploitation of black women's bodies during slavery but it is Anderson, the black pimp, (Clarke Peters) whose physical violence towards the young white girls is that most often represented. Mortwell's control and commodification of Simone for sexual satisfaction should be recognized – to use bell hooks' phrase – as 'constituting an alternative playground' (hooks, 1992: 23), where those who are established in positions of dominance due to their gender or racial group or economic power can claim their power over subordinate groups. It is a way of playing with the difference embodied in the Other from the safety of a confirmed, hegemonic position. Although Simone may be said to be in control in some respects, she is ultimately an object for sexual commodification as she does not have authority over Mortwell or her clients but has to make do with some degree of power over George. bell hooks locates Simone's lack of sexual agency in her representation as a mammy-type character but this is inappropriate in the British context where the mammy figure does not have the same historical force in Britain as it does in the USA (hooks, 1992: 74). However, the important point that hooks is making here is that the character of Simone undergoes a desexualization which does have a degree of correspondence with that of the mammy figure but is also clearly rather different. The figure of the black prostitute is – like the mammy – a desexualized black female inasmuch as she is not an object of desire but there to service or care for white people.

As with Sapphire, it is Simone's sexuality which is under investigation, the object of the white male gaze. Here, though, unlike Sapphire, Simone's background is concealed: she is another black female character who is 'deracinated' and deprived of cultural and historical reference points. The only information given about her family is that her father beat her as a child: her only relationship to black people in the film is brutally economic. Simone performs a range of 'deviant' sex often with black men but has no congress with other blacks, no visible black community with whom she may be identified.

Simone's racial isolation also contributes to her diminution as a real threat to the 'natural' order of white male dominance. The anxiety stimulated in men by women's sexuality is especially acute when considered in terms of black and white sociosexual relations. Blackness in itself connotes 'difference': when the subject is also a woman, the difference is heightened. The danger signified by all sexualized women is displaced onto her 'Otherness': it is also intensified by the portrayal of all the women as embittered, uncooperative – except when coerced – and unloving towards men.

The apparent 'motivation' for Simone's and Cathy's lesbian relationship is the brutality they suffer at the hands of the men who regulate their lives – both Mortwell and Anderson are implicated in this, as well as the clients the women serve. The possibility that the women might simply have preferred to have a sexual relationship with each other is denied, as this would be disruptive of the normative heterosexual relationship: their difference is doubly inscribed as perverse – because it is female centred sexual expression, and because it is between black and white. Thus the narrative serves to pathologize Simone in four areas: as a black, as a lesbian, as a prostitute and as a woman. These four elements are drawn from the repertoire of fantasies which sees the black/female/lesbian as the sign of anomalous sexuality and as a sexual and social threat which needs to be controlled.

The young white females in *Mona Lisa* are rather differently placed. In both medical and legal discourses, the pubescent female is seen as potentially sexually threatening and liable to bring about her own destruction unless her sexual behaviour is monitored and her body 'protected'. In the scenes where George goes to collect his teenage daughter from school, he drives along the route she follows home like a kerb-crawler, and invites her into his car: these scenes parallel the way in which the girls and women looking for business in King's Cross enter the cars of their prospective clients. This similarity is emphasized because George's daughter bears a physical resemblance to the young prostitutes he encounters in his attempts to find and 'save' Cathy. In fact the men appear to view prostitution as the natural development for the female child, and give themselves permission to punish the women relentlessly for their supposed failure to satisfy men. The pimps have a dual role though, because at the same time as beating 'their girls', they are there to protect them: and George is there to save them and make honest women of them.

Simone becomes his territory in his fantasies: for him she is both sexually knowing and virginal – her standard sexual uniform is white satin underwear – and it is the knowledge of her sexual performances with Anderson which ultimately alerts him to what is constructed as her sexual duplicity. She will have sex with Anderson – presumably for financial gain, but possibly due to coercion – and she will have a relationship with a young white woman, but she will not emotionally engage with George, a white heterosexual, working class male. Unable to understand her motivation for the choices she has made, George attributes her reluctance to have a sexual relationship with him to his being 'the wrong colour', the only explanation that he can imagine.

George sees Simone participating in a sexual act with Anderson in a video watched by him and his friend, Thomas. There is an association between animal imagery, sexuality and blackness which is a persistent and recurring feature of eighteenth century racism that is echoed in *Mona Lisa*.[7] Simone, the 'tall thin black tart', describes Anderson, her former pimp, as 'an animal born in a butcher's shop'.

The racist notion of the affinity between black males and animals in general and gorillas in particular, is invoked in *Mona Lisa* as the link between the animalistic images of the black people engaging in oral rather than 'normal' sex, and sexual deviancy and danger is embedded in the text and interwoven with the image of a voracious, cannibalistic black woman. Sex here is dangerous because it is about a black women consuming the penis, the concretization of castration anxiety: in order to forestall that anxiety the narrative progresses in such a way as to deny the possibility of that desire being realized. hooks sees this scene as representing a 'postmodern sexual practice' in which the 'masturbatory voyeuristic technologically-based fulfilment of desire is more exciting than actually possessing any real Other' (hooks, 1992: 23). It is open to discussion as to whether watching is more exciting than participating but in an era of Aids, it is clearly safer to look than to engage in sexual activity itself. hooks' comment would be equally applicable to the discussion of Leo's fetishistic scopophilia as discussed in chapter 5. During the playing of the video, Thomas remarks to George, 'you used to tell a joke about a randy gorilla'.[8] It is important that George gains knowledge of Simone's past through looking at a video. It replicates that 'knowledge' that white people have gained through texts, rather than through direct, intimate experience. It is a knowledge constructed from fragments which are then forced to take on the appearance of coherence. Here, as Claire Pajaczkowska remarks, 'George needs to discover whatever it is that she does behind closed doors. Mystery was unbearable for the man and was transformed, through narrative, into mastery' (Pajaczkowska and Young, 1992: 205). The knowledge is gained through the look, which is indicative of power: so even though George is a dupe, a working class man with limited access to power, there are still certain areas where he is in control.

WORKING CLASS OTHERNESS

There is much that is unspoken in *Mona Lisa*: the sense of implicit contrast of lifestyles between black and white, male and female, working class and middle class is present but under-elaborated. Class is addressed through the identification of dissimilar and divergent patterns of behaviour amongst working class and middle class people:

> It addresses the audience as a rather smug middle class, with a sense of moral superiority of having culture whilst the proletarians have only pornography, detective stories and high street shopping, of having careers or unalienated work whilst others have only semi-criminal ways of earning a living, and of having family life or love whereas the others have only sadistic and debased sexualities.
>
> (Pajaczkowska and Young, 1992: 208)

Whilst I would argue that there are positions of identification other than that of middle class white male offered by the text, there is a sense that the divergent worlds marked by class perspectives only meet in the realm of economic exchange and exploitation, and a sense that morality and 'proper' forms of (sexual) behaviour are the province of the middle classes. Connected to this is the notion, often a feature of white British cinema, that racism and irrational prejudice is not practised by middle class men: as previously argued, it is working class youths and sexually frustrated white women who are characterized as the perpetrators of racial prejudice.

CONCLUSION

Mona Lisa depicts relationships formed in ignorance and fear by the classes which constitute the underworld, dependent for its existence on what are seen as the excremental elements of London low-life. These relationships are formed through economic necessity, are based on individual need and greed and occur in isolation. It is not only Simone who lacks a community, there is no sense of group identity or responsibility unless it is motivated by the possibility of financial gain. This makes the film a fitting emblem of the ethos of the 1980s when Margaret Thatcher informed us that there was no such thing as society.

Cinematic narratives emerge from historical processes and discourses external to the cinema and *Mona Lisa* may be viewed as a narrative of racial, sexual and class interaction in Britain at that particular historical conjuncture. It was made in the middle of Thatcher's term as Prime Minister, a period which saw the notion of consensus politics transformed into the hegemony of the radical right, an era when Britain temporarily regained its entitlement to be called 'Great' through an imperial adventure in the southern reaches of the Atlantic ocean – a rather different Atlantic connection to that which was established during the eighteenth century, but one which enabled some sections of the population to once again feel 'masterful' and in control.

One of the central tenets identified as 'new' in the racist discourse which emerged during the late 1970s, is the racialization of cultural difference and the contention that a nation is an indivisible unit with no significant divergences in the national character to disrupt the sense of shared culture. Although, according to some commentators, the new racism does not use biological differences as a foundation for separatism, I would argue those crude scientific discourses frequently lurk just below the surface, albeit with a shift of emphasis to an instinctual notion of difference. This instinctiveness – allegedly possessed by all 'races' – maintains that it is 'natural' for different racial groupings to want to keep cultural cohesion through homogeneity and any attempt to resist that is the result of misguided intellectualization (Barker, 1981). This racialization of culture is a discourse in which black film-makers are implicated since *Pressure* (1974), *Black Joy* (1977), *Burning an Illusion* (1981) and *Playing*

Away (1986) are not focused on dismantling or deconstructing the discourse of 'race' but are centred on attacking racism. Such an approach was certainly appropriate during the 1960s, 1970s and early 1980s but demographic shifts, a shifting of the political terrain, increasing disillusionment with organized politics and a recognition of the complex position in which black diasporean people are placed, means that cinematic priorities have had to be rethought.

What might be termed in conservative discourses a 'national culture' evolves in highly complex ways through 'dynamic patterns of syncretism' (Gilroy, 1987: 13), and inevitably makes use of, and is intertwined with, material from several cultures. It is useful to bear that statement in mind when considering black film-makers in Britain. To posit an exclusively black or exclusively white mode of expression or articulation of gender issues is to emphasize the differences between black and white at the expense of an adequate analysis of differences which exist within those racial groups: I would emphasize here that the continual use of the black/white binarism in this book should not be seen as being based on a presumption of the acceptance of 'race' as a category or of racial essentialism.

The final chapter which follows will summarize the main issues and arguments presented in this book. There will also be a discussion of ways of analyzing the representation of racial and gender identities in British film and indications of further potentially fruitful areas of study.

Chapter 8

'Race', identity and cultural criticism

One of the concerns of this study has been to indicate some of the significant omissions in previous analyses of 'race' and representation in British cinema and to reveal the extent to which racial and sexual difference structures critical perspectives. I have argued that it is necessary to trace Britain's colonial past in order to elucidate this process, and demonstrated that this approach has not been adequately developed in previous analyses of British film. Little has been written regarding the racialized discourses of British cinema from 1959 to 1986, and, as I have argued in my prefatory remarks, where studies have raised issues of 'race' these have most frequently been concerned with negative and positive images and elaborations thereof. In discussing history and colonial discourse, the racialization of sexuality and gender, and their implication in British cinematic practice I have tried to challenge the assumptions and absences in conventional feminist film analyses. I have argued that it is necessary to recognize the ways in which histories are repeated, enacted and permeate contemporary cultural production. Thus, I have analysed and discussed films on the basis that a cinematic text cannot be attributed exclusively to those directly involved in its production but should be analysed as part of a complex web of inter-related experiences, ideas, fantasies and unconscious expressions of desire, anxiety and fear that need to be located in their historical, political and social contexts.

In this concluding chapter, I elucidate the potential of black feminist cultural analyses and examine the absence of black women and the ways in which they may be considered as Other for both black men and white people. I go on to summarize why I have felt it necessary to embark on this project through an examination of how 'whiteness' is under-elaborated in cultural analysis. I then argue that

white film-makers have continually constructed black women and
men as Other and attempt to account for this using psychoanalytic
theory. Throughout this study I have been concerned with both the
presence and absence of black women and tried to account for their
problematic status in the work of black and white male film-makers.
The question of how the work of black film-makers might be
addressed is discussed in some detail in order to clarify points made
elsewhere in this book about black subjectivities and cultural
criticism. The final section suggests some further areas where
critical debate and scholarly research would be of benefit in the
development of this field of study.

THE WORK OF BLACK FEMINIST CRITICISM

One of the central concerns of this study has been to attempt to
establish a conceptual framework for the study of racial difference
in the cinema which is able to engage with issues of gender and
sexuality. Crucially the impetus for discussing all the films has been
the conspicuous lack of critical feminist voices prepared to consider
colonialism's implication in the construction of notions of
femininity and sexuality in British cinema. The separation of issues
relating to 'race', gender and class and the privileging of one over
another has contributed to the lack of attention to the points at which
these politically constructed categories intersect. Although I have
argued for a consideration of the interconnections of gender and
'race', I have not posited that there is any advantage to be gained
from thinking of them as the same. The constant juxtaposition of
gender, 'race' and class should not lead to a presumption that they
are reducible to one another. Rather, I have argued in chapter 2 that
it is evident from close examination of the history of 'race-thinking'
that it is inextricably bound up with questions of gender and
sexuality, as well as social class and I argue that that point needs to
be recognized in order to demystify and deconstruct contemporary
discriminatory critical practices.

In chapter 1, I indicated that black feminists have consistently
drawn attention to European history's construction of black women
as hypersexual, or as desexualized characters, there to serve the
interests of white women and men. In the field of visual culture,
whilst there is not yet a significant body of academic black feminist
film criticism in Britain, African–Americans bell hooks and
Michelle Wallace in particular have made constructive observations

regarding white feminist cultural theorists' avoidance of discussing the specificities of racial privilege and subordination embedded in gender issues (hooks, 1991 and 1992; Wallace, 1993).

Representations of white women have often served to support and legitimate the narcissistic illusion of the centrality of white masculine, middle class identity through their acceptance of patriarchal/heterosexual conventions and lifestyles. A critical perspective which analyses the role of white women in terms of their ethnicity as well as their gender would give fresh insight into their instrumentality in such texts. It is the case that where white feminists have analysed the sociosexual colonial matrix, they have emphasized the similarity of their positioning by white men, with that of black or 'primitive' people. They have stopped short of more detailed analysis of their relative power and shifting status within that matrix. As I indicated in chapters 2 and 3, at times white women were active participants in the oppressive regimes instituted under slavery and colonialism and postcolonialism, even whilst they were subordinated in other spheres. Further, such oscillating moments of access to power were differentiated according to the white woman's sexual and social status. The point I wish to argue here is that it has not been my intention to construct a hierarchy of oppression but to suggest that a more reflective critical practice needs to be developed in order to analyse the complex ways in which these systems of oppression may be destabilized.

In chapter 1, I suggested that one aspect of the dominant form of white feminism which is important in regard to black women's absence from cinematic representation is the continued use of the 'dark continent' trope, the metaphorical status of which serves to naturalize a whole set of ideas about Africa, its inhabitants and its diaspora. For, example Mary Ann Doane (1991), although she problematizes the term, continues to use it in a way which perpetuates its mythic status. Similarly, Ella Shohat (1991) points to the ways in which the term elides the land and the people and ascribes the 'dark continent' and its peoples hypersymbolic status. This is an important point to reiterate since I argue that there has been white feminist overinvestment in the gender component of the 'dark continent', which has resulted in the virtual elimination of the racial and colonial implications. Thus this most racialized of sexual metaphors has become synonymous with the concerns of white women.

Particular importance in this study has been accorded to the way in which European history has constructed black female sexuality and femininity, characterizing women of African descent as 'lacking' those 'feminine' qualities which have been attributed to white European women. The function of both black and white women in cinema is most often sexualized, and for each of them, their representational status is frequently that of repositories for the continuation of their respective 'races'. For black women, conventional patriarchal and Eurocentric notions of femininity have been particularly problematic. This stems from being doubly inscribed with Otherness, as black and female.

The focus on black women as somehow inhibiting black political progress is a theme I have identified with reference to *Pressure* in chapter 6 and *Burning an Illusion* in chapter 7. When it comes to black male productions, audiences are presented with scenarios which regard the male expression of oppression and political resistance as being the representative black experience. This black masculinist view of the problematic position of black women is also evident in Fanon's *Black Skin, White Masks* (1986). In this psychoanalytic account of the processes which contribute to Negrophilia and Negrophobia, it is evident that Fanon concentrates on male experiences. Indeed, echoing Freud's 'dark continent' comment in relation to white women, Fanon confesses that he knows little about black women's psychosexuality (Fanon, 1986: 177). The chapters in *Black Skin, White Masks* which discuss 'The Woman of Color and the White Man' and 'The Man of Color and the White Woman' attribute quite different significance to the relations foregrounded in the titles. The 'woman of colour' is said to be motivated by self-hatred, and by a contempt of black people in general, and of black men in particular; she is greedy, wishing to deny her social and racial origins in exchange for social and economic status. On the other hand, black men's sexual relationships with white women are represented as political acts, stealing and tainting the white woman – conceptualized purely in terms of her status as the white man's possession – as an act of revenge on white men.

Michelle Wallace charts the logic of such an analysis of the powerplay of black/white sexual relations. In response to Eldridge Cleaver's homophobia in *Soul on Ice* where Cleaver equates black male homosexuality with reactionary self-hatred, Wallace states:

if *a black man were doing the fucking* and the one being fucked were a white man, the black male homosexual would be just as good a revolutionary as a black heterosexual male, if not a better one . . . . If whom you fuck, indicates your power, then obviously the greatest power would be gained by fucking a white man first, a black man second, a white woman third and a black woman not at all. The most important rule is that *nobody* fucks you.

(Wallace, 1979: 68)

It would seem to be the case then that images of, and allusions to, black male heterosexual performance are linked to political and social autonomy and function as a verification and consolidation of black masculinity. To be, or to feel impotent – whether sexually or socially – is equated with a loss of masculinity. In the films which I have discussed that focus on black life – *Pressure* (1974), *Black Joy* (1977) and, initially at least, *Burning an Illusion* (1981) – for black men, as I have already suggested, black women are potential inhibitors of male political progress, being concerned with the acquisition of material wealth and social prestige rather than serving and saving the 'race'. Thus black women, due to the disturbance they provoke, remain cinematically peripheral.

In the white-authored texts considered here, I have pointed out that white men derive their status from their assumed superior relation to black men: white women may be used to confirm this status and to emphasize their heterosexuality. Where black women have been portrayed by white film-makers in Britain, the black woman is frequently sexualized, objectified and associated with both the primal and the inappropriately oversophisticated (meaning over-civilized). The latter is signified in *Leo the Last* (1969) through Salambo's wearing of wig and make-up and in *Mona Lisa* (1986) through Simone's use of stockings, corsets, whips and so on. She is designated the origin of perverse forms of sexual behaviour as is the case with the eponymous *Sapphire* (1959), and the black woman who invites Kathy to an act of troillism in *Flame in the Streets* (1961). There is a sense in which Sister Louise in *Pressure* (1974) may be included here because of her involvement in male-dominated politics and her seduction of the much younger, and sexually naive Tony.

Within a supremacist representational schema, black women are marginal. Unlike black men, black women represent no *present* threat to established hierarchies of privilege, since black women have so little political and social power; however, black women represent a *potential* threat, a danger yet to come since they –

because of their responsibility in continuing the black 'race' – carry the future dissidents against subordinate status. Unlike white middle class women whose 'capture' confers prestige on the 'captor', black women's sexual and racial Otherness has only exotic or economic value for white men. The question of desire across racial lines is then difficult to broach since it entails relinquishing so much.

In the films I have analysed, black women are figures in the dramas of racial difference played out in the arenas of competing masculinities. The approach in these texts seems to embody Amiri Baraka's contention that 'there are black men and white men, then there are women [and the] battle really is between white men and black men.' (quoted in bell hooks, 1982: 97) This is, arguably, the case not only in regard to cinematic production but also in regard to cultural criticism, especially in Britain where black women have not made the impact in the academic and cultural establishment which they appear to have had in the USA.

Wallace situates black women at the bottom of the social hierarchy in the USA, and looking at images of black women in the films discussed would seem to confirm this low status. In their texts, black male directors and writers seem to have found it difficult to accord black women economic independence, autonomy or agency without problematizing their status as mothers or as politicized black individuals. With regard to the films discussed here, where black women are present in British films they are portrayed by white film-makers as victims, purveyors of transgressive sexuality or emblematic silent bystanders, and as politically naive and assimila-tionist by black male directors and writers: most frequently, though, they are marginal or absent. Black male film-makers, in resisting the hegemony of middle class white men, should not seek to relocate that hegemony elsewhere, but to work towards gender equity within their cultural practices.

Black feminists' interrogations of black male prerogative in defining black subjectivity and the identification of masculinist analyses of the struggle for political and social autonomy and freedom have been crucial in critiquing essentialist notions of blackness. I would not wish to claim that only black women have the authority to advance understanding of the complexities of 'race', sexuality and gender in cultural forms, but I do think it is necessary for black women to assert themselves in the academy as elsewhere. Due to the cultural constructions of gender and racial differences, attitudinal differences do occur in terms of what are seen as the priorities for critical attention and analysis. Although nothing is guaranteed by the presence of black women film-makers or critics, it is important for them to be empowered to make more interventions in the construction and criticism of images in Britain.

RACIAL IDENTITIES, REPRESENTATION AND CULTURAL ANALYSIS: THE SUBJECT OF SILENCE

White identity has managed to assume a normativeness which has left it underinterrogated and part of what I have been concerned with here has been to indicate the extent to which constructions of notions of whiteness are available for analysis in a variety of films. In regard to contemporary cultural practices, Cornel West has identified the need to defamiliarize whiteness as an important political project and he urges that black cultural critics:

> must investigate and interrogate the other of Blackness– Whiteness. One cannot deconstruct the binary oppositional logic of images of Blackness without extending it to the contrary condition of Blackness/Whiteness itself . . . what is needed [is] to examine and *explain* the historically specific ways in which 'Whiteness' is a politically constructed category parasitic on 'Blackness'.
>
> (West, 1990: 29)

Indicated here is the way in which analyses of racial and cultural identity have come to revolve around 'blackness' as the object of fascination leaving unspoken issues of differentiated white ethnicities. Having argued against essentialist positions in regard to questions of 'race' and subjectivity, I would say that it is necessary for white cultural critics to address the ways in which questions of ethnicity and racial difference are structured into texts and their analyses. However, it is especially important for black people to become involved in the analysis of media and culture and to produce knowledge and cultural theory in order to challenge the hegemony of white and male critics.

In her discussion of 'Whiteness as Absent Centre', Claire Pajaczkowska has indicated that the 'emotional state produced by denial is one of blankness' and it is this blankness which helps to sustain White identity as normal and as undefined (Pajaczkowska and Young, 1992: 202). The blankness at the centre of the denial of racism, colonialism and imperialism serves to obscure a set of contradictory actions and fantasies which are often unconscious, and are manifested in the representations created of the African Other: representations which are the projections of the 'good' and 'bad' split off parts of the self as I argued in chapter 1. This blankness of whiteness is the consequence of an identity without a centre since its existence acquires meaning only because of its relationship with the Other. Acknowledging how the idea of blackness constructs the idea of whiteness, just as the notion of femininity assists in the construction of the idea of masculinity is a small but significant step in demystifying those processes.

Stallybrass and White articulate this interdependency of opposi- tional terms and its consequences thus:

> the 'top' attempts to reject and eliminate the 'bottom' for reasons of prestige and status, only to discover, not only that it is in some way frequently dependent upon the low-Other . . . but also that the top *includes* that low symbolically, as a primary eroticized constituent of its own fantasy life. The result is a mobile, conflictual fusion of power, fear, and desire in the construction of subjectivity: a psychological dependence upon precisely those others which are being rigorously opposed and excluded at the social level.
>
> (Stallybrass and White, 1986: 5)

Being dependent or 'parasitic' on the notion of Otherness for a conceptualization of the self is problematic for both self and Other. The recognition of the self in the Other remains at root an alienated identity, an 'identity-in-Otherness'. Self-determination is a precon- dition for self-recognition or self-conscious identity. This assertion of self-determination may be thought to require that the Other – literally the Other's otherness – be negated or cancelled. Where this 'identity-in-the-Other' is racially predicated or defined by racialized discourses, the drive to self-consciousness may result in the negation or reduction of the racial Other, the Other's exclusion (Goldberg, 1993: 59).

As has been argued in chapter 2 and demonstrated throughout this work, there is a long historical tradition of black people being constituted by whites as:

> the fantasy of a fantasy – not cold, pure, clean, efficient, indus- trious, frugal, rational (that is, not the pantheon of anal-negative

ego traits which are the *summum bonum* of the bourgeois order) but rather warm, dirty, sloppy, feckless, lazy, improvident and irrational, all those traits that are associated with Blackness, odor and sensuality.

(Kovel, 1988: 61)

These fantasies which emerge from the psychical mechanisms of repression and projection are recognized at a popular, common sense level by many black people who see themselves as 'scapegoats' for white society's problems which arise regarding, for example, housing, crime and unemployment.

Those who embody Otherness and difference are often the focus for the projection of white societies' rages, fears and anxieties. Thus the actions of the insurgent 'natives' in films such as *Sanders of the River* (1935), *Song of Freedom* (1936), *Men of Two Worlds* (1947) and *Simba* (1955) are not motivated by rationality but by its antithesis: superstition and magic, often embodied in the figure of the witch doctor. White viewers' sense of self-importance is continually confirmed and enhanced, and in their viewing of films such as *Sanders of the River* (1935), *Song of Freedom* (1936), *Men of Two Worlds* (1947), *Simba* (1955) and so on, are encouraged to view themselves as morally and culturally superior to the 'primitive' black masses. Not only are these films still regularly shown on television but other, more contemporary images of African 'primitiveness' are standard televisual and journalistic fare (Reeves and Hammond, 1989; Twitchin, 1988). For those whose relationship to Africa is a textual one, the knowledge and information gained not only from films and television but also from school history and geography books, anthropological discourses and other colonialist perspectives will have a cumulative effect on their perceptions of racial Otherness.

I have shown how, in all the white-authored films examined, with the possible exception of *Leo the Last* (1969), there are elements of centuries old racialized discourses comprised of a set of assumptions about black people: black male sexuality as a threat to white womanhood and cultural superiority; black intellectual inferiority and fecklessness; and, derived from that, unmotivated irrational behaviour as the natural state of blackness. I have argued that in many white film-makers' depictions of black people there are sets of values and attitudes towards 'race' and sexuality which have their roots in long-established ideologies. The traces of these ideologies are evident in film texts where black people are annihilated, criminalized and labelled as sexually deviant, and where sexual behaviour is monitored and regulated. The perceived threat is consistently contained or diminished by rendering black people invisible, infantile, desexualized or by eliminating black subjects from texts altogether.

Racial conflict often provides a backdrop against which the main white protagonists work out their emotional, sexual or social relationships. I would argue that is so in *Sapphire* (1959), *Flame in the Streets* (1961), *Leo the Last* (1969), *Absolute Beginners* (1986), *Scandal* (1988) and *Mona Lisa* (1986). Whiteness is thus either overvalued – particularly as in the earlier texts examined – or over elaborated or both, whilst blackness is devalued or underelaborated or appropriated for cultural self-enrichment.

The illusory sense of a superior, coherent identity needs constant reassurance of its fantasized supremacy and centrality and many of these narratives perform that function. This security is, of course, spurious and thus constantly under threat because it is in reality highly dependent on its fantasized conceptualizations of Otherness to sustain that sense of coherence and of pre-eminence. White filmmakers need to be aware that avoiding issues of white racial identities whilst focusing on – or ignoring – black people merely serves to confirm the authority of white (masculine) supremacy and allows the assumption of an all-seeing, all-knowing position, which replicates the imperial I/eye.

Where the problematization of notions of racial and cultural identity is happening, it is not in what exists of 'mainstream' British cinema, where white film-makers such as Neil Jordan, David Leland, Tony Garnett, Ken Loach, and Mike Leigh have made minimal contributions to exploring the complexities of images of racial and sexual difference.[1] It has been black film-makers and cultural analysts who have made the crucial intervention of inserting racial and ethnic identity onto the cultural and cinematic agenda in Britain: with the possible exception of *Leo the Last*, white racial identity has not been systematically and consciously explored in a similar way to black identities. Significant debates have taken place in respect of gender and identity but there is still a limited amount of material which deals with white ethnicity in film in the British context. Useful to consider in the context of a discussion about similarities and differences in the concerns of black and white filmmakers is Richard Dyer's assertion regarding Paul Robeson's cross cultural reception: 'there are discourses developed by whites in white culture and by blacks in black culture which make different sense of the same phenomenon' (Dyer, 1986: 70). For example, black people are often shown as being out of place in Britain by both black and white film-makers. In many of the white-authored texts discussed here, black people are seen as intrinsically 'different' and as 'not belonging here' – see especially my analyses of *Song of Freedom* (1936), *Men of Two Worlds* (1946), *Sapphire* (1959), *Flame in the Streets* (1961). That sense of not belonging is also articulated in films where black people have made a creative input but with a crucial difference. In *Pressure* (1974), *Black Joy* (1977), *Burning an Illusion* (1981) and *Playing Away* (1986) black people's disaffection is – either explicitly or implicitly – brought about by white people's racism. Where white racism is portrayed by white film-makers, it is invariably depicted as the behavioural/psychological abberation of a particular individual: rarely is racism seen as systemic or institutionalized, or as an aspect of white, male middle class identity.

BLACK FILM, THEORY AND CULTURAL CRITICISM

In the opening chapter, I talked of a shift in ways of conceptualizing black identity: this has been a crucial component of discussions about black cultural production. During the 1980s, debates about black people, representation and history centred around absences and invisibility, and cultural activists sought to redress imbalances by rewriting the histories through both practical and theoretical work (Young, 1993: 80). This critique has consisted not only of pointing out and coming to terms with absences, it has also consisted of evaluations of the ways in which black people have been made visible and in particular how media discursive practices have been a major component in determining and defining the 'problem' of blackness. For black film-makers, struggling against such representations, the perceived necessity for creating 'accurate' images is understandable.

Through the construction of a black identity which has as its reference points the cultures of both the colonized and the colonizer, one textual strategy has been to create characters which appear to conform to white European stereotypes but which may also be read as a set of masculine identities designed to be the antithesis of white male propriety. Such characters may be found in *Pressure* (1974), *Black Joy* (1977), *Burning an Illusion* (1981) and *Playing Away* (1986). The attempt to replace 'negative' images constructed by white film-makers with 'positive' ones amounts to a 'counter-mythology' as explicated by Albert Memmi. However, it is still the case that 'In the midst of revolt, the colonized continues to think, feel and live against and, therefore, in relation to the colonizer and colonization' (Memmi, 1990: 205). Crucially those images, born out of a protest against the colonizers' representations, are defined in relation to them.

To a significant extent, black identities in Britain have been adopted as modes of resistant self-identification and political affiliation in order to counter the hegemony of Eurocentrism and racist ideologies and practices relating to difference. For black film-makers, identity – as structured through the experience of the subordination and inferiorization of colonialism – is an important issue. The mode of discussing identity and blackness has developed in ways which can be differentiated from those associated with whiteness.

Defining identity as being a coherent sense of self, both on an individual and group level, it is the threat of that dissolution of self-constructed identity which fuels racial supremacy, homophobia and misogyny. As previously discussed, identity is about having a sense of belonging, about recognizing what 'we' have in common with some people and what differentiates 'us' from others. This may be an identity constructed in order to fit in with the demands of a particular community but nonetheless, it retains a potency which is continually exploited by those who have a stake in the maintenance of absolutist notions of ethnicity and racial authenticity. The feelings of 'belongingness' which develop as a result of these group identifications may well be illusory since individual identities are not necessarily fixed or consistent, and there are occasions when the different aspects of individual subjectivities are in conflict with each other. The relationship between 'our' constructed group or cultural identity and those of 'Others' is often one in which the realities of that other group's experiences and cultural values seem to be 'alien' to 'our' own.

In his analysis of xenophobia, Memmi points to the interdependence of the subjective positions constructed through the prism of colonialism (Memmi, 1990: 196–7). However as a direct relationship between diaspora peoples and the experience of colonialism recedes, to what extent do issues of identity need to be reconceptualized? As I have argued in chapter 6, the idea of diaspora is one which is made from fragments of identity derived from a colonial construction, so where does that leave the notion of a diaspora aesthetic? Again, the necessity of opposition in the first instance is shaped and formed by the experience of marginality and the discourse is developed in direct relation to its opposite. It should be remembered that it was globalized racism which created the necessity for the supranational flag of diaspora and cultural nationalism.

As I have argued throughout, white people have seen the black Other as an object of and for investigation, and the subject of 'race' relations discourse. In contrast to the effacement and naturalizing of their ethnic location by white film-makers, black cultural practitioners have continually examined their position as specifically black subjects within white cultures. Black film-makers' constant self-analysis and the investment in carrying out such analyses begins to explain the intensity of debates about black film within black communities and the desire to construct and develop critical and interpretive frameworks such as Third Cinema and post-colonial critiques.[2] An important point to consider here is the extent to which the field itself has become a significant aspect of the cultural and critical life of Britain; black culture has become less marginal, more self-confident, more clear about the need to articulate self-determined critical analysis. There has been no equivalent theoretical debate regarding racial identities amongst white film-makers and theorists in this country. Thus, there is a sense in which black film may be placed as a discrete practice in British cinema as is suggested by the title of ICA Document 7, *Black Film, British Cinema*, since there is a marked difference in approach to the issue of racialized identities. This difference is centred around how black and white people have located themselves ethnically.

Some of the fiercest debates about black cultural politics and artistic expression have centred on the appropriateness or otherwise of what are characterized as Eurocentric textual strategies and modes of analysis. The approach used in this study has been to attempt to modify what are often casually referred to as 'Eurocentric' theories of culture by recasting them through the prism of 'race'. I have not advocated a refusal of theories the provenance of which is Europe in favour of an Afrocentric mode of analysis. The position which regards black cultural 'authenticity' as a desirable objective raises the question of racial essentialism. Through essentialism, whether strategic or otherwise, difference is seen: 'not in a positional way, but in a mutually exclusive, autonomous, and self-sufficient one. And it is therefore unable to grasp the dialogic strategies and hybrid forms essential to the diaspora aesthetic' (Hall 1992: 29). Anti-essentialist critical interventions should provide more insight than those which exclusively privilege class, 'race', gender or sexual orientation because they avoid the fixity of monolithic essentializing critical discourses, and are able to analyse the interconnections and 'dialogic strategies'.

The development of black feature film production in this country has been marked by its scarcity and its marginal status. An important part of a consideration of any film is its critical reception in both mainstream and academic publications. When the black film and video workshops came into existence during the early 1980s many discussions were initiated which were concerned with questions of identity, cultural authority and authenticity and the objectives of engaging with critical discourse. Black film having previously been denied a critical space became the subject of debate much of which was confined to the work of a small number of metropolitan-based film and video organizations. Those black-authored texts which have sought to challenge both realist conventions and some of the essentialist orthodoxies of an emergent black protonationalism were the main focus of critical work. In black cultural criticism and intellectual exchanges, non-realist, 'experimental' texts have been privileged and subsequently a canon of significant black texts has emerged. Discussions which became public through academic and intellectual debate and publications did not consistently address in detail films focused on black life like *Pressure* (1974), *Black Joy* (1977), *Burning an Illusion* (1981) or *Playing Away* (1986): it has been an objective of this study to place these films as part of the context for subsequent developments in black film practices.

CONCLUSION

Cultural production, the dissemination of historical information and the pursuit of knowledge in western Europe should be understood and analysed within a framework which recognizes the centrality of racial difference in the construction of colonial and post-colonial black and white identities. The small number of critical accounts of British cinema which have addressed racial concerns have tended to privilege 'race' without adequately exploring or indicating the place of gender, sexuality and class. With regard to the latter, although I have attempted to draw attention to the ways in which class is implicated in the interactions depicted on screen, I am aware that this analysis has been uneven. I have not, for example explored in detail how class operates in various exchanges of dialogue in *Sapphire* (1959) where differences in social status amongst the black characters are displayed in order to illustrate the liberal belief in the essential sameness of black and white people. A more sustained and detailed analysis of these kinds of interaction would be welcome.

During the course of this study, I have referred to both African–American and white North American cultural theorists and critics although I have voiced some reservations about the applicability of some of the work. Such 'cultural borrowings' are inevitable given that much of the work on images of blackness and whiteness has been focused on North American cinema. The vastness of the North American film industry, North America's cultural centrality, the burgeoning African–American feminist literature, and the development of African–American and black British diasporic sensibilities have also contributed to it being necessary to rely on a black North American input. Increasingly though, the differences in approach and in historical circumstances in regard to racism and colonialism have become apparent and whilst I do think it both necessary and productive to draw on cultural criticism from the USA, it is desirable that a feminist praxis that recognizes the specificity of British experiences be nurtured. This would involve going beyond the basic thinking of black women as the victims of white and male oppressors to considering when and how images of black women are used and the ways that they are implicitly and explicitly contrasted with white women. It would also entail thinking in more detail about how white women's and men's racial identity may be coded or unconsciously structured into a text, when there are few or no significant black characters present.

Given black women's central role as economic linchpins in the development of western Eurocapitalism – as producers, as 'breeders', as labourers, as wet-nurses and so on – black women's actual presence and significance cannot easily be cast aside. Yet it is still the case that few films give prominent roles to women of African descent in either North American or British cinema. The potentially transgressive seductions between men, between white man and black woman, and black woman and white woman are not realized in most mainstream narratives. As previously indicated, there has long been an association between 'race' and sex and it is notable that sexual relationships between black and white people are still rarely openly discussed on film: the subject still arouses fierce debate and controversy in both black and white communities and this is reflected in the content and treatment of the issue in films by both blacks and whites. The avoidance of serious, reflective discussions about such relationships generally is underlined by the prohibitions associated with overt interracial sexuality on film. It seems that interracial sexual activity is still contentious in a racist society: if the sexual activity is homoerotic and interracial, then it is virtually unspeakable. The prohibition of this aspect of sexual behaviour is reflected in the absence or superficial nature of portrayals of such relationships on the screen. Two recent examples of exceptions to the interdiction on interracial homosexual relationships are *My Beautiful Launderette* (1985), and *Young Soul Rebels* (1991).

Ideas about racial and sexual difference have long been a part of British intellectual thought. There are other factors which come into play, not least those of class, and sexual orientation and expression which make for a complex matrix of possibilities of interaction. Whatever the basis on which discussions about identity or cultural diversity are made it is the question of the distribution of power with which we have to grapple, together with an understanding of how cultural politics are articulated through and with the everyday politics of the distribution of power, of everyday injustice and racism. In the face of the escalation of reactionary political forces, and the continuation of racism and fascism which represent dangerous threats to the development of progressive social forces, people need cultural practices which question and stimulate. Proposing that the conventions or signifying practices of film be changed is not in itself an adequate strategy since spectators' existing belief systems may still restrict their perceptions. There needs to be a multiplicity of discursive practices which serve to disrupt the stability of deeply held beliefs, and a continual public and social questioning of imagery and representations to which people have become habitualized.

Problematizing realism is a useful activity as it represents a significant critique of assumptions about truth, impartiality and the nature of reality, and because it brings into conscious view much that has been unconsciously assimilated regarding aesthetic judgements about film. As previously argued, contemporary critical discourses on textual practices have implied that the way to subvert the fixity and truth claims of realism is not to mimic them by producing 'black' versions but to attempt to strike up new relations between viewer and text.

As regards audiences, how the desires of black viewers may or may not differ in absolute terms from those of white audiences, or how this concept of 'black spectatorship' might be fractured or differentiated along class, gender and generational lines, is just beginning to be investigated within British cultural studies. Questions of audience are marginalized from much theoretical work on black film, so the matter of pleasure and identification become peripheral: there is also the question of mainstream, popular cinema and black audiences' relation to that, not to mention televisual forms.

The material conditions in which films are produced also need to be considered, not as apologies for poor work but in order to be able to understand adequately how a text acquires meaning in the context in which it is produced and consumed. Also the possibilities of realist strategies as radical interventions should be broached. Of course a politics of deconstruction seeks to challenge the validity and dominance of particular ways of making sense which exclude and marginalize other forms: nonetheless there has to be a recognition of the pleasures afforded by realism and Hollywood-style cinema.

However, as has been pointed out by Stuart Hall in his discussion of documentary photography:

> the current critical orthodoxy has somewhat trivialized the argument about documentary realism by assimilating all 'realisms' (which one ought to be at pains to discriminate and differentiate) into one great essential so-called 'realist discourse.'
>
> (Hall, 1992a: 111)

No textual practice is inherently reactionary or progressive. It is much more complex than that: bell hooks puts it thus: 'The issue is really one of standpoint. From what political perspective do we dream, look, create, and take action?' (hooks, 1992: 5). That political perspective may be articulated from a multiplicity of 'standpoints', using media to document and interrogate the transformations of identity that affect those designated as Other, living in a society where they have been inferiorized for centuries.

Despite the eagerness to subscribe to post-structuralist accounts of reality, it is necessary to retain a grasp on social/material reality, which is, after all, what most people live by. Viewers bring to texts their personal and cultural knowledge which mediates their perception of the 'reality' depicted on screen. Even if it is accepted that there is no direct access to that which is called 'the real', that there is nothing outside discourse or representation, it is still the case that many texts encourage conclusions about historical events and particular issues. The struggles over representation and the demand for positive images to counteract the debilitating effects of negative ones is grounded in everyday experience of the reality of racism, sexism, homophobia, notions of 'perfect' bodies and so on.

In regard to black film, I would argue that the deployment of discursive practices which speak of the 'reality' of lived experience is legitimate as a strategy for documenting events, perspectives and perceptions. Such forms articulate the concerns of many black people for whom the reconstruction of the past and the structuring of the present seems to necessitate a certain amount of mythmaking.

I have argued that examining texts for negative and positive images is not in itself the most productive model for attempting to understand images since such analyses are unable to address adequately the complex processes which occur at the sites of the production and consumption of images of blackness and whiteness. It is, however, still necessary to examine images in racialized terms whilst noting the necessity for a continued interrogation of the binary oppositions of black and white. To deny that blackness and whiteness still have significance as ontological symbols is to deny the existence of the many ways that racism operates in contemporary British society.

The production of arts and culture in Britain is structurally inscribed with questions of racism and sexism, discrimination, domination and subordination, forged in the period of colonialism. Thus, all such work is inscribed with questions of power. The power relations embedded in the right to look or not to be looked at constitute the politics of cultural production and ensure that film-making and the resulting critical work is a crucial political activity.

Notes

INTRODUCTION

1 I was fortunate to catch *Leo the Last* – which is not available through the National Film Archive or on video – at the Barbican Arts Centre, London when they held a 1960s season.

CHAPTER 1

1 Originally published in 1973 by Viking Press.
2 It should be noted that each of those books refer to films made in the USA.
3 However, in his introductory psychoanalytic discussion of stereotypes, Sander L. Gilman points to the difference between the pathological need to stave off anxiety through the institution of crude stereotypes and the general need to stereotype which he maintains, exists in us all. Stereotyping, then, does not have to entail negative consequences (Gilman, 1985: 11).
4 Note that, in the following list, the single quotation marks enclosing problematic terms are mine.
5 For a detailed historical description of British legislation and policy in the colonies, see Fernando Henriques (1974); for a history of relations between black and white people during slavery in the British Caribbean, with special reference to women, see Hilary McD. Beckles (1989).
6 There are a number of factors which have led to the camera's obsession with white women's faces which are demonstrated through extended close-ups, soft focus lenses and so on. The valorization of individualism, the aestheticization of white feminine beauty, the notion that the face is the gateway to the soul – all these points have contributed to the lingering close-up caress of the film camera as the ultimate accolade for aspiring female stars.
7 Quoted by Ivan Ward in his introduction to Kovel (1988), *White Racism: A Psychohistory*, p. xli.
8 It should be noted that Jonathan Rutherford makes a similar point in a book he is writing on Englishness and male sexuality.

9 The relationship between the economic and psychic realms is discussed in Ivan Ward's comprehensive introduction to Joel Kovel's *White Racism* (1988).

10 In a more recent short piece about black cinema, MacCabe criticizes what he characterizes as the modernist project of both *Handsworth Songs* (1986) and *Passion of Remembrance* (1986), as well as what he sees as the realist confines of *Playing Away* (1986). Only the last of these films falls within the scope of this book but I should like to note here how MacCabe feels it necessary to locate each of these texts within an identifiable Eurocentric discourse. Reference is made to their potential respective audiences without an allowance that these audiences may not be as irredeemably separated as he indicates (MacCabe, 1988).

11 For an essay which indicates the potential of using Gramsci to think through issues of 'race', see Stuart Hall (1986b).

CHAPTER 2

1 Racism is not totally dependent on these phenotypical characteristics as some manifestations of anti-Semitism demonstrate. However, there is often a biological/physiological underpinning to anti-Jewish sentiments. See Sander L. Gilman (1985: 31-35).

2 See Frantz Fanon (1986), chapter 4.

3 The Swedish botanist Carl Linne, or Linnaeus (1707–1778) is an important figure here, as it was he who set about collecting and categorising plants, subsequently constructing similar taxonomies for humans, in which alleged racial characteristics were used to map the inferior and the superior 'races'. Peter Fryer quotes part of Linne's taxonomy for homo sapiens:

> *H. Europaei.* Of fair complexion, sanguine temperament, and brawny form . . . Of gentle manners, acute in judgement, of quick invention, and governed by fixed laws.
> *H. Afri.* Of black complexion, phlegmatic temperament, and relaxed fibre . . . Of crafty, indolent, and careless disposition, and are governed in their actions by caprice.
>
> Fryer (1984: 166)

4 The term 'pseudoscience' is problematic since it implies the possibility of a 'real' science, which is truthful and objective, and exists outside of ideology.

5 For a specific exploration of the interconnections between 'race', gender and nature/culture, see Haraway (1992).

6 For a discussion of eighteenth century debates about beauty and 'race' see David Dabydeen (1985: 41).

7 For some historical accounts, see James Walvin (1973: 208); Paul B. Rich (1986); for sociologically orientated work about post-war settlement and inter-racial relations, see, for example, K. L. Little (1948); Sheila Patterson (1963); and Clifford Hill (1965), especially

chapter 6.

8 Note though that the fact of African nakedness may be, at least in part, attributable to fantasy since there is evidence to suggest that elaborately dyed and printed cloth and jewellery were widely used in West Africa during the period of European exploration: I am grateful to Stella Osoba for pointing this out to me.

9 This is in spite of Elizabeth I's proclamation demanding that all 'black-amoors' be sent back to Africa as there were too many in England. See Peter Fryer (1984: 10). There is also of course, the case of Shakespeare's play *Othello*.

10 Walvin argues that:

> Whiteness and purity had become even more important since the accession of the Queen for they were the symbol of the Queen's beauty, and a manifestation of the purity of virginal, queenly government.
>
> (Walvin, 1973: 23)

11 Associations between animals and black people were plenty; for example, a pupil of Linnaeus', Reaumur, related the details of an experiment in which a rabbit was supposed to have fertilized a hen and produced chicks covered with fine hair instead of feathers. Dire inferences were drawn from this incident and he noted that 'one would have reason to think that the Moors had a rather strange origin' (quoted in Fryer 1987: 179).

12 These anxieties about 'race' and sex abound in North American film in particular: D. W. Griffith's *The Birth of a Nation* (1915) is a classic depiction of the fear of interracial sexual relations.

13 For an indication of the fascination for investigating and viewing the Otherness of black anatomy and sexuality, see Sander Gilman's account of Sarah Bartmann, the 'Hottentot Venus'. When she died in 1815, it became possible for those who paid to stare at her exposed body in exhibitions across Europe and to see her genitalia on display in the Musee de l'Homme in Paris (Gilman, 1985: 76–108).

14 For a discussion of eugenics and its place in Fabian socialism see, G. R. Searle (1981). For a critique of 'new racism' and its use of eugenics and social Darwinism see Martin Barker (1981) and Stephen Jay Gould (1981), and for the explicit use of photography to support eugenicist beliefs see David Green (1986).

15 For more on this issue, see Sander Gilman (1985: 76–108). Currently representations circulate in relation to Aids where black female and male prostitutes are seen as contaminators, spreading moral and physical decay through European and North American men: see Simon Watney (1990: 89–106).

16 In North American cinema, see for example, Tina Turner in *Mad Max: Beyond the Thunderdome* (1985) or Grace Jones in *Vamp* (1986) or virtually any of the black women who have appeared in James Bond films. There is also a way using black femininity and deviance through the use of black iconography in the film *Something Wild* (1986). For a comprehensive analysis of this film (directed by Jonathan Demme), see

Cameron Bailey (1988: 28–40).

CHAPTER 3

1 Raymond Williams notes the ambiguities and uncertainties which have accrued to the term 'imperialism'. In the late nineteenth century, imperialism was usually defined as 'primarily a political system in which colonies are governed from an imperial centre' (Williams, 1988: 159). However, imperialism also has a set of meanings where the emphasis is on the economic rather than the political, thus the term connotes 'an economic system of external investment and the penetration and control of markets and sources of raw materials' (ibid.: 159–160). In the context of this book, the emphasis is on the former meaning, rather than the latter.

   There are several variations on this genre of film and literature: of particular note is the representation of the Indian sub-continent and its peoples. This is, however, outside the scope of this book.

2 For various approaches to this question, see J. A. Hobson (1988) and V. I. Lenin (1933): see also Walter Rodney (1988), especially 147–201.

3 For example, Henry Morton Stanley, the renowned writer and explorer explained to a group of Birmingham traders in 1878:

> There are forty million naked people beyond that gateway [to the Africa that *he* had opened up] and the cotton spinners of Manchester are waiting to clothe them . . . and the ministers of Christ are zealous to bring them, the poor benighted heathen, into the Christian fold.
>
> (quoted in Davidson, 1984: 172)

4 However, these texts should not be thought of as ideologically homogeneous tracts as there is often evidence of contradictory feelings about the Empire and the demands it made, particularly on young men: see Joseph Conrad's *Heart of Darkness* (1989) for example which is, broadly speaking, anti-imperialist but suffused with imperial rhetoric. In his concluding chapter, Joseph Bristow (1991) discusses some of the ambivalences in writing of the late nineteenth century. For debates conducted amongst Victorians, see Christine Bolt (1971); for an informative account of Conrad's stance on imperialism as evidenced in his writings, see Benita Parry (1983); for an introduction to, and references for the role of the Pan-African movement in the 1920s and 1930s, see Peter Fryer (1984), and Walter Rodney (1988); a leading Pan-Africanist who came to Britain whose work is relevant here is George Padmore, (1936).

5 Torgovnick's use of 'we' and 'they' is problematic since it serves to reinforce the Euro-American dominant cultural status in determining who is 'us' and who is 'them'. Torgovnick attempts to justify it thus:

> The 'we' as I use it in this section basically denotes the 'we' that imagines a primitive 'them', a cultural 'we' . . . I use the we strategically, to prevent myself and my reader from backing away, too easily, from the systems of us/them thinking that structure all discourse

about the civilized and the primitive . . . But at times . . . that 'we' is intended to produce a sense of discomfort or misfit. The 'we' is necessary to expose a shared illusion: the illusion of a representative primitive 'them' as opposed to a monolithic unified, powerful 'us'.

(Torgovnick, 1990: 6)

Unfortunately, the effect of using that 'we' is to consolidate white European dominance as the extent to which her desire to make 'us' feel uncomfortable will be experienced as helpful by those who have always felt excluded from the academic 'we' is questionable.

6 For a cogent analysis of the metaphoric status of this comparison between black people and women, see Nancy Leys Stepan (1990: 38-57).

7 For more on the formation and consolidation of ideas about masculinity and dependency in the Victorian era, see Catherine Hall (1992).

8 A substantial body of critical work which engages with gender and racial relations, the realm of the psyche and the material aspects of British colonialist and imperialist cinema has not been established. However, much productive analytical work has been carried out on nineteenth century literature. For more detailed analysis in this subject area, see Brian Street (1975); Benita Parry (1983); Patrick Brantlinger (1988); Joseph Bristow (1991). For work on cultural forms other than literature, see John Mackenzie (1984), and for an exploration of the links between white English public school life, masculinity and the literature and films of Empire, see Jeffrey Richards (1973).

9 Both the association of animal imagery with black women and the inferior model of colonization offered by the Belgians are evident in Joseph Conrad's *Heart of Darkness* (1989: 80).

10 These ideas about the massed 'native' Other were also the mainstay of the Western genre of North American cinema where the confrontation would be between Native American and Euro-American.

11 For examples of some of the films affected by censorship in Kenya and Northern Rhodesia in the 1940s, see Rosaleen Smyth (1983: 346, note 28).

12 Harold Moody was founder of the League of Coloured People in 1931.

13 For an examination of Paul Robeson's cross-over appeal, see Richard Dyer (1986).

14 For example, in the casting of African-American Denzil Washington as a former black soldier from London in *For Queen and Country* (1988) and similarly, Forrest Whittaker in *The Crying Game* (1992).

15 See Dyer (1986). Interestingly, in a biography of Robeson, it is claimed that he felt that *The Song of Freedom* was the 'first true one he has done about that continent [Africa]' (Foner, 1978: 31).

16 This title must surely refer to Robeson's earlier theatrical success in Eugene O'Neill's play, *The Emperor Jones* (1924) and in the film of the same name, made in 1933. See Richard Dyer (1986), chapter 2 'Paul Robeson: Crossing Over' for a comparison between the film and stage versions of O'Neill's text.

17 The issue of 'colour casting' is a fraught one, not always consistent and

more noticeable in North American popular cinematic and photographic images. Dark skinned women are more likely to be asexual nurturing 'mammies' or 'red hot' sexualized mammies: either way they are frequently derisory characters. An example of the former would be Hattie MacDaniels' character in *Gone With the Wind* (1939), and Louise Beavers in Sirk's *Imitation of Life* (1959): for a recent example of the latter see the character of Delores played by Delores Hall in *Lethal Weapon 3* (1990) directed by Richard Donner.

18 See Richard Dyer (1986: 98) for a discussion of how Robeson was seen as the embodiment of male Africanness.

19 See Bogle (1991) especially chapter 3 'The 1930s: The Servants' for a descriptive account of this predominantly North American tradition.

CHAPTER 4

1 The issue of language constructed within a discourse of 'race' is difficult: it is hard to discuss events, issues, material and attitudes without using terms which are problematic. One way of indicating unease with particular terms is to place them in quotation marks. It is difficult to remain consistent about this and at times it may seem as though virtually everything needs to be thus placed. Generally speaking, I problematize terms when they are first used and trust that the reader will remember not to take them at face value.

2 In 1951 there were approximately 15,300 settlers from the Caribbean in Britain: ten years later that figure had risen to 171,800: see James Walvin (1984: 111).

3 There were also at least two black film-makers active during the early 1960s. Lloyd Reckord, who was an actor as well as a director made *Ten Bob in Winter* (1963) and Lionel Ngakane made a short film about two children who get lost together, a black girl and a white boy, *Jemima and Johnny* (1964) (Givanni, 1992).

4 James Walvin comments:

> Throughout the 1919 riots, sexual jealousy had been an open element in the response of white mobs to the Negroes . . . . Although difficult to prove, it would seem that interracial sexual relations and the hostile response towards them constitute one of the most important ingredients in the slow germination of English racialism, from the sixteenth century to the twentieth.
>
> (Walvin, 1973: 208)

5 The term 'mulatta' is derived from 'mule'. The mule is the progeny of a horse and a donkey which is generally infertile. This comparison stemmed from the belief that 'negroes' and 'caucasians' were separate species and that any children which resulted from sexual union between the two 'races' would be infertile. The confusion between the human 'races' and animal species is thus consolidated in the use of mulatto/mulatta. For a discussion of how 'mixed-race' subjects have been regarded in Britain, see Paul B. Rich (1986), chapter 6.

6 The Reverend Clifford Hill's poll, carried out in north London asked 'would you approve of your sister or your daughter marrying a coloured man?' and 91% of respondents said they would not agree. Note that the question is constructed around the sexual vulnerability of the woman. Reverend Hill had appeared on a radio programme and been asked this question regarding his own daughter. He replied that, all other things being equal, he would have no objections and promptly received a large number of abusive letters, threats on his life and a burning cross in his front garden. It was this experience which prompted him to conduct this extensive sociological survey.

7 For example, see the film reviews by Penelope Gilliat, *The Observer* (17 September 1961) and Eve Perrick *The Daily Mail* (14 September 1961).

8 For example, see Richard Hoggart (1959: 203ff.) regarding his distrust of 'Americanization'. See also Paul Gilroy (1987: 160ff.) for a discussion of the nexus of class, 'race' and gender in regard to dance and music starting in the 1950s.

9 In the USA such attitudes were institutionalized through being enshrined in the juridical process, backed by legislation which was informed by scientific and anthropological discourses on racial difference:

> It shall hereafter be unlawful for any white person in this State to marry any save a white person, or a person with no other admixture of blood than white and American Indian. For the purpose of this chapter, the term 'white person' shall apply only to such person as has no trace whatever of any blood other than Caucasian; but persons who have one sixteenth or less of the blood of the American Indian and have no other non-Caucasic blood shall be deemed to be white persons.

> (Virginia Code Ann. Section 20–54, 1960, quoted in Henriques, (1974: 25)

For an examination of the juridical and legislative definitions of blackness in the USA in relation to *Imitation of Life* (1959); see Lauren Berlant (1991). For a detailed study of Britain's legislative processes regarding the identification of the racial subject, see Fernando Henriques (1974).

10 See for example Pauline Hopkins 'miscegenation, either *lawful* or *unlawful*, we do not want', quoted in Hazel Carby (1985: 274); see also W. E. B. Du Bois, 'We believe it the duty of the Americans of Negro descent, as a body, to maintain their race identity until this mission of the Negro people is accomplished, and the ideal of human brotherhood has become a practical possibility.' Quoted in Anthony Appiah (1985: 24).

11 In the late 1940s through the 1950s there were a number of Hollywood films which had as their motif, a 'mixed-race' female subject who passes or attempts to pass for a white woman. The female protagonists of these films were classic examples of the 'tragic mulatta' stereotype which is more a feature of North American than of British popular

culture. In *Pinky* (1949), *Lost Boundaries* (1949), *Showboat* (1951), *Kings Go Forth* (1958), *Night of the Quarter Moon* (1959) and *Imitation of Life* (1959) all the tragic mulattas were played by white actors.

12 There are various ways in which it may be said that 'white people' pass for 'black'. In attempting to emulate 'authentic' 'black' music or street culture for example. There are also a number of instances of white people living as black in order to make a point about racism. Probably the most well known of these is John Howard Griffin's account *Black Like Me* (1984). Again, through the treatment that Griffin takes in order to make him look 'black' and which needs 'topping up' every so often, the white male takes control of his colour, and enables him to become his mirror self. Without wishing to undermine his commitment to his political project or underestimate the dangers he encountered, it does indicate that black people's own articulation of their experiences of racism are not enough: they have to be authenticated by a white man.

13 It is interesting to note that in her discussion of both versions of *Imitation of Life*, E. Ann Kaplan insists that Peola and Sarah Jane 'pretend' to be white, without justifying her implied assertion that they are 'really' black (Kaplan, 1992: 165).

14 It has to be said that when I have shown this scene to students, it has often been the subject of much incredulous laughter, as have other scenes in the film. There are times, however, when the whole film has evoked some painful memories for those who had seen it when it was originally released.

15 There is a curious scene in *Sapphire* where an austerely dressed W. P. Sergeant Cook who is characterized as a non-heterosexualized, masculinized policewoman, is disgusted by the thought of having to visit 'Babette's', the exotic underwear shop from which Sapphire's red underskirt was bought.

16 See also Sheila Patterson (1963: 249).

17 For an earlier account of racial attitudes in Britain which contains some interesting examples of racialized discourse in the press, see K. L. Little (1948). See also Clifford S. Hill (1965) who attributes at least some of the blame for racial problems to media sensationalism.

18 See Klaus Theweleit (1990) for examples of the use of such imagery by officers in the German Freikorps.

19 The Act restricted the right of entry into Britain of those who came from the New Commonwealth: those who held passports not issued in Britain had to have work permits in order to come here (Walvin, 1984).

20 Although the Labour Party – then in opposition – declared its disagreement with the underlying principles of the Bill, the tone and level of debates about immigration in the period leading up to the Bill's enactment cemented the belief that not only was such legislation desirable from all political perspectives, it was also inevitable that it should be brought in. Subsequent events demonstrated that the promises made whilst in opposition did not have to be kept. Although Labour promised to repeal the 1962 Act when they came to power, successive Labour governments, in their bids to maintain popular support, brought

in some of the harshest immigration legislation enacted in this country (Walvin, 1984).

21 See Terry Lovell (1990), where she makes a similar point.

22 For an elaboration on this narrative schema, see Stephen Neale (1987: 20ff.).

CHAPTER 5

1 The name Salambo is interesting for its closeness to Sambo which although it is a Hausa (from the north of Nigeria) family name, came to be used by Europeans as a generic term for Africans. *Salammbo* is also the title of an orientalist novel by Gustave Flaubert about a foreign mercenary who falls in love with the eponymous young daughter of the King of Carthage.

2 Torgovnick does initially problematize her use of 'we' but does not sustain her self-reflexivity on the matter. It is still the case that the equation of 'we' with the non-black, 'non-primitive self' privileges and normalizes whiteness and excludes other readers from the text.

3 This use of the contrast between the savage and the civilized brings to mind David Dabydeen's (1985) critical account of the use of black people in the work of the artist William Hogarth.

CHAPTER 6

1 For a schematic account of developments in television and representations of black people, see Angela Barry (1988): for a collection of critiques and examples of fictional representations, see various sections in Daniels and Gerson (1989).

2 This film is a record of a public meeting held at the West Indian Students' Centre in which African–Americans James Baldwin and Dick Gregory discuss aspects of black politics in the USA and their relevance to black people elsewhere. Also discussed is the role of white liberals in black political struggle. See Horace Ove quoted in Pines (1992: 121).

3 It is also worth noting that there were several television situation comedies which had black characters or dealt with 'race' during this period. Some of these were later developed as films: see, for example, *Love Thy Neighbour* (1973) and *Rising Damp* (1980).

4 Jean-Louis Comolli and Jean Narboni (1976). This essay, published originally in *Cahiers du Cinéma* no. 216 (October, 1969), was translated and appeared in *Screen*, volume 12 number 1 (Spring, 1971).

5 See Claudia Jones (1985), 'An End to the Neglect of the Problems of Negro Women!' written in 1949. For a more recent indication of the range of black women involved in British political struggle in Britain, see Claudette Williams (1993).

6 See Michele Wallace (1979: 160–167). Sister Louise's actions also resonate with Stokely Carmichael's declaration that 'The only position of women in SNCC [Student Non-violent Coordinating Committee] is prone.' (quoted in Michele Wallace, 1979: 7).

7 Although in many senses, his activities have been considered as marginal, Michael X remains an interesting figure, not least because his political trajectory was in some ways similar to Malcolm X. For a short article on Michael de Freitas (Michael X) see The *Guardian* Education tabloid, 2 March 1993: 2–3.

8 See Philip Oakes in the *Sunday Times*, 18 July 1976 and 29 January 1978. In 1976 when the Notting Hill Carnival erupted in violence – typically characterized as riots by the press – Ove's film was referred to on a number of occasions due to its articulation of the experiences of disaffected black youth. See the *Daily Mail* letters page of 4 September 1976 and *New Society* of 9 September 1976.

9 Although there have been several accounts documenting racism in the juridical system and problematic 'race relations' in general, more media attention has been given to those works which support the dominant views on 'race' and crime. For critical accounts of the role of the law in supporting racism, see for example: Stuart Hall *et al.* (1978); Lee Bridges (1983); Cecil Gutzmore (1983); Chris Mullard (1973); Dilip Hiro (1973).

10 It is worth noting how influential feminist perspectives analysed the family as the prime site of women's oppression and how black women responded to this, pointing to black family life as a sustaining, nurturing environment where the importance of kinship is emphasized. See, for example, Michele Barrett (1980). For a critique of this position, see Hazel V. Carby (1986: 214).

11 Referring to the North American context, Cornel West notes how: 'Black peoples' quest for validation and recognition occurred on the ideological, social and cultural terrains of other non-Black peoples' (West, 1991: 26).

12 See, for example in the North American context, Daniel Moynihan's report, *The Negro Family: The Case for National Action* (Office Planning and Research, US Department of Labor, 1965). For the deployment of similar ideas in Britain, see especially Kenneth Pryce (1979).

CHAPTER 7

1 I am not claiming that the old ideologies have remained unchanged across two hundred years: however, racist ideologies, like much else, do not progress in a neat linear fashion and several forms may co-exist. For those at the sharp end, 'newness' is not an issue.

2 For further discussion of the history and politics of black hairstyling, see Kobena Mercer (1991).

3 This was, of course, after World War II but before the USA took centre stage politically and culturally.

4 Sade Adu is a singer, popularly known as 'Sade' and Roland Gift was at the time lead singer with Fine Young Cannibals.

5 Graham Fuller in conversation with Neil Jordan and David Leland, *Guardian* (28 August 1986).

6 See, for example, Diana Ross's star vehicle *Mahogany* (1975), Eddie Murphy's box office hit *Trading Places* (1983) and notably, Whoopi Goldberg's not very successful *Fatal Beauty* (1987) in which her love scene with the white male protagonist was edited out after adverse reactions to the scene. More recently, there does seem to have been a slight shift, notably in Spike Lee's *Jungle Fever* (1992).

7 Shakespeare's *Othello* also offers a number of examples of this set of associations. See Ben Okri (1988) and also Ruth Cowhig (1985).

8 This motif is invoked in the Tarzan cycle of books and films but also in the film *King Kong* (1933). For an extended discussion of Tarzan and the racial significance of apes, see Marianna Torgovnick (1990), chapter 2. For a detailed analysis of apes and their importance in North American culture and their relationship to sex and 'race', see Donna Haraway (1992: 160ff.).

CHAPTER 8

1 Neil Jordan's drama of sexual duplicity and masculine sexual identity, *The Crying Game* (1992) is an exception, which, in spite of its problematic refusal to engage with the politics of racial difference raised by the casting of two black men in pivotal roles, does at least suggest the possibility of less rigid sexual binarisms.

2 See, for example, the public debates on Black Audio's *Handsworth Songs* (1986), (Mercer and Julien, 1988: 16–17). For issues relating to Third Cinema, see Solanas and Getino (1976), Cham and Andrade-Watkins (1988), and Pines and Willemen (1989).

Bibliography

Abrams, P. (1968) *The Origins of British Sociology*, Chicago: University of Chicago Press.

Afro-Caribbean Mental Health Association (1989) 'Mental Health Services to the Afro-Caribbean Community in West Lambeth: a Survey Report', London: Afro-Caribbean Mental Health Association.

Althusser, L. (1988) *Essays on Ideology*, London: Verso.

Amos, V. and Parmar, P. (1982) 'Resistances and Responses: the Experience of Black Girls in Britain' in A. MacRobbie, and T. MacCabe (eds) *Feminism for Girls*, London: Routledge and Kegan Paul.

Amos, V. and Parmar, P. (1984) 'Challenging Imperial Feminism', in *Many Voices, One Chant: Feminist Review*, number 17.

Anderson, B. (1991) *Imagined Communities*, London: Verso.

Appiah, A. (1985) 'The Uncompleted Argument: Du Bois and the Illusion of Race', *Critical Inquiry*, number 12, Autumn: 21–37.

Armes, R. (1978) *A Critical History of British Cinema*, London: Secker and Warburg.

Attille, M. and Blackwood, M. (1987) 'Black Women and Representation' in C. Brunsdon (ed.) *Films for Women*, London: BFI: 202–9.

Auty, M. and Roddick, N. (1985) *British Cinema Now*, London: BFI.

Bailey, C. (1988) 'Nigger/Lover – The Thin Sheen of Race in *Something Wild*' in *Screen: the Last 'Special Issue' on Race?*, volume 29, number 4, Autumn: 28–40.

Bailey, D. A. and Hall, S. (1992) 'The Vertigo of Displacement: Shifts within Black Documentary Practices' in *Critical Decade: Black British Photography in the 80s*, Ten Photo Paperback, volume 2, number 3, Spring: 14–23.

Baldwin, J. (1988) 'A Talk to Teachers' in R. Simonson and S. Walker (eds) *Multi-cultural Literacy: Opening the American Mind*, Minnesota: Graywolf Press.

Barker, M. (1981) *The New Racism*, London: Junction Books Ltd.

Barr, C. (ed) (1986) *All Our Yesterdays: 90 Years of British Cinema*, London: BFI.

Barrett, M. (1980) *Women's Oppression Today*, London: Verso.

Barry, A. (1988) 'Black Mythologies: the Representation of Black People on British Television' in J. Twitchin, (ed.) *The Black and White Media Book: Handbook for the Study of Racism and Television*, Stoke-on-Trent: Trentham Books: 83–102.

Beckles, H. McD. (1989) *Natural Rebels: A Social History of Enslaved Black Women in Barbados*, London: Zed Books.

Belsey, C. (1980) *Critical Practice*, London: Methuen.

Ben-Tovim, G. and Gabriel, J. (1987) 'The Politics of Race in Britain, 1962–79: a Review of the Major Trends' in C. Husband, (ed.) *'Race' in Britain: Continuity and Change*, London: Hutchinson: 142–68.

Bennett, T. *et al.* (eds), (1989) *Culture, Ideology and Social Process: a Reader* London: B. T. Batsford Ltd and Open University Press.

Berlant, L. (1991) 'National Brands/National Body: Imitation of Life' in H. J. Spillers, (ed.) *Comparative American Identities: Race, Sex and Nationality in the Modern Text*, New York and London: Routledge: 110–40.

Bertram, G. C. L. (1958) 'West Indian Immigration', London: The Eugenics Society.

Bhabha, H. K. (1983) 'The Other Question...' in *Screen*, volume 24, number 6, November/December: 18–36.

Bhabha, H. (1987) 'Interrogating Identity' in L. Appignanesi (ed.) *Identity: the Real Me*, ICA Documents 6, London: ICA: 5-11.

Bhabha, H. (1987) 'What Does the Black Man Want?' in *New Formations*, number 1, Spring: 118–24.

Bhabha, H. (1988) 'The Commitment to Theory' in *New Formations*, number 5, Summer: 5–24.

Black Health Workers and Patients Group (1983), 'Psychiatry and the Corporate State', in *Race and Class*, volume 25, number 2, Autumn: 49–64.

Bland, L. (1984) 'Look Out for the Good Time Girl: Dangerous Sexualities as Threat to National Health' in Formations Editorial Collective (eds) *Formations of Nation and People*, London: Routledge Kegan Paul.

Bobo, J. (1988) '*The Color Purple*: Black Women as Cultural Readers', in E. D. Pribram (ed.) *Female Spectators: Looking at Film and Television*, London: Verso: 90–109.

Bogle, D. (1980) *Brown Sugar: Eighty Years of America's Black Female Superstars*, New York: Da Capo.

Bogle, D. (1988) *Blacks in American Films and Television: An Illustrated Encyclopedia*, New York: Simon and Schuster Inc.

Bogle, D. (1991) *Toms, Coons, Mammies, Mulattoes and Bucks: An Interpretative History of Blacks in American Films*, New York: Continuum.

Bolt, C. (1971) *Victorian Attitudes to Race*, London: Routledge and Kegan Paul.

Bonner, F. *et al.* (eds) (1992) *Imagining Women: Cultural Representations and Gender*, Cambridge: Polity.

Bordwell, D. and Thompson, K. (1990) *Film Art: An Introduction*, New York: McGraw-Hill.

Brantlinger, P. (1988) *Rule of Darkness: British Literature and Imperialism*, Ithaca: Cornell University.

Bridges (1983), 'Policing the Urban Wasteland' in *Race & Class: British Racism: The Road to 1984*, volume 25, number 2, Autumn: 31–47.

Bristow, J. (1991) *Empire Boys: Adventures in a Man's World*, London: HarperCollins Academic.

Brown, J. (1977) *Shades of Grey: Police/West Indian Relations in Handsworth*, London: Cranfield Police Studies.

Brunsdon, C. (ed.) (1987) *Films for Women*, London: BFI.

Bryan, B. *et al.* (1985) *The Heart of the Race: Black Women's Lives in Britain*, London: Virago.

Bush, B. (1981) 'Blacks in Britain: the 1930s' in *History Today*, September.

Byars, J. (1991) *All That Hollywood Allows: Re-Reading Gender in 1950s Melodrama*, London: Routledge.

Carby, H. (1985) '"On the Threshold of Woman's Era": Lynching, Empire, and Sexuality in Black Feminist Theory', *Critical Inquiry*, number 12, Autumn: 262–77.

Carby, H. (1986) 'White Woman Listen! Black Feminism and the Boundaries of Sisterhood' in Centre for Contemporary Cultural Studies (eds) *The Empire Strikes Back: Race and Racism in 70s Britain*, London: Hutchinson University Library.

Cashmore, E. (1979) *Rastaman*, London: Allen and Unwin.

Centre for Contemporary Cultural Studies (1986) *The Empire Strikes Back: Race and Racism in 70s Britain*, London: Hutchinson University Library.

Cham, M. B. and Andrade-Watkins, C. (eds), (1988) *BlackFrames: Critical Perspectives on Black Independent Cinema*, Cambridge, Massachusetts: Celebration of Black Cinema, Inc. and MIT Press.

Cohen, P. (1988) 'The Perversions of Inheritance: Studies in the Making of Multi-Racist Britain' in P. Cohen and H. S. Bains (eds) *Multi-Racist Britain*, Basingstoke: MacMillan Education Ltd.

Cohen, P. (1988) 'Tarzan and the Jungle Bunnies: Class, Race and Sex in Popular Culture' in *New Formations*, number 5, Summer: 25–30.

P. Cohen and H. S. Bains, (eds) (1988) *Multi-racist Britain*, Basingstoke: MacMillan Education.

Cohen, P. and Gardner, C. (eds) (1982) *It Ain't Half Racist, Mum*, London: Comedia.

Cohen, S. (1972) *Folk Devils and Moral Panics: The Creation of the Mods and Rockers*, London: MacGibbon and Kee.

Collins, J. *et al.* (eds) (1993) *Film Theory Goes to the Movies*, New York: Routledge.

Collins, P. H. (1991) *Black Feminist Thought: Knowledge, Consciousness and the Politics of Empowerment*, New York: Routledge.

Commission for Racial Equality (1979), 'Youth in a Multi-Racial Society: The Urgent Need for New Policies: "The Fire Next Time"' London: Commission for Racial Equality.

Comolli, J. and Narboni, J. (1976) 'Cinema/Ideology/Criticism' in B. Nichols, (ed.), *Movies and Methods*, Berkeley: University of California Press: 23–30 (originally published in 1969).

Conrad, J. (1989) *Heart of Darkness*, London: Penguin, (originally published in 1902).

Cowhig, R. (1985) 'Blacks in English Renaissance Drama and the Role of Shakespeare's Othello' in D. Dabydeen (ed.) *The Black Presence in English Literature*, Manchester: Manchester University Press: 1–25.

Cripps, T. (1977) *Slow Fade to Black: The Negro in American Film*, Oxford: Oxford University Press.

Cripps, T. (1993) *Making Movies Black: The Hollywood Message Movie from World War II to the Civil Rights Era*, Oxford: Oxford University Press.

Curran, J. and Porter, V. (eds) (1983) *British Cinema History*, London: George Weidenfeld and Nicolson Ltd.

Dabydeen, D. (ed.) (1985) *The Black Presence in English Literature*, Manchester: Manchester University Press.

Dabydeen, D. (1985) *Hogarth's Blacks: Images of Blacks in Eighteenth Century English Art*, Denmark and Surrey: Mundelstrup.

Daniels, T. and Gerson, J. (eds) (1989) *The Colour Black: Black Images in British Television*, London: BFI.

Davidson, B. (1984) *The Story of Africa*, London: Mitchell Beazley.

Davis, A. (1981) *Women, Race and Class*, London: The Women's Press.

Dent, G. (ed.) (1992) *Black Popular Culture*, Seattle: Bay Press.

Diawara, M. (1988) 'Black Spectatorship: Problems of Identification and Resistance' in *Screen: The Last 'Special Issue' on Race?'* volume 29, number 4, Autumn: 66–80.

Diawara, M. (ed.) (1993) *Black American Cinema*, New York: Routledge.

Doane, M. A. (1991) *Femmes Fatales: Feminism, Film Theory, Psychoanalysis*, New York: Routledge.

Donaldson, L. E. (1992) *Decolonizing Feminisms: Race, Gender and Empire Building*, London: Routledge.

Duane, P. and Mackenzie, J. (eds) (1986) *Imperialism and Popular Culture*, Manchester: Manchester University Press.

Durgnat, R. (1970) *A Mirror for England*, London: Faber and Faber.

Dyer, R. (1986) *Heavenly Bodies: Film Stars and Society*, New York: St Martin's Press.

Dyer, R. (1988) 'White' in *Screen: The Last 'Special Issue' on Race?'* volume 29, number 4, Autumn: 44–65.

Dyer, R. (1993) *The Matter of Images: Essays on Representations*, London: Routledge.

Eagleton, T. (1992) *Literary Theory: an Introduction*, Oxford, UK and Cambridge, USA: Blackwell.

Ellis, J. (1988) *Visible Fictions: Cinema, Television, Video*, London: Routledge.

Erens, P. (ed.) (1990) *Issues in Feminist Film Criticism*, Indiana: Indiana University Press.

Fanon, F. (1986) *Black Skin, White Masks*, (translated by Charles Lam Markmann), London: Pluto Press, (originally published in 1952).

Ferguson, R. (1973) 'Women's Liberation has a Different Meaning for Blacks' in G. Lerner (ed.) *Black Women in White America: a Documentary History*, New York: Vintage Books: 587–92.

Ferguson, R. *et al.* (eds) (1991) *Out There: Marginalization and Contemporary Cultures*, New York: The New Museum of Contemporary Art.

Foner, P. S. (1978) *Paul Robeson Speaks: Writings, Speeches, Interviews: 1918–1974*, London: Quartet.

Foucault, M. (1977) *Discipline and Punish: The Birth of the Prison*, London: Penguin Books.

Foucault, M. (1980) *Power/Knowledge: Selected Interviews and Other Writings, 1972–1977* (translated by Colin Gordon, Leo Marshall, John Mepham, Kate Soper), New York: Pantheon Books.

Freud, S. (1938) *Totem and Taboo: Resemblances between the Psychic Lives of Savages and Neurotics*, Harmondsworth: Pelican Books.

Freud, S. (1977) *On Sexuality* (translated by James Strachey), Harmondsworth: Penguin Books.

Freud, S. (1984) *On Metapsychology: The Theory of Psychoanalysis* (translated by James Strachey), Harmondsworth: Penguin Books.

Freud, S. (1985) *Civilization, Society and Religion* (translated by James Strachey), London: Penguin Books.

Freud, S. (1986) *Historical and Expository Works on Psychoanalysis* (translated by James Strachey), London: Penguin.

Friedan, B. (1963) *The Feminine Mystique*, New York: W. W. Norton.

Friedman, L. (ed.) (1993) *British Cinema and Thatcherism*, London: UCL Press.

Fryer, P. (1984) *Staying Power: The History of Black People in Britain*, London: Pluto Press.

Fryer, P. (1987) 'Pseudo-scientific Racism' in D. Gill, and L. Levidow, (eds) *Anti-racist Science Teaching*, London: Free Association Books.

Fusco, C. (1988) *Young British and Black: A Monograph on the Work of Sankofa Film/Video Collective and Black Audio Collective*, New York: Hallwalls/Contemporary Arts Center.

Fusco, C. (1989) 'About Locating Ourselves and Our Representations' in *Third Scenario: Theory and Politics of Location*, Framework 36: 7–14.

Gaines, J. (1988) 'White Privilege and Looking Relations: Race and Gender in Feminist Film Theory' in *Screen: The Last 'Special Issue' on Race?'* volume 29, number 4, Autumn: 12–27.

Gamman, L. and Marshment, M. (eds) (1988) *The Female Gaze: Women as Viewers of Popular Culture*, London: Women's Press.

Garrison, L. (1980) *Black Youth, Rastafarianism and the Identity-Crisis in Britain*, London: ACER.

Gates Jr, H. L. (1989) *Figures in Black: Words, Signs and the 'Racial' Self*, New York and Oxford: Oxford University Press.

Genovese, E. D. (1976) *Roll Jordan, Roll: The World the Slaves Made*, New York: Vintage Books.

Giles, P. (1993) 'History With Holes: Channel Four Television Films of the 1980s' in Friedman, L. (ed.) *British Cinema and Thatcherism*, London: University College Press: 70–91.

Gilman, S. L. (1985) *Difference and Pathology: Stereotypes of Sexuality, Race and Madness*, Ithaca: Cornell University Press.

Gilman, S. L. (1987) 'The Origins of Psychiatric Photography' in *The

Mind, York: Impressions Gallery of Photography: 5–15

Gilroy, P. (1987) *There Ain't No Black in the Union Jack*, London: Hutchinson.

Givanni, J. (1992) *Black Film and Video List*, London: BFI.

Gledhill, C. (ed.) (1991) *Stardom: Industry of Desire*, London: Routledge.

Gledhill, C. (ed.) (1992) *Home Is Where the Heart Is: Studies in Melodrama and the Woman's Film*, London: BFI.

Goldberg, D. T. (ed.) (1990) *Anatomy of Racism*, Minneapolis: University of Minnesota Press.

Goldberg, D. T. (1993) *Racist Culture: Philosophy and the Politics of Meaning*, Cambridge, Massachusetts and Oxford, UK: Blackwell.

Gould, S. J. (1981) *The Mismeasure of Man*, New York: W. W. Norton and Company.

Green, D. (1984) 'Classified Subjects' in *Ten 8*, number 14: 30–7.

Green, D. (1986) 'Veins of Resemblance: Photography and Eugenics', in P. Holland, *et al.*, (eds) *Photography/Politics 2*, London: Comedia/Photography Workshop: 9–21.

Griffin, John Howard (1984) *Black Like Me*, London: Grafton.

Gutzmore, C. (1983) 'Capital, "Black Youth" and Crime' in *Race and Class*, volume 25, number 2, Autumn: 13–30.

Haggard, H. R. (1979) *King Solomon's Mines*, London: Octopus Books, (originally published in 1885).

Haggard, H. R. (1991) *She*, Oxford: Oxford University Press, (originally published in 1887).

Hall, C. (1992) *White, Male and Middle Class: Explorations in Feminism and History*, Cambridge: Polity Press.

Hall, S. (1984) 'Reconstruction Work', *Ten 8*, number 16: 2–9

Hall, S. (1986a) 'New Ethnicities' in K. Mercer, and I. Julien, (eds) *Black Film, British Cinema*, ICA Documents 7, London: ICA: 27–30.

Hall, S. (1986b) 'Gramsci's Relevance for the Study of Race and Ethnicity' in *Journal of Communication Inquiry*, volume 10 number 2, Summer.

Hall, S. (1987) 'Minimal Selves' in L. Appignanesi (ed.) *Identity: The Real Me*, ICA Documents 6, London: ICA: 44–8.

Hall, S. (1989) 'Cultural Identity and Cinematic Representation' in *Third Scenario: Theory and Politics of Location*, Framework 36: 68–81.

Hall, S. (1990a) 'Cultural Identity and Diaspora' in J. Rutherford (ed.) *Identity: Community, Culture, Difference*, London: Lawrence and Wishart: 222–37.

Hall, S. (1990b) 'The Whites of Their Eyes: Racist Ideologies and the Media' in M. Alvarado, and J. O. Thompson, (eds), *The Media Reader* London: BFI: 7–23.

Hall, S. (1992a) 'Reconstruction Work: Images of Post War Black Settlement' in *Critical Decade: Black British Photography in the 80s*, Ten 8 Photo Paperback, volume 2, number 3, : 106–13.

Hall, S. (1992b) 'What is this "Black" in Black Popular Culture?' in G. Dent (ed.) *Black Popular Culture*, Seattle: Bay Press: 21–33.

Hall, S. *et al,*. (1978) *Policing the Crisis: Mugging, the State, and Law and Order*, Basingstoke: Macmillan.

Hansberry, L. (1969) 'The Negro in American Culture' in C. W. E. Bigsby (ed) *The Black American Writer*, Florida: Everett/Edward.

Haraway, D. (1992) *Primate Visions: Gender, Race and Nature in the World of Modern Science*, London: Verso.

Harding, S. (1986) *The Science Question in Feminism*, Milton Keynes: Open University Press.

Henderson, B. (1985) 'The Searchers': an American Dilemma' in B. Nichols (ed.) *Movies and Methods: Volume II*, Berkeley: University of California Press: 429–49.

Henriques, F. (1974) *Children of Caliban: Miscegenation*, London: Secker and Warburg.

Hill, J. (1986) *Sex, Class and Realism: British Cinema 1956-1963*, London: BFI.

Hill, C. (1965) *How Colour Prejudiced is Britain?*, London: Gollancz.

Hiro, D. (1973) *Black British, White British*, Harmondsworth: Penguin.

Hirsch, M. and Keller, E. F. (eds) (1990) *Conflicts in Feminism*, New York: Routledge.

Hobson, J. A. (1988) *Imperialism: a Study*, London: Unwin Hyman, (originally published in 1938).

Hoggart, R. (1959) *The Uses of Literacy*, Harmondsworth: Penguin.

hooks, b. (1982) *Ain't I a Woman! Black Women and Feminism*, London: Pluto.

hooks, b. (1984) *Feminist Theory: From Margin to Center*, Boston, Massachusetts: South End Press.

hooks, b. (1989) *Talking Back: Thinking Feminist – Thinking Black*, London: Sheba Feminist Press.

hooks, b. (1991) *Yearnings: Race, Gender, and Cultural Politics*, London: Turnaround.

hooks, b. (1992) *Black Looks: Race and Representation*, London: Turnaround.

Husband, C. (ed.) (1987) *'Race' in Britain: Continuity and Change*, London: Hutchinson University Library.

Hyam, R. (1991) *Empire and Sexuality: The British Experience*, Manchester: Manchester University Press.

Jacobus, M. *et al.* (eds) (1990) *Body/Politics: Women and the Discourses of Science*, New York and London: Routledge.

James, W. and Harris, C. (eds) (1993) *Inside Babylon: The Caribbean Diaspora in Britain*, London: Verso.

JanMohamed, A. R. (1985) 'The Economy of Manichean Allegory: The Function of Racial Difference in Colonialist Literature' in *Critical Enquiry*, number 12, Autumn: 59–87.

Jewell, K. S. (1993) *From Mammy to Miss America and Beyond: Cultural Images and the Shaping of US Social Policy*, London: Routledge.

Johnston, C. (1985) 'Women's Cinema as Counter-Cinema' in B. Nichols, (ed.) *Movies and Methods*, Berkeley: University of California Press: 208–17.

Jones, C. (1985) 'An End to the Neglect of the Problems of Negro Women!' in B. Johnson (ed.) *'I Think of My Mother': Notes on the Life and Times of Claudia Jones*, London: Karia Press

Jordan, W. (1974) *The White Man's Burden: Historical Origins of Racism in the United States*, New York: Oxford University Press.

Julien, I. and Mercer, K. (1988) 'Introduction: De Margin and De Centre' in *Screen: The Last 'Special Issue' on Race?'* volume 29, number 4, Autumn: 2–11.

Kaplan, E. A. (1983) *Women and Film: Both Sides of the Camera*, London and New York: Methuen.

Kaplan, E. A. (1992) *Representation and Motherhood: The Mother in Popular Culture and Melodrama*, London: Routledge.

Kovel, J. (1988) *White Racism: a Psychohistory*, London: Free Association Books.

Kuhn, A. (1985) *The Power of the Image: Essays on Representation and Sexuality*, London: Routledge and Kegan Paul.

Laplanche, J. and Pontalis, J. B. (1988) *The Language of Psychoanalysis* (translated by Donald Nicholson-Smith), London: Karnac Books.

Lapsley, R. and Westlake, M. (1988) *Film Theory: An Introduction*, Manchester: Manchester University Press.

Larkin, A. S. (1988) 'Black Women Film-makers Defining Ourselves: Feminism in Our Own Voice' in E. D. Pribram (ed.), *Female Spectators: Looking at Film and Television*, London: Verso: 157–73.

Lawrence, E. (1986a) 'Just Plain Common Sense: the "Roots" of Racism' in Centre for Contemporary Cultural Studies (eds) *The Empire Strikes Back: Race and Racism in 70s Britain*, London: Hutchinson: 47–94.

Lawrence, E. (1986b) 'In the Abundance of Water the Fool is Thirsty: Sociology and Black Pathology' in Centre for Contemporary Cultural Studies (eds) *The Empire Strikes Back: Race and Racism in 70s Britain*, London: Hutchinson: 95–142

Leab, D. J. (1975) *From Sambo to Superspade: The Black Experience in Motion Pictures*, London: Secker and Warburg.

Lenin, V. I. (1933) *Imperialism, the Highest Stage of Capitalism: A Popular Outline*, London: Lawrence and Wishart, (originally published in 1917).

Little, K. L. (1948) *Negroes in Britain*, London: Kegan Paul, Trench, Trubner and Co. Ltd.

Lovell, T. (1983) *Pictures of Reality: Aesthetics, Politics and Pleasure*, London: BFI.

Lovell, T. (1990) 'Landscapes and Stories in 1960s British Realism' in *Screen*, volume 31, number 4, Winter: 357–76

MacCabe, C. (1985) *Theoretical Essays: Film, Linguistics, Literature*, Manchester: Manchester University Press.

MacCabe, C. (1986) 'Black Film in 80s Britain' in K. Mercer and I. Julien (eds) *Black Film, British Cinema*, ICA Documents 7, London: ICA: 31–2.

MacKenzie, J. (1984) *Propaganda and Empire: The Manipulation of Public Opinion, 1880–1960*, Manchester: Manchester University Press.

Mannoni, O. (1985) *Freud: The Theory of the Unconscious*, London: Verso.

Martin, E. (1990) 'Science and Women's Bodies: Forms of Anthropological Knowledge' in M. Jacobus, *et al.* (eds) *Body/Politics: Women and the Discourses of Science*, New York and London: Routledge: 69–82.

Mast, G. and Cohen, M. (eds) (1985) *Film Theory and Criticism: Introductory Readings*, New York and Oxford: Oxford University Press.

Memmi, A. (1990) *The Colonizer and the Colonized*, (translated by Howard Greenfield), London: Earthscan Publications, (originally published in 1957).

Mercer, K. (1986a) 'Recoding Narratives of Race and Nation' in K. Mercer and I. Julien (eds) *Black Film, British Cinema*, ICA Documents 7, London: ICA: 4–14.

Mercer, K. (1986b) 'Imaging the Black Man's Sex' in P. Holland *et al.* (eds) *Photography/Politics: Two*, London: Commedia Publishing Group: 61–9.

Mercer, K. (1988) 'Diaspora Culture and the Dialogic Imagination: the Aesthetics of Black Independent Film in Britain', in M. B. Cham and C. Andrade-Watkins (eds), *BlackFrames: Critical Perspectives on Black Independent Cinema*, Cambridge, Massachusetts: Celebration of Black Cinema, Inc. and MIT Press: 50–61.

Mercer, K. (1991) 'Black Hair/Style Politics' in R. Ferguson *et al.* (eds) *Out There: Marginalization and Contemporary Cultures*, New York: The New Museum of Contemporary Art: 247–65.

Mercer, K. and Julien, I. (1988) 'Race, Sexual Politics and Black Masculinity: A Dossier', in R. Chapman and J. Rutherford (eds) *Male Order: Unwrapping Masculinity*, London: Lawrence and Wishart: 97–164

Metcalf, A. and Humphries, M. (eds) (1985) *The Sexuality of Men*, London: Pluto Press.

Millett, K. (1972) *Sexual Politics* London: Rupert Hart-Davis.

Milne, T. (1989) *The Time Out Film Guide*, London: Penguin Books.

Mitchell, J. (1971) *Woman's Estate*, Harmondsworth: Penguin Books.

Modleski, T. (1988) *The Women Who Knew Too Much: Hitchcock and Feminist Theory*, London and New York: Routledge.

Morrison, T. (1987) *Beloved*, New York: Plume.

Moynihan, D. (1965) *The Negro Family: the Case for National Action*, Office Planning and Research, US Department of Labor.

Mullard, C. (1973), *Black Britain*, London: Allen and Unwin.

Mulvey, L. (1985), 'Visual Pleasure and Narrative Cinema' in B. Nichols (ed.) *Movies and Methods, Volume II*, Berkeley: University of California Press: 303–14.

Neale, S. (1987) *Genre*, London: BFI.

Nichols, B. (ed.) (1976) *Movies and Methods*, Berkeley: University of California Press.

Nichols, B. (ed.) (1985) *Movies and Methods: Volume II*, Berkeley: University of California Press.

Oakley, A. (1974) *Housewife*, Harmondsworth: Pelican.

Okri, B. (1988), 'Leaping Out of Shakespeare's Terror: Five Meditations on Othello' in K. Owusu *Storms of the Heart: an Anthology of Black Arts and Culture*, London: Camden Press: 9–18.

Ove, H. (1988) 'Going to Meet the Man' in K. Mercer and I. Julien (eds) *Black Film, British Cinema*, ICA Documents 7, London: ICA: 57.

Owusu, K. (1986) *The Struggle for Black Arts in Britain: What Can We*

Consider Better Than Freedom?, London: Commedia.

Owusu, K. (ed.) (1988) *Storms of the Heart: an Anthology of Black Arts and Culture*, London: Camden Press.

Padmore, George (1936) *Africa: How Britain Rules Africa*, London: Wishart Books.

Pajaczkowska, C. and Young, L. (1992) 'Racism, Representation, Psychoanalysis' in J. Donald and A. Rattansi. *'Race', Culture and Difference* London: Sage: 198–221.

Parry, B. (1983) *Conrad and Imperialism: Ideological Boundaries and Visionary Frontiers*, London: Macmillan.

Patterson, S. (1963) *Dark Strangers: A Study of West Indians in London* Harmondsworth: Pelican.

Pieterse, J. N. (1992) *White on Black: Images of Africa and Blacks in Western Popular Culture*, New Haven and London: Yale University Press.

Pines, J. (1975) *Blacks in Film: A Survey of Racial Themes and Images in the American Film*, London: Studio Vista.

Pines, J. (1981) 'Blacks in Films: The British Angle' in *Multi-racial Education*, volume 9, number 2, Spring.

Pines, J. (1988) 'The Cultural Context of Black British Cinema' in M. B. Cham and C. Andrade-Watkins (eds), *BlackFrames: Critical Perspectives on Black Independent Cinema*, Cambridge, Massachusetts: Celebration of Black Cinema, Inc. and MIT Press: 26–36.

Pines, J. (1991) *Representation and Blacks in British Cinema*, London: BFI Education booklet.

Pines, J. (ed.) (1992) *Black and White in Colour: Black People in British Television Since 1936*, London: BFI.

Pines, J. and Willemen, P. (eds) (1989) *Questions of Third Cinema*, London: BFI.

Pratt, M. L. (1985) 'Scratches on the Face of the Country; or, What Mr Barrow Saw in the Land of the Bushmen', in *Critical Inquiry*, volume 12, Autumn: 119–43.

Pribram, D. (ed.) (1988) *Female Spectators: Looking at Film and Television*, London: Verso.

Pryce, K. (1979) *Endless Pressure*, Harmondsworth: Penguin.

Reeves, M. and Hammond, J. (eds) (1989) *Looking Beyond the Frame: Racism, Representation and Resistance*, Oxford: Links Publications.

Rex, J. (1973) *Race, Colonialism and the City*, London and Boston: Routledge and Kegan Paul.

Rich, P. B., (1986) *Race and Empire in British Politics*, Cambridge: Cambridge University Press.

Richards, J. (1973) *Visions of Yesterday*, London: Routledge and Kegan Paul Ltd.

Richards, J. and Aldgate, A. (1983) *Best of British: Cinema and Society*, Oxford: Basil Blackwell.

Roach, J. and Felix, P. (1988) 'Black Looks' in L. Gamman and M. Marshment (eds) *The Female Gaze*, London: Women's Press: 130–42.

Rodney, W. (1988) *How Europe Underdeveloped Africa*, London: Bogle L'Ouverture Publications.

Roper, M. and Tosh, J. (eds) (1991) *Manful Assertions: Masculinities in Britain Since 1800*, London: Routledge.

Rowbotham, S. (1973) *Woman's Consciousness, Man's World*, Harmondsworth: Pelican.

Rugg, A. (1984) *Brickbats and Bouquets: Black Woman's Critique: Literature, Theatre, Film*, London: Race Today Publications.

Rutherford, J. (ed.) (1990) *Identity: Community, Culture, Difference*, London: Lawrence and Wishart.

Said, E. W. (1985) *Orientalism*, Harmondsworth: Penguin.

Said, E. W. (1993) *Culture and Imperialism*, London: Chatto and Windus.

Sayer, S. and Jayamanne, L. (1987) *'Burning an Illusion'* in C. Brunsdon (ed.) *Films for Women*, London: BFI: 86–90.

Searle, G. R. (1981) 'Eugenics and Class' in C. Webster (ed.) *Biology, Medicine and Society 1840–1940*, Cambridge: Cambridge University Press: 217–42.

Shohat, E. (1991) 'Gender and the Culture of Empire: Toward a Feminist Ethnography of the Cinema' in *Quarterly Review of Film and Video*, volume 13: 45-84.

Simmonds, F. N. (1992) *'She's Gotta Have It*: The Representation of Black Female Sexuality on Film' in F. Bonner *et al.* (eds), *Imagining Women: Cultural Representations and Gender*, Cambridge: Polity Press: 210–20.

Sivanandan, A. (1983) 'Challenging Racism: Strategies for the '80s', in *Race & Class: British Racism: The Road to 1984*, volume 25, number 2, Autumn: 1–11.

Smith, G. A. (1987) *When Jim Crow Met John Bull: Black American Soldiers in World War II Britain*, London: I. B. Tauris and Co. Ltd.

Smyth, R. (1983) 'Movies and Mandarins: the Official Film and British Colonial Africa' in J. Curran, and V. Porter (eds) *British Cinema History*, London: Weidenfeld and Nicholson: 129–43.

Snead, J. (1994) *White Screens, Black Images: Hollywood From the Dark Side*, New York: Routledge.

Solanas, F. and Getino. O (1976) 'Towards a Third Cinema' in Nichols, B. (ed.) *Movies and Methods*, Berkeley: University of California.

Solomos, J. *et al.* (1986) 'The Organic Crisis of British Capitalism and Race: the Experience of the Seventies' in Centre for Contemporary Cultural Studies (eds) *The Empire Strikes Back: Race and Racism in 70s Britain*, London: Hutchinson: 9–46.

Solomos, J. (1988) *Race and Racism in Contemporary Britain*, London: MacMillan.

Spillers, H. J. (ed.) (1991) *Comparative American Identities: Race, Sex and Nationality in the Modern Text*, New York and London: Routledge.

Stallybrass, P. and White, A. (1986) *The Politics and Poetics of Transgression*, Ithaca: Cornell University Press.

Stam, R. and Spence, L. (1985), 'Colonialism, Racism and Representation: an Introduction' in B. Nichols (ed.) *Movies and Methods, Volume II*, Berkeley: University of California Press: 632–48

Stepan, N. L. (1982) *The Idea of Race in Science: Great Britain (1800–1960)*, London: MacMillan.

Stepan, N. L. (1990) 'Race and Gender: the Role of Analogy in Science' in

D. T. Goldberg (ed.) *Anatomy of Racism*, Minneapolis: University of Minnesota Press.

Stott, R. (1989) 'The Dark Continent: Africa as Female Body in Haggard's Adventure Fiction' in *Feminist Review*, number 32, Summer: 69–89.

Street, B. (1975) *The Savage in Literature: Representations of 'Primitive' Society in English Fiction 1858–1920*, London: Routledge and Kegan Paul.

Stuart, A. (1988) '*The Color Purple*: In Defence of Happy Endings' in L. Gamman and M. Marshment (eds) *The Female Gaze*, London: Women's Press: 60–75.

Tagg, J. (1989) 'Power and Photography – a Means of Surveillance: the Photograph as Evidence in Law' in T. Bennett *et al.* (eds), *Culture, Ideology and Social Process: a Reader*, London: B. T. Batsford Ltd and Open University Press: 285–307.

Tarr, C. (1985) '*Sapphire, Darling* and the Boundaries of Permitted Pleasure' in *Screen* volume 26, number 1: 50–65.

Theweleit, K. (1990) *Male Fantasies: Women, Floods, Bodies, History*, Cambridge: Polity.

Torgovnick, M. (1990) *Gone Primitive: Savage Intellects, Modern Lives*, Chicago and London: University of Chicago Press.

Twitchin, J. (ed.) (1988), *The Black and White Media Book: Handbook for the Study of Racism and Television*, Stoke-on-Trent: Trentham Books.

Vaughn, J. (1959) 'The Dark Continent in the Wrong Light' in *Films and Filming* January: 10.

Vieler-Porter, C. (1992) in J. I. Givanni (ed.), *Black Film and Video List*, London: BFI: 238.

Wallace, M. (1979) *Black Macho and the Myth of the Superwoman*, London: John Calder.

Wallace, M. (1990) *Invisibility Blues: From Pop to Theory*, London: Verso.

Walvin, J. (1973) *Black and White: The Negro and English Society 1555–1945*, London: Allen Lane.

Walvin, J. (1984) *Passage to Britain: Immigration in British History and Politics*, Harmondsworth: Penguin.

Ware, V (1992) *Beyond the Pale: White Women, Racism and History*, London: Verso.

Washington, M. H. (1987) *Invented Lives: Narratives of Black Women 1860–1960*, New York: Anchor Press.

Watney, S. (1990) 'Missionary positions: AIDS, Africa, and Race' in R. Ferguson *et al.* (eds) *Out There: Marginalization and Contemporary Cultures*, New York: New Museum of Contemporary Art: 89–106.

West, C. (1991) 'The New Cultural Politics of Difference' in R. Ferguson *et al.* (eds) *Out There: Marginalization and Contemporary Culture*, New York: New Museum of Contemporary Art.

White, M. (1992) 'Ideological Analysis and Television' in R. C. Allen (ed.) *Channels of Discourse, Reassembled*, London: Routledge: 161–202.

Willemen, P. (1990) 'Review of *Sex, Class and Realism: British Cinema 1956-1963* by John Hill' in M. Alvarado and J. O. Thompson (eds), *The Media Reader*, London: BFI: 105-110.

Williams, C. (1993) 'We are a Natural Part of Many Different Struggles:

Black Women Organizing' in Winston James and Clive Harris (eds) *Inside Babylon: The Caribbean Diaspora in Britain*, London: Verso: 153–178.

Williams, R. (1988) *Keywords: A Vocabulary of Culture and Society*, London: Fontana.

Wollen, P. (1982) *Readings and Writings: Semiotic Counter-Strategies*, London: Verso.

Young, L. (1990) 'A Nasty Piece of Work: A Psychoanalytic Study of Sexual and Racial Difference in *Mona Lisa*' in J. Rutherford (ed.) *Identity: Community, Culture, Difference*, London: Lawrence and Wishart: 188-206.

Young, L. (1991) 'Representation and British "Racial Problem" Films' in *Women: A Cultural Review*, volume 2, number 1, Spring: 40–51.

Young, L. (1993) 'Identity, Realism and Black Photography' in M. Sealy (ed.) *Vanley Burke: A Retrospective*, London: Lawrence and Wishart.

Young, L. (1994) 'Mapping Male Bodies: Thoughts on Gendered and Racialized Looking' in N. Salaman (ed.), *What She Wants: Women Artists Look at Men*, London: Verso: 39-50.

Young, R. (1990) *White Mythologies: Writing History and the West*, London: Routledge.

Films Cited

Films are British unless otherwise indicated.
Absolute Beginners (Julien Temple: 1986)
Babylon (Franco Rosso: 1980)
Baldwin's Nigger (Horace Ove: 1968)
The Birth of a Nation (D. W. Griffith: 1915: USA)
Black Joy (Anthony Simmons: 1977)
Britannia Hospital (Lindsay Anderson: 1982)
Burning an Illusion (Menelik Shabbazz: 1981)
The Cook, The Thief, His Wife and Her Lover (Peter Greenaway: 1989)
Countryman (Dickie Jobson: 1982)
The Crying Game (Neil Jordan: 1992)
Dreaming Rivers (Martine Attille: 1988)
The Drum (Zoltan Korda: 1938)
Fatal Beauty (Tom Holland: 1987: USA)
Flame in the Streets (Roy Baker: 1961)
For Queen and Country (Martin Stellman: 1988: USA/UK)
The Four Feathers (Zoltan Korda: 1939)
Gone With the Wind (Victor Fleming: 1939: USA)
Handsworth Songs (John Akomfrah: 1987)
Heavens Above! (John Boulting: 1963)
Imitation of Life (Douglas Sirk: 1959: USA)
Jemima and Johnny (Lionel Ngakane: 1964)
Jungle Fever (Spike Lee: 1993: USA)
Kings Go Forth (Delmer Daves: 1958: USA)
King Solomon's Mines (Robert Stevenson: 1937)
King Solomon's Mines (J. Lee Thompson: 1985: USA)
The L-Shaped Room (Bryan Forbes: 1962)
Lethal Weapon 3 (Richard Donner: 1990: USA)
Leo the Last (John Boorman: 1969)
Look Back in Anger (Tony Richardson: 1959)
Looking for Langston (Isaac Julien: 1988)
Lost Boundaries (Alfred L. Werker: 1949: USA)
Love Thy Neighbour (John Robins: 1973)

Mad Max: Beyond the Thunderdome (George Miller/George Ogilvie: 1985: Australia)
Mahogany (Berry Gordy: 1975: USA)
Men of Two Worlds (Thorold Dickinson: 1946)
Mona Lisa (Neil Jordan: 1986)
My Beautiful Launderette (Stephen Frears: 1985)
Night of the Living Dead (George Romero: 1969: USA)
Night of the Quarter Moon (Hugo Haas: 1959: USA)
The Passion of Remembrance (Isaac Julien and Maureen Blackwood: 1986)
Personal Services (Terry Jones: 1987)
Pinky (Elia Kazan: 1949: USA)
Playing Away (Horace Ove: 1986)
Pool of London (Basil Dearden: 1950)
Pressure (Horace Ove: 1974)
The Proud Valley (Pen Tennyson: 1939)
Raiders of the Lost Ark (Steven Spielberg: 1981)
Rhodes of Africa (Berthold Vietel: 1936)
Rising Damp (Joe McGrath: 1980)
Room at the Top (Jack Clayton: 1959)
Sanders of the River (Alexander Korda: 1935)
Sapphire (Basil Dearden: 1959)
Scandal (Michael Caton-Jones: 1988)
Scrubbers (Mai Zetterling: 1982)
She's Gotta Have It (Spike Lee: 1986: USA)
Showboat (George Sidney: 1951: USA)
Simba (Brian Desmond Hurst: 1955)
Something Wild (Jonathan Demme: 1986)
The Song of Freedom (J. Elder Willis Wills: 1936)
A Taste of Honey (Tony Richardson: 1961)
Ten Bob in Winter (Lloyd Reckord: 1963)
To Sir, With Love (James Clavell: 1966)
Trading Places (John Landis: 1983: USA)
Vamp (Richard Wenk: 1986: USA)
Young Soul Rebels (Isaac Julien: 1991)

Index